CW00923976

B/11
16

Color Management for Logos

A Comprehensive Guide for Graphic Designers

RotoVision

A RotoVision Book

Published and distributed by RotoVision SA

Route Suisse 9

CH-1295 Mies

Switzerland

RotoVision SA

Sales & Editorial Office

Sheridan House, 114 Western Road

Hove BN3 1DD, UK

Tel: +44 (0) 1273 72 72 68

Fax: +44 (0) 1273 72 72 69

www.rotovision.com

10 9 8 7 6 5 4 3 2 1

ISBN: 978-2- 88893-021-1

RotoVision Art Director: Tony Seddon

Creative Directors: John T. Drew and Sarah A. Meyer

Book Design: Matt Woolman

Book Layout and Production: Matt Woolman, Chris Malven, Jason Taylor

Acuity Color System: John T. Drew and Sarah A. Meyer

Diagrams and Illustrations: John T. Drew, Sarah A. Meyer, Matt Woolman, and Chris Malven

Typeface: Trade Gothic Family

Text © 2006 John T. Drew and Sarah A. Meyer

Acuity Color System ©2006 John T. Drew and Sarah A. Meyer. For more information about Acuity 1.0 contact John T. Drew at jdrew@fullerton.edu or Sarah A. Meyer at sameyer@csupomona.edu

Reprographics in Singapore by ProVision Pte.

Printed in Singapore by Star Standard Industries (Pte) Ltd.

Color

Management

for

Logos

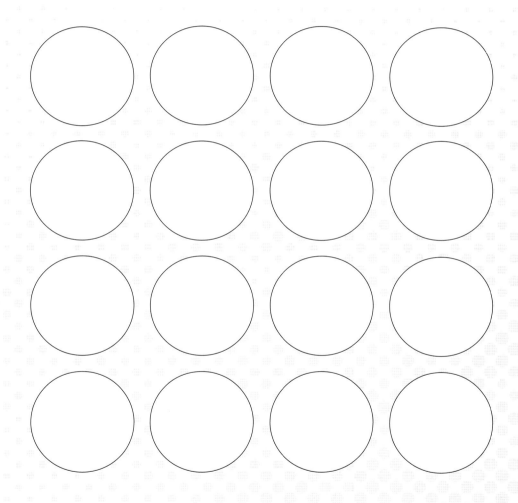

John Drew & Sarah Meyer

One Fine Day

Restless gophers push up through the dirt and sniff the air.

Relentless pennywhistlers play Irish jigs.

Armies of gray soldiers with black helmets march off to war.

A thousand red flowers open in the field.

A small wooden cart pulled by oxen

makes its way slowly over a winding dirt road.

A fish swims to the surface

breaking the calm reflection

then descends into the gloom.

A man removes his wristwatch,

An alligator slides up out of the brown

water onto the muddy shore.

A bird glides overhead,

first appearing as a moving shadow on the ground.

A mushroom cloud appears on the cover of *Life* magazine.

A man stands in the road in the sunlight and

transforms his baggy blue pants into an evening dress.

John Randolph Carter

For our daughters, Olivia and Gustava, who have shown a tremendous amount of patience; Frank and Elaine Meyer (grandparents of our daughters); Colonel Mark C. Bane Jr., their great-grandfather; and the late great Mark C. Bane III, their great-uncle.

Contents

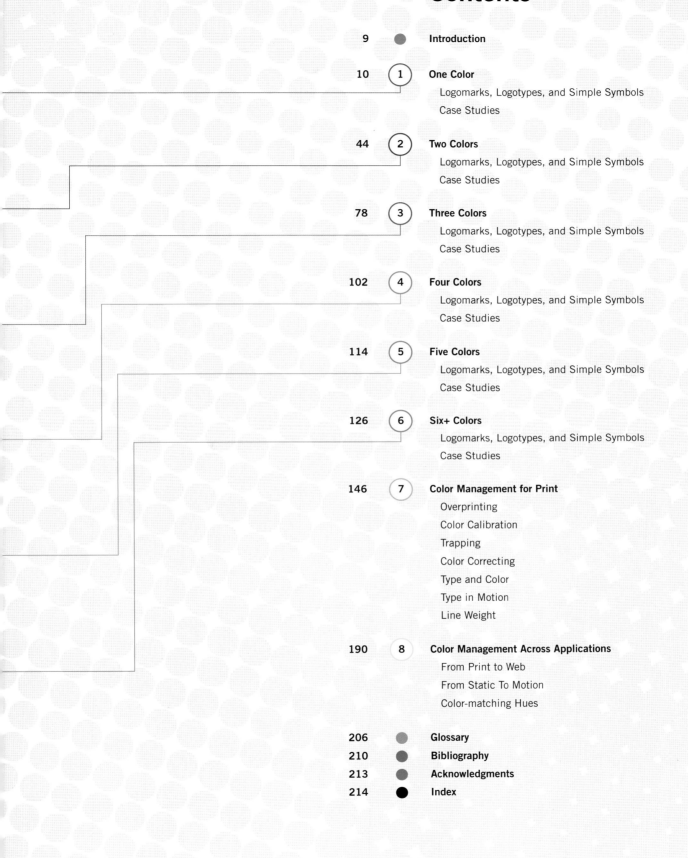

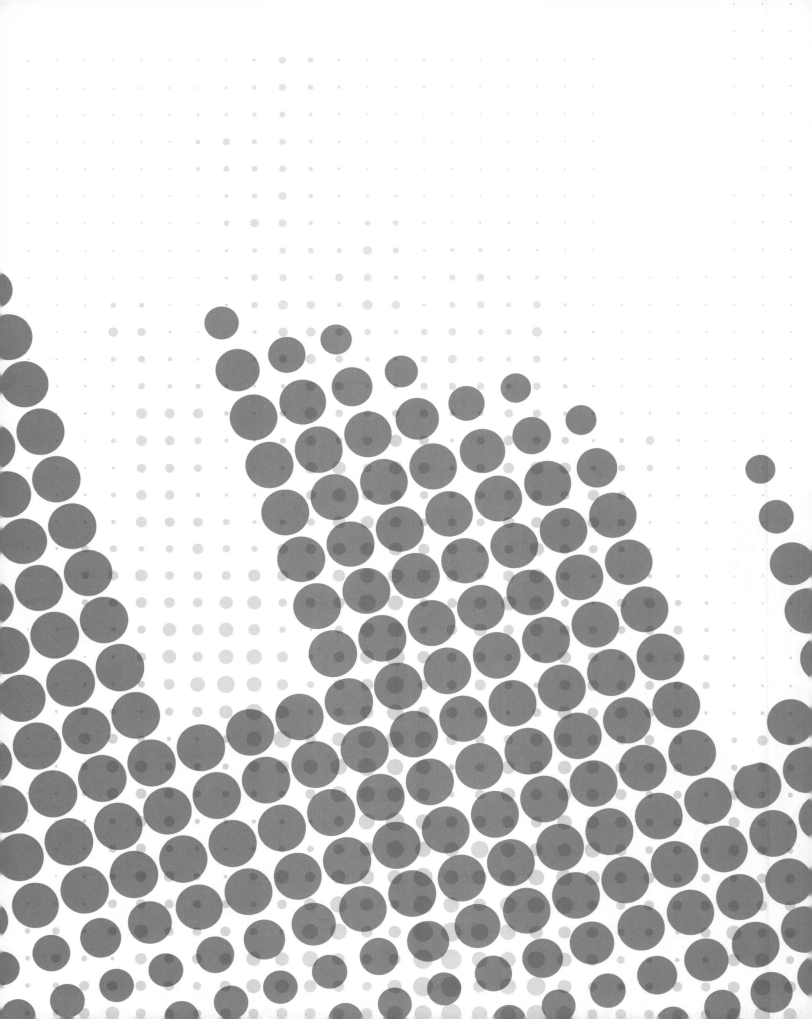

Introduction

In 1990, we set out to answer a simple question: "Does color have an effect on readability/legibility and, if so, can it be measured?" The answer is yes. Through our research, we also found that color has psychological/learned behavioral effects associated with its use. The bibliography sums up the path we have taken over the last 16 years in conducting our research. We have compiled an enormous amount of data from diverse fields in order to answer the question. The bibliography for this book was also used for our previous title, *Color Management: A Comprehensive Guide for Graphic Designers* (RotoVision, 2005).

The dynamics of practical color use are intrinsic to the process of solving a graphic design problem. Without color, the marks that humankind creates go unnoticed. Logos and the shapes they take are an important aspect of a given outcome, but color is the force that holds the mark together and engages and transfixes the viewer over diverse applications.

Color sells a product. It has both physical shape and psychological/learned behavioral attributes that can communicate well beyond the size, shape, and scope of the mark. Color has the ability to transform and translate meaningful messages so that responses can be measured.

Color Management for Logos is a unique body of consolidated information that demonstrates both pragmatic and technical color issues involved in logo design today, including how to display marks in subtractive, additive, and 3-D color space for rendering. Through the use of more than 1,000 visually stimulating logomarks, showcased in print-based, motion, environmental, and interactive graphics, *Color Management for Logos* gives the reader technical know-how, as well as inspiration for logo design. These inspirational marks are placed in context through analysis of the design problem solved, the brand represented, and the application of the system and identity over diverse media.

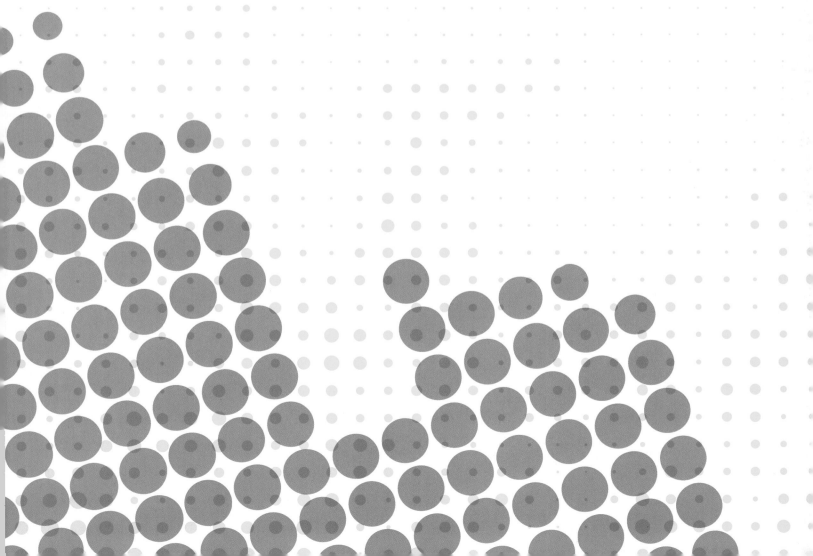

1 One Color

The world's best logomarks, logotypes, and simple symbols are designed first as a one-color mark. Color sells a product. The term "one-color mark" may seem like an oxymoron, but think of it as a matter of versatility. Logos should work in any given situation, whether being transmitted by fax or being seen on the Web. From the initial sketch to the finished mark, versatility must always be a primary objective. The logo objectives should be applied not only to color, shape, form, tone, and texture, but also to the context for branding purposes. Objectives should include any foreseen and unforeseen budgetary constraints.

It is a tall order to predict how a mark will be used in the future, but logomarks, logotypes, and simple symbols have longevity like no other graphic-design product. If designed correctly, a mark will stand the test of time. Through careful observation, research, and knowledge of color management, a logo created today can be passed down from generation to generation, no matter the business or corporation.

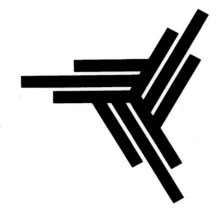

United African Companies
Studio: Essex Two

Associative Color Response:
· prestigious, strong: black

Color Scheme: one hue

In this logomark, a modular system consisting of three shapes that are rotated and repeated three times is an excellent way of constructing a mark with a corporate feel.

The Mazing Show
Designer: Art Chantry

Associative Color Response:
· percussive, expressive: black

Color Scheme: one hue

This expressive logotype is carried out through the manipulation of font, the constellation of letterforms, and the choice of typeface. These three factors combined add up to a playfully expressive mark. In most cases the look and feel of a logotype is established by the font/fonts used—font choice is almost always the primary signifier.

Estrus Records 1
Designer: Art Chantry

Associative Color Response:
· strong, powerful: black

Color Scheme: one hue

The typographic manipulation of this logotype is a metaphor to depict the meaning of estrus (being sexually excited and the ability to conceive). This is brought about through the expanded capital letterform "E" and the upward angle of the mark. The outlined letterform "E" operates both as male and female.

G Force Snowboards
Designer: Art Chantry

Associative Color Response:
· heavy, basic: black

Color Scheme: one hue

Here the interplay between font, texture, and placement creates a dynamic mark that is carried out through simile. Note how the letterforms in "force" progressively collide into and overlap each another. The texture found in the mark creates motion from left to right.

Mudhoney
Designer: Art Chantry

Associative Color Response:
· mysterious: black

Color Scheme: one hue

The manipulation of font and placement creates an energetic mark that represents a crazed madness. Today any letterform or font can be converted into vector art. This ability gives designers tremendous flexibility to create logotypes that are unique and relate to the subject matter.

Smash Hits
Designer: Art Chantry

Associative Color Response:
· anger, fear, nightmares: black

Color Scheme: one hue

The manipulation of letterforms creates a simile-based metaphor that is both expressive and direct. In almost all cases, texture creates a visual magnet, pulling in the reader to discover additional content-based information.

EUROPE

MAMBOMANIA

Joe Junk
Designer/Illustrator: Lanny Sommese

Associative Color Response:
· powerful, mysterious: black

Color Scheme: one hue with gray tones—conveyed through line work

Substitution is one of the most powerful tools a designer can use to create an effective logomark or logotype. The scale at which substitution is used should relate directly to content. In this case, a huge amount of substitution is used in order to convey the idea of junk.

Hüsker Dü
Designer: Art Chantry

Associative Color Response:
· despairing, depressing: black

Color Scheme: one hue with gray tones—conveyed through line work

This simile-based manipulation is created through the use of texture and distortion. Texture is used, through line work, to create a mark in a downward direction, whereas distortion (overextending and compressing letterforms) is used to reinforce the concept.

Hugs/ReVital
Studio: Essex Two

Associative Color Response:
· winter: black

Color Scheme: one hue

Thickness of line is critical when constructing logomarks such as this. Too thin and the mark will fall apart when used at small sizes; too thick and the mark will look clumsy at any size. A logomark or logotype is as good as its weakest link, and in this case the line work will be the first to disappear at a distance. Test the mark to determine the smallest size it can be used without loss of line work. If the mark holds up at half an inch, it is good.

Europe
Designer: Art Chantry

Associative Color Response:
· cold, classic: black

Color Scheme: one hue

Having an excellent type library can lead to unique and appropriate content. Spending time at a university library or national archive may be out of fashion, but it is the most productive way of discovering forgotten typefaces. With today's technology, fonts that are not in current print can be rejuvenated through software applications such as Macromedia's Fontographer, or created into vector art.

TEGA 1
Designer: Tanya A. Ortega
Art Director: John T. Drew

Associative Color Response:
· pristine, pure: blue-green

Color scheme: one hue

The Tega logotype is an experimental design for a fly-fishing outfitting company. The loop of the "g" is extended horizontally to emulate a floating fly-fishing line, and a geometric shape is used to attach and compress the spatial arrangements within the latter half of the mark. This effective technique solidifies numerous letterforms into a cohesive whole.

Mambomania
Designer: Art Chantry

Associative Color Response:
· magical: black

Color scheme: one hue

The mambo, which Perez Prado originated in the late 1940s, is a Cuban dance similar to the rumba. Two halves—a forward and a backward step—define the basic pattern of the dance. The Mambomania logotype loosely reflects these steps, with the up and down balls indicating the rhythm of the dance. The cross bar of each capital letterform "A" is extended horizontally to indicate the side movement of a mambo dancer's hips. This retro logotype is truly kinetic.

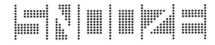

Savannah Hill

pure**burn**™

Loosenut Films
Designer: Art Chantry

Associative Color Response:
· heavy, solid: black

Color Scheme: one hue with shades of gray

The gray hues in this logomark are accomplished through a continuous-tone line screen. Only one ink is laid down on press, and gray is achieved through tinting (line screen). An irony-based metaphoric mark is accomplished through the formal execution of binary opposition.

Folklife Festival
Designer: Art Chantry

Associative Color Response:
· noble: black

Color Scheme: one hue

The Folklife Festival logotype is very kinetic. This is achieved by placing the logotype on an upward angle, using an italic typeface, and using a drop shadow to create a 3-D illusion on a 2-D plane. These three techniques add up to create a wonderfully executed mark.

Snooze
Designer: Savio Alphonso
Art Director: Theron Moore

Associative Color Response:
· spatial, mysterious: black

Color Scheme: one hue

The logotype consists of grouped circles that form the letters of the word Snooze. This makes the mark intriguing because the viewer has to decipher not only the form of the letters, but also the form of the word.

Savannah Hill
Designers: Kristin Sommese and Lanny Sommese
Studio: Sommese Design

Associative Color Response:
· soft, subdued, quiet: mid-range pink-red

Color Scheme: one hue with shading

This elegant logomark is beautifully executed through the use of a reductive illustration reinforced with texture. In most cases, quality marks are reduced to the essential elements needed to communicate. An overly complicated mark leads to ambiguity, confusion, and an overall lack of interest. There are exceptions to this rule, however. In this case, the mark is beautifully reduced to the essential elements to create a superior mark.

WF
Designer: Shiho Mizuno
Art Director: John T. Drew

Associative Color Response:
· mature growth, nature: dark green

Color Scheme: one hue

Economy of line coupled with gestalt (i.e., the whole is greater than its parts) often creates a mark that has intrigue and interest. Analyzing the structure of the letterforms creating the logotype yields insight into how individual parts can be manipulated and/or eliminated to create intrigue. This allows the audience to engage with the mark through their imagination and fill in the rest of the story.

Roxio: Pure Burn
Designer: Stefan G. Bucher
Studio: 344

Associative Color Response:
· dark, death, powerful: black

Color Scheme: one hue

This simple logomark is well executed through the duplication and multiple perspectives. A formal technique celebrated by Cubist artists, and popularized by the likes of Picasso, multiple perspectives add intrigue and uniqueness to a mark.

Kowalgo Holding Co.
Designer: Art Chantry

Associative Color Response:
· powerful: black

Color Scheme: one hue

The boldness of this mark coupled with a sans-serif letterform makes a logo that can be used at any size. This mark could be reduced down to the size of a pencil eraser or smaller and still stay visually intact. This is achieved by an acute awareness of the form/counterform relationships found within the mark.

Moe
Designer: Art Chantry

Associative Color Response:
· life, basic: black

Color Scheme: one hue

The hand-rendered letterforms of the Moe logotype embody uniqueness unsurpassed by any type-foundry font. The kinetic energy achieved through hand rendering is superb; this is an excellent technique to create variation and stylistic differences.

Serious Robots
Designer/Art Director: Scott Pridgen

Associative Color Response:
· forces, military: mid-green

Color Scheme: one hue

Choosing the right color for a logomark or logotype is as important as the shape or typefaces used. This logotype is divided into two parts, opposing stillness with motion. This duality creates a kinetic mark by juxtaposing an object that is static with one that appears to be moving. Motion is achieved by the choice of font and the italic cut of this font.

Enovation Computers
Designer: Pelying Li
Art Director: John T. Drew

Associative Color Response:
· lively, energetic: high-chroma blue

Color Scheme: one hue

A 3-D illusion on a 2-D plane is always a good starting point when creating a mark. The 3-D illusion opens up the active white space exponentially, fooling the eye into believing that it can not only move from side to side but also move in, out, through, and around an object. A 3-D illusion works best when juxtaposed with a 2-D object (flat)—in this example, the name of the company.

Glen Moore
Designer: Art Chantry

Associative Color Response:
· spatial, percussion: black

Color Scheme: one hue

Creating a logotype by hand (i.e., off the computer), is as important today as it has ever been. The uniqueness of form often cannot be achieved through a filter or set action found within contemporary graphic design applications. Constant experimentation with the physicality of form, both on and off the computer, is the only way to master it.

Meet Market
Designer/Art Director: Scott Pridgen

Associative Color Response:
· intense, aggressive: high-chroma red

Color Scheme: one hue

The Meet Market logomark uses texture in a highly interesting way. Texture is used both as an indexical reference and as a visual magnet to draw attention to itself. The color red is also used in an indexical manner, to indicate a butcher's seal and to reference red meat.

FARISI

TERRAVIDA COFFEE

ORIVO

burma

Farisi 1
Designer: Saied Farisi

Associative Color Response:
· exhilarating, stimulating: dark orange

Color Scheme: one hue

The fluidity of line and kinetic energy of this logotype are achieved through the thick and thin relationships. This is an excellent hand-rendered technique for creating logomarks or logotypes, and is particularly effective when coupled with an appropriate choice of color.

Via 101
Studio: AdamsMorioka

Associative Color Response:
· powerful, heavy: black

Color Scheme: one hue

The Via 101 logotype is a simplistic mark that is anatomically conceived so that the logo can be used at any size. This true monoweight typeface is an excellent specimen for viewing at a distance. The letterforms and line weight are exactly the same thickness, creating only one visual angle. If a typeface that has thick and thin relationships is used, multiple visual angles will be created; this means that different parts of the typographic anatomy will disappear at different distances.

TerraVida Coffee
Studio: Hornall Anderson Design Works

Associative Color Response:
· basic: black

Color Scheme: one hue with tinting (created by a textural halftone screen)

The TerraVida Coffee logotype uses substitution and texture. Substitution is used within the "A" and "V" of TerraVida (coffee leaves). The scale of substitution is subdued in comparison with many of the other marks found within this book. The texture symbolizes the caffeine "buzz" associated with drinking coffee, and resembles the burlap sacks used to ship coffee beans.

Orivo
Studio: Hornall Anderson Design Works

Associative Color Response:
· powerful, heavy, strong: rust brown

Color Scheme: one hue

A weight change within a logotype can create an excellent focal point, engender movement, and demonstrate how a company's name should be pronounced.

Canestaro
Designer: Javier Cortes

Associative Color Response:
· classic, invulnerable: red

Color Scheme: one hue

The classically formal relationships and symbolism used within this mark communicate longevity. In some cases, it is best to have a logomark that is purposely designed to look as though it has been around for decades. In this context, age equates to the quality of the food and the profitability of the business.

Burma
Designer: Art Chantry

Associative Color Response:
· cold, classic: black

Color Scheme: one hue

A unique logotype can be created by hand manipulation, by vector manipulation, or by using an unusual font—and this is the case with the Burma mark. The extension of many of the anatomical parts found within the logotype creates an unusual composition—meant to resemble the Myanmar (Burmese) script—that is eloquently defined.

Sommese Design
Designers/Art Directors: Kristin Sommese and Lanny Sommese
Studio: Sommese Design

Associative Color Response:
· stimulating: high-chroma red

Color Scheme: one hue

The Sommese Design mark was created to represent the two partners of this design firm—a husband-and-wife partnership. The logomark represents the concept of putting two heads together to produce shocking results. The color red was used to reinforce this idea.

Co Architects
Studio: AdamsMorioka

Associative Color Response:
· dignity, mature: high-chroma blue

Color Scheme: one hue

Varying the weight distribution within this logotype places emphasis on "Co" over "Architects"—an excellent technique to emulate the inflections found within speech patterns. The use of capital letterforms gives the appearance of a stable environment. This, coupled with the choice of color, reinforces the idea of a dignified and mature business.

Union
Designer: Mark Raebel
Studio: Arsenal Design

Associative Color Response:
· magical: black

Color Scheme: one hue

This intriguing logomark uses repetition to represent the idea of union. The circle/ball, located in the center of the mark, has two reflection points that have two ovals rotating around it. This is enclosed by a white square surrounded by a black one. Typographically, the word "union" is repeated twice horizontally and twice vertically. Repetition coupled with pattern or sequence is an excellent technique for uniting and solidifying marks.

Yujin Ono 1
Designer: Yujin Ono
Art Director: John T. Drew

Associative Color Response:
· security, service: dark blue

Color Scheme: one hue

Reducing a logomark to its essential elements is an effective technique for creating quality marks. In most cases, a highly reductive mark will engage the viewer by virtue of gestalt, suggestion, and the viewer's imagination. In this case, the human form is highly active, communicated through four simple shapes. The line work has a severe thick-and-thin relationship to help create a 3-D illusion on a 2-D plane—this adds to the perceived activity.

Yujin Ono 2
Designer: Yujin Ono
Art Director: John T. Drew

Associative Color Response:
· mature growth: dark green

Color Scheme: one hue

Repetition of form is an excellent way to create a logomark. In the Ono mark, one basic shape is repeated to form Yujin's last name. This gives continuity and consistency to the structure of the mark, which is reinforced by the use of one color.

7-Year Bitch
Designer: Art Chantry

Associative Color Response:
· expensive: black

Color Scheme: one hue

This Art Chantry mark parodies the expression "seven-year itch." This humorous mark is unusual because of the number of signifiers used to communicate the concept (seven). Substitution is used (flames in place of hair) to communicate desire; an empty martini glass to signify being impaired; a young naked woman to communicate both desire and past youth; a ribbon to communicate a trophy; "7-year bitch" to signify being married; and the swirling line work and bubbles to communicate being drunk. This number of signifiers is extremely hard to control, but Art Chantry has done a masterful job.

Western Coffee Shop
Designer: Art Chantry

Associative Color Response:
· distant: black

Color Scheme: one hue

The Western Coffee Shop logotype is an excellent example of a 3-D mark. This is carried out through repetition of form and two-point perspective. The 3-D illusion is amplified by juxtaposing "Western" (3-D) against "Coffee Shop" (flat).

Oktoberfest
Designer: Art Chantry

Associative Color Response:
· powerful, heavy: black

Color Scheme: one hue

The Oktoberfest logomark uses an interesting visual hierarchy. The three figures within the mark are monoweight, bold graphics, and are meant to be seen first. The typography found in the mark is a tertiary element that at a distance, or when used at smaller sizes (less than 1 inch), will collapse on itself, becoming unreadable. This is caused by the small number of counterforms found within the selected font.

Pitch and Groove Records
Designer: Art Chantry

Associative Color Response:
· mysterious, heavy: black

Color Scheme: one hue

Using multiple perspectives is an interesting formal technique to create intrigue within 3-D logomarks. In the Punch and Groove logomark, these perspectives juxtaposed with one another create an unorthodox coexistence.

Gartal
Designer/Art Director: Saied Farisi

Associative Color Response:
· rich, elegant: dark red

Color Scheme: one hue

This interesting logomark is an excellent example of a harmonious relationship between the mark and typeface chosen. When creating a congruous relationship between two elements, harmony is achieved through formal likeness. Note the thick-and-thin relationships, sharpness, and crispness of line, similarity of arcs, and repetition of form.

Penn State Jazz Club 1
Designer: Kristin Sommese
Art Director/Illustrator: Lanny Sommese
Studio: Sommese Design

Associative Color Response:
· mysterious, magical: black

Color Scheme: one hue

This playful logomark is a superb example of the interplay between form and counterform. By using simile-substitution, a lively and energetic mark that symbolizes the freedom of jazz is created.

Búho
Designer: Carlo Irgoyen
Art Director: John T. Drew

Associative Color Response:
· powerful, elegant: black

Color Scheme: one hue

In the Búho logomark, Carlo Irgoyen uses sequential repetition of form to create a simplistically beautiful mark. Repetition of form creates visual consistency.

Watts
Designer: Art Chantry

Associative Color Response:
· basic, strong: black

Color Scheme: one hue

In this unusual logotype, distressing is created through the use of repetition; the forms lose their integrity of shape as they are repeated. Kinetic energy is achieved by placing the repeated forms at different intervals; this erratic movement amplifies the grittiness of the mark.

Tough Stuff
Designer: Art Chantry

Associative Color Response:
· powerful, strong: black

Color Scheme: one hue

In the Tough Stuff mark, simile is used within the letterforms of "Stuff" to communicate the meaning of the mark. If all the letterforms had been knocked off the pre-existing horizontal plane, the mark would not be a simile, nor would it communicate the meaning. Opposition is used to create the simile; radically placed type—"STU" is juxtaposed with stationary type—"FF."

One Louder Records
Designer: Art Chantry

Associative Color Response:
· invulnerable: black

Color Scheme: one hue

In today's design environment, it is easy to jump on the computer to generate a design solution. However, uniqueness of form is most often carried out by hand. Understanding the physicality of form and how to generate it in many diverse media will enrich the ultimate solution.

Modular system logo
Designer: Songlin Wu
Art Director: John T. Drew

Associative Color Response:
· strong, invulnerable: black

Color Scheme: one hue

This modular system mark creates consistent kinetic energy by repeating and rotating the wedge shape clockwise three times.

Saint Patrick's Massacre
Designer: Mark Raebel
Studio: Arsenal Design

Associative Color Response:
· Saint Patrick's Day: high-chroma green

Color Scheme: one hue

In the Saint Patrick's Massacre logomark, symbolism is used (the sword and pierced clover) to communicate the concept. Icon, symbol, and index are excellent tools for designers to help generate an image bank of reference material for any job, especially marks.

Estrus Records 2
Designer: Art Chantry

Associative Color Response:
· basic, cold, classic: black

Color Scheme: one hue

In the E-snail logomark, xerography is used to create the distressed quality of line. This method of working was commonplace prior to the computer age, and is making a comeback today. In fact, any type of texture that can be created off the computer and then scanned in is an excellent method for distressing objects. The problem with most software filters is that they look unnatural; they tend to say "I was done on the computer" and therefore override content.

The Drags
Designer: Art Chantry

Associative Color Response:
· cold, classic: black

Color Scheme: one hue

In all software applications used by graphic designers there are canned techniques that are commonplace and trite. Drop shadows are one of the most common (I have seen a few billion in my lifetime), and if used in a stereotypical manner yield sophomoric results. If you are going to use a common technique, use it in an unusual way, as Art Chantry has for this logotype.

Ent
Designer: Francisco Ortiz
Art Director: John T. Drew

Associative Color Response:
· expensive: black

Color Scheme: one hue

When creating logotypes such as the Ent mark, the line width, when reduced to its smallest size, should not exceed .25pt for sheet-fed offset printing, and .33pt for web-fed offset printing. Dropout may occur if the line work is thinner than these specifications. For commercial silkscreen printing, the line weight should be set no thinner than .5pt.

Non
Designer: Carlo Irgoyen
Art Director: John T. Drew

Associative Color Response:
· dignity, pleasing: high-chroma blue

Color Scheme: one hue

This classically constructed logotype is pleasing to the eye and uses economy of line to construct the mark. Both the left and right stroke of the capital letterform "O" is also used for the right and left hairline stroke of the capital letterform "N" on either side of the "O." If done correctly, this kind of logotype engages the reader by asking them to use their imagination.

BSK T Big Bash
Designer: Art Chantry

Associative Color Response:
· heavy: black

Color Scheme: one hue

This psychedelic logotype is, at its core, a modular system. Twelve rectangular shapes with rounded corners are used to construct the basic mark. A "," mark is used to create the counterforms within each rectangular shape. By doing so, letterforms are created that give the mark its psychedelic look. By building a logotype in this manner, visual consistency is assured—the key component to the success of this mark.

Slowboy Records
Designer: Art Chantry

Associative Color Response:
· magical: black

Color Scheme: one hue

This wonderfully humorous logomark is anatomically organized. The shape of the boy's head is a vertical structure that harmonizes with the condensed letterforms. The overlapping of image and type just behind the ears makes them stand out, and adds to the lighthearted nature of this mark.

The Capitol Club
Designer: Art Chantry

Associative Color Response:
· strong: black

Color Scheme: one hue

This logomark uses condensed letterforms to reinforce the idea, through simile (vertical columns), of the word "capitol." This substitution is quite abstract, but aids in the construction of the mark. When using substitution, the scale in which it can be used and the level of abstraction (on a scale from obvious to obscure) make up the inflections found within each individual mark.

Hoot Nite
Designer: Art Chantry

Associative Color Response:
· noble, night: black

Color Scheme: one hue

This mark demonstrates how a reductive illustration can be used to create logos. The way in which the mouth is illustrated, and the placement of the box for "hoot night," helps to convey its humorous demeanor.

Chuckie-Boy Records
Designer: Art Chantry

Associative Color Response:
· mysterious: black

Color Scheme: one hue

This logomark was designed for Chuckie-Boy Records, an alternative record company based in Seattle, Washington. In most cases, creating an anatomically correct illustration yields boring results. The basic inflection of any illustration is brought to bear through the push and pull of line work.

Deck
Designer: Brendan Cosgrove
Art Director: John T. Drew

Associative Color Response:
· authoritative, credible: dark blue

Color Scheme: one hue

The logotype Deck, designed by Brendan Cosgrove, is an excellent example of gestalt. This is a highly effective technique for engaging the audience—viewers must use their imagination to fill in the rest of the information.

Rez
Designer: Savio Alphonso

Associative Color Response:
· heavy, basic: black

Color Scheme: one hue

The Rez logotype is a visual metaphor of its meaning—a denotative mark that is superbly executed. Looking up the definition of a word that directly or indirectly relates to the subject is an excellent method for conceptual direction. Many words found within the dictionary have seven or eight definitions, each of which can act as a conceptual primer to foster a visual outcome.

Mass
Designer: Carlo Irgoyen
Art Director: Theron Moore

Associative Color Response:
· strength, sober: high-chroma blue

Color Scheme: one hue

The choice of typeface is outstanding to fit the content and meaning of the logotype. A typographic portrait of "Mass," this mark is beautifully conceived.

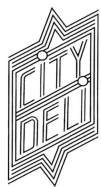

Rhubärb Pharmaceuticals
Designer: Tarun Deep Girdher

Associative Color Response:
· strength, sober: high-chroma blue

Color Scheme: one hue

This dignified logomark creates a pleasing, mature, and provoking statement. Sobering in its execution, the stair-step arrangement creates a counterbalance relationship activating the visual hierarchy.

City Deli
Designer/Art Director/Illustrator:
Lanny Sommese
Studio: Sommese Design

Associative Color Response:
· elegant: black

Color Scheme: one hue

The line work found within this mark, coupled with the choice of color, creates a beautiful and elegant mark that is cohesive and visually consistent. Skewing the mark activates the kinetic energy upward.

Gateway Medical
Designer/Illustrator/Art Director:
Lanny Sommese
Studio: Sommese Design

Associative Color Response:
· elegant, prestigious: black

Color Scheme: one hue

This masterfully executed mark incorporates a wonderful 3-D illusion. When creating an outlined mark, logomark, or logotype, it is important to consider the line width. The minimum line width is .25pt for sheet-fed lithography, .33pt for web-fed lithography, and .5pt for commercial silkscreen printing.

Black Panther
Designer/Illustrator: Lanny Sommese
Art Director: Kristin Sommese
Studio: Sommese Design

Associative Color Response:
· spatial, prestigious: black

Color Scheme: one hue

In general, creating illustrative logomarks that have kinetic energy requires that the illustration not be photorealistic. As seen here, creating a mark that is lively and energetic requires exaggeration of form.

i-Copack
Designer: Linda Liejard

Associative Color Response:
· devotion, credible: dark blue

Color Scheme: one hue

The i-Copack logomark is an excellent example of a reductive mark. The qualitative measure of a mark is directly related to the designer. Understanding the skill sets one possesses is critical in matching the stylistic treatment needed to produce quality.

Estrus Records 3
Designer: Art Chantry

Associative Color Response:
· night, life: black

Color Scheme: one hue

As shown in the Estrus Records logomark, the thickness of line work is excellent for presenting the mark at smaller sizes. When creating a mark that has line work, test the mark by printing the logo as small as it will go. If the line work falls apart prior to the mark being half an inch, the thickness of line will need to be increased.

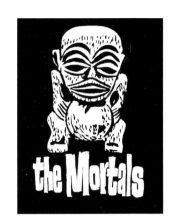

bossa:nova
Designer: Stefan G. Bucher
Studio: 334

Associative Color Response:
· basic: black

Color Scheme: one hue

The bossa:nova logomark is a superb example of harmonizing the typeface chosen with the mark created. Note how all anatomical parts within the mark have a curvilinear basis and how this relates to the structure of the typeface, including the width to spatial arrangements.

Unit G Design
Designer: Tanya A. Ortega

Associative Color Response:
· heavy: black

Color Scheme: one hue

This wonderful logotype is an excellent example of joining two dissimilar letterforms into a cohesive whole. This is solidified by the interplay between the loop of the lowercase "g" and the stroke of the lowercase "u"—the loop of the "g" looks as though it is wrapping its leg around the upper ankle of the "u."

The Holidays: Seattle
Designer: Art Chantry

Associative Color Response:
· powerful: black

Color Scheme: one hue

In this example, the typeface chosen harmonizes superbly with the illustrative mark. Note how the ears and left side of the cat have the same basic wedge shapes as the forms and counterforms found within the font.

Homo Habilis Records
Designer: Art Chantry

Associative Color Response:
· school: black

Color Scheme: one hue

Adding line work often helps to create kinetic energy to a mark.

The Mortals
Designer: Art Chantry

Associative Color Response:
· basic, heavy, powerful: black

Color Scheme: one hue

Harmonizing the typeface with the mark helps to create a cohesive logo that will stand the test of time. No matter how crudely the image is drawn, if the underpinning structure is sound the quality of the mark will be apparent to the viewer.

Estrus Records 4
Designer: Art Chantry

Associative Color Response:
· heavy: black

Color Scheme: one hue

Creating harmony through a perceived action creates unity of form. Note how the person is leaning on the six round balls, pushing the letterforms to become italic.

Arlington International Festival of Racing
Studio: Essex Two

Associative Color Response:
· prestigious: black

Color Scheme: one hue

Gestalt is one of the most effective techniques for logo design.

The Who
Studio: Essex Two

Associative Color Response:
· basic, powerful: black

Color Scheme: one hue

The Who logotype is an outstanding example of hand-rendered typography. Hand-rendered typography can create a unique form, resulting in a mark of merit.

Ace Chain Link Fence
Studio: Essex Two

Associative Color Response:
· strong: black

Color Scheme: one hue

In the A logotype, the underpinning structure of the mark is symmetrical, making the interlocking forms the focal point. If the line work that created the "A" were asymmetrical, the emphasis and hierarchy would change, thereby diminishing the importance of the interlocking shape.

447
Studio: Essex Two

Associative Color Response:
· heavy, strong: black

Color Scheme: one hue

The form/counterform relationship, coupled with the gestalt aspects within this logotype, is quite amazing. Placement of form plays an important role in understanding the spatial arrangement so that gestalt can take place effectively.

Szechwan
Studio: modern8

Associative Color Response:
· heavy, strong: red

Color Scheme: one hue

Texture plays an important role in understanding and navigating our environment. No matter how slight, texture acts as a visual magnet.

Urban Shopping Center
Studio: Essex Two

Associative Color Response:
· basic, invulnerable: black

Color Scheme: one hue

Substitution is a tried and true technique for developing effective logomarks, and this case is no exception. Note how the simile of form helps to create a cohesive mark.

Jessica L. Howard
Designer: Jessica L. Howard
Art Director: John T. Drew

Associative Color Response:
· lively, pleasing: high-chroma blue

Color Scheme: one hue

In this asymmetrical logomark, note how the line work seems fluent and natural. This is achieved by devising a measuring stick (a nonstandardized ruler) made from the most common spatial arrangement found within the original mark. This unit of measurement is then subdivided to create a unique ruler to examine and adjust the spatial arrangements. If used correctly, this ruler ensures quality of form/counterform relationships.

First Health
Studio: Essex Two

Associative Color Response:
· heavy, expensive: black

Color Scheme: one hue

When using a commonly recognized symbol, it is best to execute it in a unique way so that the mark does not look trite. In this case, the bottom-right part of the heart is shifted to create a tangent point. This allows the eye to move in and out of the mark, creating interest.

Thunk
Designer: Art Chantry

Associative Color Response:
· basic: black

Color Scheme: one hue

Repetition of form coupled with texture and off-registration creates a wonderfully kinetic mark. Note how the outline surrounding the mark is incomplete (degraded and disfigured), allowing the eye to pass freely in and out of the mark—this adds to the kinetic energy.

Crafted With Pride In U.S.A.
Studio: Essex Two

Associative Color Response:
· basic, elegant: black

Color Scheme: one hue

In almost every case, creating a modular system to generate a mark will yield a corporate look. The mark (star) is created by using three lines of the same thickness. The three lines are shortened by the same degree, and then rotated to form the star. The more consistency applied within the underpinning structure, the cleaner the mark will look.

Procter & Gamble: Spanish
Studio: Essex Two

Associative Color Response:
· basic, powerful, heavy: black

Color Scheme: one hue

In the square sun logomark, repetition of line coupled with scale is used to create agitation within the mark, imparting visual interest.

TAD
Designer: Art Chantry

Associative Color Response:
· powerful, basic, heavy: black

Color Scheme: one hue

This logotype, created through the process of xerography, is an excellent example of texture creating visual interest. To create a line quality that is degraded, adjust the toner setting and dramatically scale the image up and down when copying.

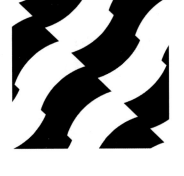

centraal
museum

wereldwijd
worldwide

Fat Rooster 1
Designer: Brenda Cox
Art Director: John T. Drew

Associative Color Response:

· serene, quiet, authoritative,
credible, devotion, security,
service, classic, conservative,
strong, dependable, traditional,
informed, professional: dark blue
· producing, healing, tasty, growing,
fire, warm, cleanliness, happy,
cheerfulness, childlike, sunrise,
harvest, friendly, loud, pride,
wholehearted: high-chroma orange

Color Scheme: one hue

Color plays an invaluable role in
the meaning, interpretation, and
physicality of form. Through the
use of different hues a mark can be
reinterpreted for specific needs.

Color has a direct bearing on the
distance at which an object can be
seen. The dark-blue hue is more
visible at a distance than the red
and orange hues. In fact, the dark
blue is 20% more visible than the
orange hue in average daylight.
(Dark blue: 79.63; high-chroma red
75.72; high-chroma orange 57.71;
these numbers are calculated from
white, white being 100.) This may
not seem that great a difference.
However, as the viewing distance
increases so does the viewing gap
between hues. For example, at 100
yards an object can be seen in the
dark-blue hue, and if the object was
the same size in all respects other
than its hue (orange) the object
would only be seen from a distance
of up to 80 yards.

Fat Rooster
Designer: Brenda Cox
Art Director: John T. Drew

Associative Color Response:

· brilliant, intense, energizing, sexy,
dramatic, stimulating, active,
cheer, joy, fun, aggressive, hope,
powerful, warm, overflowing,
compassion, heat, hot, fire: high-
chroma red

Color Scheme: one hue

Kristin
Designer: Irene Marx

Associative Color Response:

· exhilarating, inspiring, provoking:
dark orange

Color Scheme: one hue

This asymmetrical mark is an
excellent example of positioning the
focal points, in a triadic relationship,
so that the eye is drawn completely
through the mark. The hand and feet
act as focal points, each performing
as one of the three corners within
the triad.

Kleinpeter
Designer: John R. Kleinpeter
Art Director: John T. Drew

Associative Color Response:

· strong, invulnerable: black

Color Scheme: one hue

This modular-system logomark is
achieved using a single shape. The
shape is flipped and spaced apart
using the same form, creating an
energetic and consistent mark.

**Centraal Museum: Wereldwijd
Worldwide 1**
Studio: Thonik

Associative Color Response:

· energetic, cheery: high-chroma red

Color Scheme: one hue

The Centraal Museum logotype/mark
is created through a modular
system, the letterform "c." Stepping
and repeating the letterforms
achieve visual consistency within
the mark. A reductive human figure
is created by adapting the logotype
into the mark. Note that the line work
that makes up the arms, legs, and
torso are visually consistent with the
stroke width of the letterform "c."

Engeman's Dream Works
Designer: Tom Engeman

Associative Color Response:
· powerful, basic, heavy: black

Color Scheme: one hue

Anytime a continuous-tone image is used within the logomark, a coarse halftone screen is advised. The Dreamworks logomark is an excellent example.

CMP
Studio: BBK Studio

Associative Color Response:
· cheerful: orange
· pure: blue
· fresh: green

Color Scheme: one hue

In the CMP logomark, opposition (thick to thin) is utilized to create visual intrigue.

Wildlife Center of Silicon Valley
Designer: Erika Kim

Associative Color Response:
· life, wilderness, outdoorsy: high-chroma green

Color Scheme: one hue

Inspired by the yin and yang symbol, this interwoven logomark is beautifully executed. Taking advantage of the white space found within the mark, substitution was applied to enrich content. The high-chroma green is an excellent color choice for the content (an animal rescue center).

Quirk
Designer: John Malinoski

Associative Color Response:
· youthful, exhilaration: high-chroma yellow

Color Scheme: one hue

This simile-based mark is an outstanding example of manipulating typography to suit content.

Arch
Designer: Justin Deister

Associative Color Response:
· youthful, exhilaration: high-chroma red-orange

Color Scheme: one hue

The oppositional duality presented in this mark creates an interesting juxtaposition. This complex concept is compressed into two images that are arranged by a distorted use of scale. The building is small and the flame is large—a clever use of opposition.

Nijntje
Studio: Thonik

Associative Color Response:
· cheerfulness, energizing: high-chroma orange

Color Scheme: one hue

This simplistic yet exciting logomark is an excellent example of line work that is coupled with appropriate execution of form to create an extremely legible mark.

APS Corporation
Designer: Linda Liejard

Associative Color Response:
· mature growth: dark green

Color Scheme: one hue

The APS logomark is a wonderful example of a 3-D mark using a modular system. The two-point perspective is flawlessly executed, making the illusion believable.

Zango
Studio: Hornall Anderson Design Works

Associative Color Response:
· energizing: High-chroma orange

Color Scheme: one hue

In the Zango logotype, the loop of the "g" is manipulated to imply a springlike action. This mark is incredible, especially when applied to colorful, high-chroma collateral materials. The upbeat, high-chroma-orange hue is an excellent choice to reinforce the liveliness of the mark.

Hanyang University Design Gallery
Designer: Inyoung Choi

Associative Color Response:
· dignity, dramatic: high-chroma orange

Color Scheme: one hue

The University Design Gallery logotype uses pictograms combined with geometric shapes to communicate the content of the subject matter. The high-chroma blue reinforces the prestige of the gallery.

Center for Design
Designer: Inyoung Choi

Associative Color Response:
· regal, classic, powerful: high-chroma blue-purple

Color Scheme: one hue

This modular mark is an excellent example of how to create kinetic energy within a logo. The modular unit is stepped, rotated, and repeated to create a cohesive whole. Each element is designed in a progressive manner to create a thick-to-thin relationship that fosters movement within the eye of the viewer.

Plastic Soldier Factory
Studio: Plastic Soldier Factory Pte Ltd
Designer: Audrey Koh

Associative Color Response:
· restrained, toned-down, soft, subdued, quiet, sentimental, sober, tame, domestic: mid-range pink-red
· pristine, pure, serious, cleanliness, pensive, tranquillity, lively, mellow, cheerful, clarity, consistent, great strength: blue-green

Color Scheme: one hue

This universal identity system is executed through a modular system to ensure consistency of shape and line. Although some of the psychological responses to the hues used may not seem to be appropriate for the subject matter, using high-chroma colors ensures a high level of perceived activity by the reader.

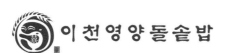

Cho-Ichon Restaurant
Designer: Inyoung Choi

Associative Color Response:
· rich, elegant, refined: dark red

Color Scheme: one hue

The dark red (burgundy) hue chosen
for this mark is reminiscent of hot
wax, and is an excellent choice—
the mark is designed as though
it is a royal seal.

Hanyang Music Research Center 1
Designer: Inyoung Choi

Associative Color Response:
· elegant, noble: black

Color Scheme: one hue

The mark design for the Hanyang
Music Research Center uses
repetition, fluidity, and 3-D aspects
within the line work to create a
beautifully executed mark that
connects to the subject matter.

Hanyang Music Research Center 2
Designer: Inyoung Choi

Associative Color Response:
· elegant, noble: black

Color Scheme: one hue

In this version of the logo for
Hanyang Music Research Center,
substitution is used effectively to
capture the spirit of the content.

Plastic Soldier Factory
Studio: Plastic Soldier Factory
Pte Ltd
Designer: Audrey Koh

Associative Color Response:
· energizing, communication,
  receptive, pride, dramatic, lively,
  exciting, bright, stimulating,
  aggressive: high-chroma orange/
  high-chroma red
· new growth, tart, fruity, acidic:
  high-chroma green-yellow

Color Scheme: one hue

This universal identity system is
executed through a modular system
to ensure consistency of shape
and line. Although some of the
psychological responses to the hues
used may not seem to be appropriate
for the subject matter, using high-
chroma colors ensures a high level of
perceived activity by the reader.

Island Sports

Island Sports
Designer: Mark Raebel
Studio: Arsenal Design

Associative Color Response:
· basic, magical: black

Color Scheme: one hue

A mascot or figurine is often an appropriate solution. In this case, the figurine has a retro feel, implying that the company has been around for decades.

Pottymouth
Studio: 86 The Onions

Associative Color Response:
· spiritual, basic: black

Color Scheme: one hue

If done correctly, texture is one of the most effective techniques to create interest. The Pottymouth logo uses three types of texture to create an interesting interplay between the mark and the typeface chosen.

Estrus Records 5
Designer: Art Chantry

Associative Color Response:
· basic: black

Color Scheme: one hue

The quality of line found in the Estrus mark is superbly executed—the mark can be reduced down to any size, and at the same time creates visual interest.

Urban Outfitters
Designer: Art Chantry

Associative Color Response:
· heavy: black

Color Scheme: one hue

The interaction of mark and typography creates an energetic logo. In this case, the italic font and the reversed type within the black bar create motion and weight that help to connect the object both formally and conceptually.

Washington State Economic Region 2
Designer: Art Chantry

Associative Color Response:
· basic: black

Color Scheme: one hue

The Region 2 mark uses a reductive illustration of a pinecone and arrowhead shield to communicate "forest"—an excellent example of using no more than two signifiers to communicate a message.

Washington State Economic Region No. 7
Designer: Art Chantry

Associative Color Response:
· basic: black

Color Scheme: one hue

The Region 7 mark also uses a reductive illustration to communicate "forest." This time, the illustration is executed in a retro style to give it the appearance of an older mark.

Holy Cow
Designer: Art Chantry

Associative Color Response:
· mysterious: black

Color Scheme: one hue

The Holy Cow mark, designed by Art Chantry, uses multiple perspectives (the double halo) to create an intriguing design.

Custom Shirt Shop
Designer: Art Chantry

Associative Color Response:
· elegant: black

Color Scheme: one hue

The Custom Shirt Shop logo uses a retro approach. The figure of the woman is positioned in such a way as to express innocence, to give the mark a fresh and clean appearance.

Brandu
Designer: Marnita Smith

Associative Color Response:
· invulnerable, heavy: gray

Color Scheme: one hue

The Brandu logotype uses texture to create visual interest. Note how all the textural elements found within the mark harmonize to help create a cohesive whole.

Newspaper section logo
Designer: Art Chantry

Associative Color Response:
· invulnerable, mysterious: black

Color Scheme: one hue

This logomark is an excellent example of matching the quality of line work to the illustration style and subject matter.

Willie Wear a Condom
Designer: Art Chantry

Associative Color Response:
· powerful: black

Color Scheme: one hue

The figurine of a condom coupled with the "blue ribbon" prize creates a humorous juxtaposition of type and image. Note the positioning of the rocket within the blue ribbon.

DeauxBoy Productions
Designer: Mike Paz

Associative Color Response:
· quality, classic, timeless: neutral gray

Color Scheme: one hue

When using a continuous-tone image for logos it is best to limit the amount of contrast within the image. By increasing the contrast and limiting the amount of tonal range, the mark will go through a fax machine faster—a more practical solution.

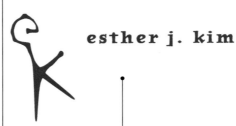

ir 1
Designer: Alex Prompongsatorn
Art Director: John T. Drew

Associative Color Response:
· refreshing, faithful, dependable:
  pastel blue

Color Scheme: one hue

To create more kinetic energy, place
the mark or letterform off-center.
This technique helps to create a
more dynamic, asymmetrical design.

Dot
Designer: Elle Osorio
Art Director: John T. Drew

Associative Color Response:
· heavy, strong: black

Color Scheme: one hue

Type reversals knocked out of solid
letterforms is an excellent technique
for creating uniqueness of form. The
form/counterform relationship found
within this logotype serves to create
a visual depiction of meaning (dot).

Sun Tzu Report
Designer: Chen Wang

Associative Color Response:
· timeless, pristine, further: neutral
  gray /blue-green

Color Scheme: one hue

This modular mark uses a step,
scale-down, and repeat pattern that
is copied and inverted.

Esther J. Kim
Designer: Esther J. Kim

Associative Color Response:
· elegant: violet

Color Scheme: one hue

The Esther Kim logotype uses
hand-drawn letterforms to create
the mark—an excellent formal
technique to create visual interest.

Photo Typo
Designer: Hiroyuki Matsuishi

Associative Color Response:
· elegant: black

Color Scheme: one hue

The hand-drawn letterforms in the
Photo Typo logotype are superbly
crafted. Note the thick and thin
relationships found within the
letterforms, and how accent marks
are utilized within the font—a
masterful job.

**California State Polytechnic
University, Pomona**
Designer: Deborah Lem
Art Director: Babette Mayer

Associative Color Response:
· powerful, elegant: black

Color Scheme: one hue

This logomark is a composite of two
indexical references found on the
university campus—a building and
orchards. If done correctly, this
is an excellent process to create
a logomark.

NATIONAL
ENDOWMENT
FOR THE ARTS

KASHOKAI

CEIS • College of Education and
Integrative Studies

Sonia Luque
Designer: Sonia Luque
Art Director John T. Drew

Associative Color Response:
· refreshing, faithful, happy: pastel
  blue

Color Scheme: one hue

Using the punctuation marks and
symbols found within a font is a
good technique for creating unique
solutions. Holding down the option
key while selecting the numbers
and letters on the keyboard will
access all punctuation and symbols
associated with the font.

**The National Endowment for
The Arts**
Designers: Tom Engeman, Ned Drew,
and Richard Crest

Associative Color Response:
· powerful, strong: black

Color Scheme: one hue

The National Endowment for The
Arts logomark is a good example
of not enclosing the entire shape.
By allowing the mark to breathe,
activating the white space, the eye
can move in and out of the mark. If
the mark was enclosed, for example
a circle around an object, the white
space will not be activated.

egi
Designer: Aurieanne Lopez
Art Director: John T. Drew

Associative Color Response:
· pristine, timeless, further: neutral
  gray /blue-green

Color Scheme: one hue

Several formal techniques are
employed in the egi logotype.
Substitution of anatomical parts
within the lowercase letterform
"g," coupled with gestalt and
counterform utilization, creates an
intriguing mark. Substitution is
carried out through an expanded "~"
mark of the same font.

Kashokai
Designer: Hiroyuki Matsuishi

Associative Color Response:
· strong, taste, mature: dark red

Color Scheme: one hue

The Kashokai logotype is a unique
blend of Japanese characters and
roman alphabet to spell out the
same word. The dark-red hue is an
excellent choice of color to represent
this company.

Peace
Designer: Hiroyuki Matsuishi

Associative Color Response:
· blood, powerful, dangerous: high-
  chroma red

Color Scheme: one hue

Here, an irony-based metaphor is
created through substitution—the
guns spell out the Japanese
character for "peace."

**College of Education and
Integrative Studies
California State Polytechnic
University, Pomona**
Designer: Babette Mayor

Associative Color Response:
· elegant, strong: black

Color Scheme: one hue

Continuing on the theme found in
the California State Polytechnic
logo, indexical references to
orchards are used for the College of
Education and Integrative Studies.
The lowercase letterform "e" is
manipulated to create an organic
harmonious relationship between the
leaf and letterform used.

Morphosis Architecture Inc.
Designer: Sisi Xu
Art Director: John T. Drew

Associative Color Response:
· radiant, prestigious: dull gold

Color Scheme: one hue

The elegance of form and the subtle revelation of each letter in this mark suggest prestige, quality, and achievement. The "a" as a counterform seems to radiate out from the warm background color.

Zumaya
Designer: Shannon Ramsay

Associative Color Response:
· spatial, percussion: black

Color Scheme: one hue

This mark moves by flowing thick and thin forms around the central black core. These forms reiterate the circle through the white counterform present in the outline of the circle.

Farisi 2
Designer: Saied Farisi

Associative Color Response:
· life, mysterious: black

Color Scheme: one hue

The minimal owl is fanciful and mysterious. The eyes seem to peer into the viewer due to their imbalance of white. This effect is created through simultaneous contrast, which is most pronounced in disproportionate quantities of color.

earthed
Designer: Ivan Betancourt
Art Director: John T. Drew

Associative Color Response:
· growing, tasty: orange

Color Scheme: one hue

The meaning of this mark seems to precisely mirror the Associative Color Responses for orange. The metaphorical substitution of a leaf for the "e" further demonstrates the produce qualities associated with this mark.

The Park
Designer: Kristin Sommese
Illustrator: Lanny Sommese
Art Directors: Kristin Sommese and Lanny Sommese
Studio: Sommese Design

Associative Color Response:
· magical, noble: black

Color Scheme: one hue

This mark for a local conservation group is inviting. It fosters an awareness of the positive impact of urban green space and the precarious nature of an unprotected environment. The bird is intricately linked to the park through consistent stroke weights in both the legs and the type. Protection and caring is implied through the negative and positive hands visible in the counters of the bird's wings.

Monomen Here's How
Designer: Art Chantry

Associative Color Response:
· magical, night: black

Color Scheme: one hue

This humorous and retro logomark is designed with the human figure mooning the moon. Stacked typography is not often used because of readability concerns—it is the most unreadable configuration for roman type. However, in this mark, the vertical type helps the compositional balance and complements the retro feel.

Harbour Suites
Designer/Art Director: Scott Pridgen

Associative Color Response:
· sheltering, warm: brown

Color Scheme: one hue

The calligraphic font helps to convey a rich, warm, and rather lavish environment with an emphasis on traditional hospitality. The lushness of the brush strokes is counterbalanced by the sans-serif letterforms, giving the audience the feeling that the establishment is both inviting and professional.

Tega 2
Designer: Tanya A. Ortega
Art Director: John T. Drew

Associative Color Response:
· new, fresh: high-chroma blue-green

Color Scheme: one hue

The line quality of the mark suggests forward movement. In addition, the elimination of the thin strokes within the letterforms completes the connotation of motion by replicating what happens to type viewed at a distance. The thinnest part of the stroke is hardest to discern at a distance and will greatly diminish legibility.

Farisi 3
Designer: Saied Farisi

Associative Color Response:
· elegant, noble: black

Color Scheme: one hue

The unequal relationship between the foreground color (black) and the background color (white) within this mark helps to accentuate the eyes. This phenomenon, coupled with thick-to-thin relationships found with the line work, creates a kinetic mark.

The Catholic Campus Ministry
Designer/Art Director: Ned Drew

Associative Color Response:
· dignity, service: high-chroma blue

Color Scheme: one hue

The Catholic Campus Ministry logomark is an excellent example of harmonizing the font with the mark. This is brought about through the consistency of stroke width, not only in the font but in the mark as well. The juxtaposition of the three signifiers (cross, heart, dove) creates a symbol for the campus ministry.

Penn State Jazz Club 2
Designer: Kristin Sommese
Illustrator/Art Director: Lanny Sommese
Studio: Sommese Design

Associative Color Response:
· magical, percussion: black

Color Scheme: one hue

The elongated forms and black rectangle create a perceived banner that is reminiscent of a marching-band flag. The whimsical counterforms seem to spill from the instruments with a lyrical quality.

The Untamed Youth
Designer: Art Chantry

Associative Color Response:
· powerful, mysterious: black

Color Scheme: one hue

The cropping of the shoulder and head on the left seem to imply a coquettish revealing of the human form. Sardonic humor is expressed through the text written across the body and its disproportionate relationship to the arm.

Aquatics & Exotics Pet Store
Designer/Illustrator/Art Director:
Lanny Sommese
Studio: Sommese Design

Associative Color Response:
· pristine, cheerful: blue-green

Color Scheme: one hue

The ambiguity of the animals
illustrated in this mark is in keeping
with the variety of species available
in an exotic pet store. The blue-green
can be related to both water and
vegetative habitats. The purity of
the color bolsters the simultaneous
contrast and thereby the positive/
negative effect.

Mexican Doorbell
Designer: Art Chantry

Associative Color Response:
· death, night: black

Color Scheme: one hue

The Chihuahua has been silenced in
this humorous and sardonic mark.

The Children's Care Center
Designer/Illustrator/Art Director:
Lanny Sommese
Studio: Sommese Design

Associative Color Response:
· charming, tender: purple

Color Scheme: one hue

The Children's Care Center logomark
is emotive without being juvenile or
disrespectful of the noble work done
by childcare providers. The color
of the mark creates a tender and
sweet quality.

Lab Useful 1
Designer: Savio Alphonso

Associative Color Response:
· surging, brilliant, intense,
  energizing, dramatic: red

Color Scheme: one hue

The knockout of this simple mark
distinctly changes associative color
meaning with each ink (see also
page 37). This red carries an
intensity and energy.

Rahfar Architecture
Designer: Saied Farisi

Associative Color Response:
· elegant, meditative: purple

Color Scheme: one hue

It is important for an architectural
firm to represent itself as
dependable and trustworthy. Here,
the color helps to distinguish the
firm as a thoughtful consultancy
interested in creating classic design
that is both elegant and forward-
thinking.

Rush
Designer: Savio Alphonso

Associative Color Response
· excitement, energizing: red

Color Scheme: one hue

In placing a food product, it is crucial that the customer is aware of the product's benefits and develops loyalty through a maintained brand identity. The marketability of Rush lies in the fact that it is a caffeinated beverage. Therefore, every component of the design reiterates this key content. For example, the pixelated font (Emigre Eight) and the color convey the stimulating and subtly jarring effects of caffeine.

Huevos Rancheros
Designer: Art Chantry

Associative Color Response:
· basic, night: black

Color Scheme: one hue

The neutrality of the black color allows the illustrative quality of this humorous mark to gain prominence.

Lab Useful 2
Designer: Savio Alphonso

Associative Color Response:
· healing, tasty, growing, cheerfulness, warm: orange
· rustic, deep, rich, folksy, rooted, sheltering, durable: brown

Color Scheme: one hue

The knockout of this simple mark distinctly changes associative color meaning with each ink (see also page 36). The brown is stable and secure, and the orange produces a cheerful, gregarious response. These subtle shifts illustrate the power color holds as a message carrier.

Art Resources
Designer: Saied Farisi

Associative Color Response:
· tranquil, devoted to noble ideas: blue

Color Scheme: one hue

This logomark for a handmade rug, sculpture, and handicraft distributor features the classic lines evident in Persian antiquities and a color often associated with the market.

Diana Gonzalez
Designer: Diana Gonzalez

Associative Color Response:
· sophisticated, creative: high-chroma red-purple

Color Scheme: one hue

The playful acronym for Diana Gonzalez, graphic designer, is carefully evoked through the subtle slant of the letterforms and shift in foreground and background through the "d" and "G." This, in combination with a well-defined usage of associative color, implies that the designer has strong conceptual abilities and high energy that will yield thoughtful design.

Flux
Designer: Diana Gonzalez
Art Director: Jen Bracy

Associative Color Response:
· school, noble: black

Color Scheme: one hue

This logotype for a nonprofit organization dedicated to educating young people in careers in art and design communicates through form and color by reiterating its mission to promote continual growth and change. The metamorphosis of the font and the strength of the color support the idea that design can change the individual and the world—a noble mission.

ar
Designer: Leon Shultz-Ray
Art Director: John T. Drew

Associative Color Response:
· tranquil, dependable: pastel blue

Color Scheme: one hue

Here, the smooth transitions of each letterform reiterate the color's associative responses of calm, tranquillity, and peacefulness, while the italic, serif font choice further defines the acronym as timeless and dependable.

The X-Rays
Designer: Art Chantry

Associative Color Response:
· powerful, mysterious: black

Color Scheme: one hue

This is a provocative and powerful image that playfully builds on the concept of "X" meaning "explicit," while simultaneously censoring the frontal pose to further the mystique and pique curiosity. To further the pun, all of the mystery could be hypothetically revealed if the viewer had the fabled X-ray vision illustrated in superhero comics.

Fonds Alexandre Alexandre
Designer/Illustrator/Art Director: Lanny Sommese
Studio: Sommese Design

Associative Color Response:
· spatial, magical: black

Color Scheme: one hue

The intertwined relationship between film and art is exemplified in this logo for a collection of posters on those subjects. Each is seen as indelibly influencing the other and inseparable in content. This idea creates depth and dimensionality to the individual's artistic effort defined through the substitution of a brush and film leader for fingers of a hand.

Inter Valley Systems
Designer/Illustrator/Art Director: Lanny Sommese
Studio: Sommese Design

Associative Color Response:
· compassion, empathy: green

Color Scheme: one hue

Empathy, camaraderie, and a natural compassionate flow of energy is exemplified through the calming green color and the smooth transitions of circular shapes.

Handle With Care
Studio: Essex Two

Associative Color Response:
· basic, sober: black

Color Scheme: one hue

This mark for the US Department of Labor Accident Prevention Program creates a strong, clear, and objective statement that, if handled with care, damage can be avoided. The type and line quality of the form are also heavy and minimal, reinforcing the rather sober message.

Ferris University Bull Dogs
Studio: Essex Two

Associative Color Response:
· powerful, invulnerable: black

Color Scheme: one hue

The thick black line around the bulldog mascot creates an impressive and imposing force that is Ferris State University athletics. The stark contrast, sharp line quality, and edgy collar create a professional and yet slightly youthful mark that appeals to college ages.

Freedom Home Care
Studio: Essex Two

Associative Color Response:
· serenity, dignity: high-chroma blue

Color Scheme: one hue

The mark for Freedom Home Care, an in-home healthcare organization, epitomizes the healing hands of a calm, caring professional. Rather than repeating typical health-industry metaphors, this mark emphasizes the service, dignity, and respect that a patient deserves.

Fisk
Designer: Art Chantry

Associative Color Response:
· basic, bold: black

Color Scheme: one hue

This utilitarian mark for Fisk harks back to the aerodynamic quality of 1950s design.

Michael Stein Voice Talent
Designer: Art Chantry

Associative Color Response:
· magical, mysterious: black

Color scheme: one hue

This mark is lyrical and humorous, referencing an uncanny ability to change one's voice. The implication is made through the grainy quality of the black ventriloquist's dummy as well as the lighthearted but eerie facial expression.

Dante's Takeout
Designer/Illustrator/Art Director: Lanny Sommese
Studio: Sommese Design

Associative Color Response:
· classic, basic: black

Color Scheme: one hue

The contrasting forms create a quick read that says, "Food can be gotten here." The minimalist approach implies instant gratification through classic cuisine.

Lower Manhattan Cultural Council

Lower Manhattan Cultural Council

Designer/Art Director: Petter Ringbom
Project Management: Doug Lloyd

The Lower Manhattan Cultural Council (LMCC) brings art to downtown New York. The design studio Flat refined the LMCC's existing logo to make it more contextually appropriate and easy to use. A full identity system—including a new color palette, usage guidelines, print collateral, and marketing and communication materials—was developed to accomplish LMCC's mission.

LMCC needed a mark that would be both readable and visually interesting in order to contrast with the organization's rather cumbersome and hard-to-remember name. The identity had to create recognition for a body that has had some difficulty gaining name recognition. The line treatment of the font, as well as the cropping of the letterforms to their

essential elements, decreases the legibility (visual clarity of all parts) and thereby de-emphasizes the need to memorize the name. In contrast, the understated name increases the overall recognition of the organization as a dynamic and vital entity. In some instances, the mark is cropped to the most essential typographic elements needed for readability (speed and ease of reading). In these cases, the mark is usually juxtaposed with a completely legible tagline or the organization's full name. The designer increases brand recognition by reducing the hierarchy of the name. This concept is in keeping with the ability of many organizations to shift and redefine their corporate image through a redesigned logomark.

For example, how many people automatically associate IBM with International Business Machines or ATT with American Telegraph and Telephone? These associations are no longer necessary or appropriate. ATT moved beyond its national image through its global logomark. As an organization grows and develops, so must its visual identity.

LMCC's palette consists of three color combinations (cool gray/blue, warm gray/yellow orange, and warm gray/lime green). The colors are used interchangeably throughout the stationery system. For example, the business card is blue, the envelope is yellow, and the mailing label is green. The flexible application of the colors is playful and vibrant—a stark

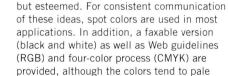

contrast to institutional colors, which typically consist of minimal color or black. Originally, pink was discussed, but the color associations were not thought to be in keeping with the LMCC's effort to promote itself as an energetic organization that was lighthearted but esteemed. For consistent communication of these ideas, spot colors are used in most applications. In addition, a faxable version (black and white) as well as Web guidelines (RGB) and four-color process (CMYK) are provided, although the colors tend to pale slightly in CMYK.

One World Challenge

Studio: Hornall Anderson

The rough, crude, and gritty nature of the logomark combined with a classic, powerful, and expansive color imbues this mark with an appropriateness of context like no other. Seemingly one with the ocean, the mark and color combinations used for collateral material, apparel, and sailing vessel are well thought out. On a 12-step color wheel, the foundation of the color palette starts with a blue-violet. Near-complementary orange is utilized for the collateral material and apparel. By using a high-chroma orange, the typography and cap "pop." (Cool colors recede and warm colors come forward, giving the design work vigorous activity through a perceived dimensionality and kinetic energy.) Blue is added to the complementary color palette to create further harmony with the sailing vessel and surrounding waters. A neutral gray is utilized to give the collateral material, apparel, and sailing vessel a timeless quality that also harmonizes well with the marine life found within the sea.

T   36% black is added to the blue-violet, shading the color so that the orange appears to have a higher chroma value than it actually does. By darkening the color, through the use of shading, the near-complementary color palette creates a greater illusion of depth.

100% Blue-Violet	100% Blue-Violet 18% Black	100% Blue-Violet 36% Black
100% Orange	100% Orange	100% Orange

As the blue-violet is darkened and receded, the orange hue is optically pulled forward.

Two Colors

One- and two-color logos are still the most commonly used today. Budgetary constraints can inspire a multitude of intriguing color palettes, be it for logomarks, logotypes, or simple symbols, as these constraints often force designers to consider alternative, more original, measures in solving a design problem. Simplifying the color palette can enhance the design direction by placing limits that facilitate superior and inspirational marks.

Simplified color palettes can control the look, feel, dimension, legibility, readability, direction, harmony, discord, and kinetic energy of a mark. The inherent energy found within a mark, and applied through color, is most often intentional. In addition, its color association and learned behavioral effects and/or psychological attributes enhance communication by amplifying the tone, texture, form, silhouette, and ultimately combine to facilitate the objectives.

MT
Designer: Anna Marie
Art Director: John T. Drew

Associative Color Response:
· new growth, regal, classic:
yellow-green (with shading) and
blue-violet

Color Scheme: two points of a
triadic color palette (tertiary hues)

The color combinations of yellow-
green and blue-violet create
a classical environment that
communicates new growth. The line
work in this logotype is exceptionally
executed to maximize the use of
gestalt.

ASPPA PAC
Studio: Bremmer & Goris
Communications

Associative Color Response:
· benevolent, compassion: red shade
· honesty, dignity: high-chroma blue

Color Scheme: primaries

This series of marks for the ASPPA
communicates confidence and
forward-thinking. The lean to the right
of each white counterform becomes
a foreground image that reiterates
progress, while the color defines
integrity. Some colors, such as the red
and blue of the United States flag,
communicate strength, solidarity,
and dignity. The slight shading of
the traditional flag red dampens the
virility and increases the trustworthy
undertones. The intensification of the
traditional flag blue creates a more
energetic and proactive composition.
These colors, with the white of the
Capitol Building, put the committee
in context.

Prevent Fire. Save Lives.
Studio: Bremmer & Goris
Communications

Associative Color Response:
· receptive: high-chroma orange
· sober: gray

Color Scheme: one hue plus neutral

The color scheme for this mark
clearly communicates fire and
ash without being blatantly
inflammatory—the antithesis of
the concept. The orange attracts the
eye and requests the audience to
soberly accept responsibility for the
prevention of fires.

ASPPA Marketplace
Studio: Bremmer & Goris
Communications

Associative Color Response:
· service: dark blue
· rich: high-chroma blue

Color Scheme: analogous

As a continuation of the ASPPA
series, this Marketplace logo
emphasizes service, professionalism,
and accessibility through a confident
color choice.

Qatar Petroleum
Designer: Tarek Atrissi

Associative Color Response:
· calm, quiet, natural: pastel green
· dignity, mature: high-chroma blue

Color Scheme: simple analogous

The choice of hues for the Qatar
Petroleum logomark is devised to
create a public image of a clean and
natural product. The use of color as
propaganda to communicate the
opposite traits of an industry is an
interesting approach—it makes
people feel good even though they
know better.

**ASPPA Pension Education and
Research Foundation**
Studio: Bremmer & Goris
Communications

Associative Color Response:
· mature growth: green shade
· healthy: yellow-orange

Color Scheme: near incongruent
with shade

ASPPA's membership comprises
a diverse group of individuals
working in the highly regulated
private pension industry. The
organization offers educational
opportunities, credentialing, and
legislative tracking and information
to its membership. The primary
organizational mark seeks to
encapsulate the mission and
communicate its desire to keep
abreast of the changing needs of
the retirement plan industry. Both
colors show the healthy growth
a successful pension fund seeks
to attain.

Cuties on Duty
Studio: Bremmer & Goris
Communications

Associative Color Response:
· fun: high-chroma pink
· neutral: black

Color Scheme: hue plus neutral

High-chroma pink is an attention-grabbing color that makes the black almost disappear. The vibrant pink exudes excitement and inspires a genial atmosphere.

Lubbock Chinese American Association: Fourth Annual Chinese Festival
Designer: Chen Wang

Associative Color Response:
· energizing, joy, fun: high-chroma red
· noble, spiritual, magical: black

Color Scheme: hue plus neutral

The color combination of red and black helps to create a fun and exciting atmosphere in which all Americans can enjoy and promote Chinese culture—red and black also symbolize traditional Chinese values. The simple flat shapes found within the mark allow for ease of printing. The posters and T-shirts for the festival were silkscreen, adding a richness of color unsurpassed by any other form of printing—in silkscreen printing the inks are more opaque and a greater ink volume can be laid down on press to produce lush colors.

Palenque
Designer: Carlo Irgoyen
Art Director: John T. Drew

Associative Color Response:
· warm, active: high-chroma red
· prestigious, strong: purple

Color Scheme: one hue plus neutral

The Palenque logomark is an excellent example of color choice. This color combination helps to create an exciting and energetic mark that also indicates, when placed in context, the atmosphere and geographical location.

Fat Rooster 2
Designer: Brenda Cox
Art Director: John T. Drew

Associative Color Response:
· thought, pride, exciting: high-chroma orange
· powerful: high-chroma blue-purple

Color Scheme: near complementary

When creating a color palette, it is often best to use a disproportionate amount of one color over another. An accent color tends to draw attention to itself by virtue of oppositional techniques. In this case, the oppositional techniques are small to large, and cool to warm colors—cool colors recede and warm colors advance. These techniques create a high degree of kinetic energy within the Fat Rooster logotype.

California State Polytechnic University, Pomona, College of Business
Designer: Babette Mayor

Associative Color Response:
· strength: high-chroma yellow-green
· prestigious: black

Color Scheme: one hue plus neutral

California State Polytechnic University, Pomona (CPP) was first established as an agricultural campus on land endowed by W. K. Kellogg, the cereal entrepreneur and Arabian horse aficionado. In honor of this history and in deference to the university's logomark, the College of Business logomark integrates a green leaf into the counterform of the lowercase "b". The green is a vibrant tint of the university's green, implying new growth, sharp business sense, and unlimited potential. These associated attributes help define the College of Business.

RPM
Designer: Carlo Irgoyen
Art Director: John T. Drew

Associative Color Response
· exhilarating, inspiring: dark orange
· authoritative, credible: dark blue

Color Scheme: complementary with shading

The RPM logotype uses a conservative color palette, through the use of shading, that denotes an authoritative tone. The logotype uses gestalt to generate interest by revealing just enough information to understand the mark without making it obvious. In most cases, to make a mark obvious is to create a logo that is trite.

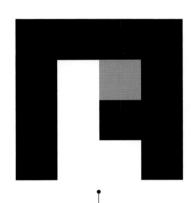

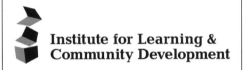

Avrek Financial Corporation
Designer: Carlo Irgoyen
Art Director: John T. Drew

Associative Color Response:
· rich, warm, strength: earth-tone orange
· lively, strength, dramatic: high-chroma blue

Color Scheme: complementary with tinting and shading

Color plays an important role in how a company wants to be viewed by the public, especially when it is dealing with an individual's personal assets. In this case, color sets the tone by making sure the audience views the company in a warm and inviting way, while at the same time making them feel secure.

BCC Custom Tile and Stone
Designer: Chad Dewilde
Studio: The Beautiful Design

Associative Color Response:
· strength, wholesome, rooted: earth tone
· honesty, strength, lively: high-chroma blue

Color Scheme: near complementary with shading

In a highly competitive market, the BCC Custom Tile and Stone logomark needs to communicate in a more direct manner than its rivals. The color palette helps soften the directness of the mark by implying the values of the company and thereby potentially capturing a greater customer base.

The Language Key
Studio: Bremmer & Goris Communications

Associative Color Response:
· new growth: high-chroma green-yellow
· neutral: gray

Color Scheme: hue plus neutral

The addition of black to the green-yellow tones down the acidic qualities and imbues the mark with a sense of new growth tempered by experience. The gray further reiterates the practicality of education in a timeless manner.

Institute for Learning and Community Development
Studio: Bremmer & Goris Communications

Associative Color Response:
· creative, unique: high-chroma violet
· new growth: high-chroma yellow-green

Color Scheme: near complementary

The purple shade gives a rich and sophisticated touch to children's playful building blocks. The green increases the depth and helps to rotate the purple forms in an upward progressive direction. In addition, the green tint suggests new growth without appearing childish.

hd
Designer: Maja Bagic
Creative/Art Directors: Davor Bruketa and Nikola Zinic

Associative Color Response:
· new growth: high-chroma yellow-green
· warm-hearted: earth-tone red

Color Scheme: near complementary with shading

Through the use of color, the "hd" logotype is a wonderful example of promoting an environmentally friendly company. It also generates a corporate image that reflects the future growth of the company.

Lubbock Chinese American Association
Designer: Chen Wang

Associative Color Response:
· powerful, elegant: black
· wise, cultured: dark gray

Color Scheme: one hue with shading (achromatic)

Designer Chen Wang used a simple achromatic color scheme to help speed recognition of the logotype. The Lubbock Chinese American Association mark uses a gray square to delineate the "L" from the "C"—an outstanding practical application of color.

A D R I S

HIDAKA PRINTING

Fishing outfitters
Designer: Edwin Alvarenga
Art Director: John T. Drew

Associative Color Response:
· pleasure, water: pastel blue-violet
· classic, regal: high-chroma blue-violet

Color Scheme: simple monochromatic

This mark, designed for a fishing outfitting company, is an excellent example of using selected hues and a simple color scheme to help convey the psychological effects associated with fishing.

Choice One Medical
Designer: Doug Herberich

Associative Color Response:
· calm, relaxed: high-chroma blue
· classic, tender: high-chroma blue-violet

Color Scheme: simple analogous

Color has context. Depending upon the industry in which the color is used, different psychological and learned behavioral effects will be associated with the color or colors used. Different environments will change our perception of the same hues and color schemes, both physically and psychologically.

Adris
Creative/Art Directors: Davor Bruketa and Nikola Zinic

Associative Color Response:
· powerful, strong: black
· classic: high-chroma blue-violet

Color Scheme: one hue with neutral

The Adris logotype is an excellent example of gestalt. In this case, the crossbar of the capital "A" is removed, making the mark interesting by engaging the audience's imagination to envision the missing part. Without the removal of the crossbar this mark would be uninteresting—the mark's story would be told in an obvious way.

Alexander Construction
Designer: Chad Dewilde
Studio: The Beautiful Design

Associative Color Response:
· complete, natural: pastel green
· pristine, serious: pastel blue-green

Color Scheme: near simple analogous with tinting

Choosing the right color palette for a company says a lot about the values the company holds dear. In this case, the use of the index images combined with the choice of colors creates the perfect company image.

Absolute
Designer: Jeff Sandford

Associative Color Response:
· strong: olive
· new growth: high-chroma yellow-green

Color Scheme: one hue with neutral

This robust logotype is a fine example of gestalt, harmony of form, and color choice. Note that the typeface chosen for "Absolute" and the "A" mark above have the same stroke width, creating harmony of form. The "A" mark is a modified "A" that is not entirely spelled out (the sum is greater than its parts), and the yellow-green and black create a powerful and dynamic color palette.

Hidaka Printing
Designer: Hiroyuki Matsuishi

Associative Color Response:
· strong: black
· intense, energizing: high-chroma red

Color Scheme: one hue with neutral

Black and high-chroma red are one of the most successful color combinations ever used. In most cases, this color combination will create a powerfully strong and energetic mark.

TRIDVAJEDAN *tržišne komunikacije d.o.o.*

Plant Zero 1
Designer: John Malinoski

Associative Color Response:
· brilliant, energizing: high-chroma red
· warm, healing: high-chroma red-magenta

Color Scheme: simple analogous

Within this color study, the legibility, readability, and psychological and learned behavioral effects can be assessed to determine which mark functions best.

When comparing the four studies, Plant Zero 1 should not be used at any distance greater than 18 to 24 inches. The two hues within this color study are a metameric pair—they have the same spectral reflectance curve (CV) in at least one light source, making it all but impossible to distinguish shape at a distance.

Plant Zero 2
Designer: John Malinoski

Associative Color Response:
· brilliant, energizing: high-chroma red
· stimulating, fun: high-chroma yellow-orange

Color Scheme: primary, secondary (random)

In Plant Zero 2, 3, and 4, the red dot can be seen at a greater distance than its counterpart. Plant Zero 3 breaks the 20% rule of thumb, however, the neutral gray is the second-most visible color at a distance. The yellow-orange is the third-most visible and the yellow-green is the least visible. At the mark's maximum distance, the red dot will be seen and nothing else. The neutral gray is roughly 15% more visible, at a distance, than the yellow-orange, and is roughly 20% more visible than the yellow-green.

Plant Zero 3
Designer: John Malinoski

Associative Color Response:
· brilliant, energizing: high-chroma red
· quality, passion: neutral gray

Color Scheme: one hue with neutral

In some cases, colors that have 20% or less CVD cannot be distinguished from one another. This is why the rule exists. However, this is not the case with Plant Zero 3.

Plant Zero 4
Designer: John Malinoski

Associative Color Response:
· brilliant, energizing: high-chroma red
· new growth, sunlight: high-chroma yellow-green

Color Scheme: near complementary

Fountain Head
Designer: John Malinoski

Associative Color Response:
· intense, energizing: high-chroma red
· new growth: high-chroma yellow-green

Color Scheme: near complementary

The color combination for this whimsical mark is a perfect metaphor for the conceptual statement being made—the psychological and learned behavioral effects of the hues harmonize with the illustration.

Tridvajedan
Designer/Art Director: Izvorka Serdarevic

Associative Color Response:
· rich, upward: high-chroma blue
· powerful, cold, classic: black

Color Scheme: one hue with neutral

The Tridvajedan logo color scheme is an ideal choice for this corporate logomark. The high-chroma blue juxtaposed with the black letterforms creates a strong, classic, and upward-moving mark.

DEVELOPMENT PARTNER
PILOT PROGRAM

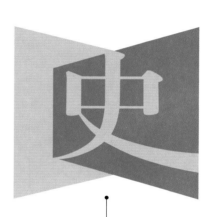

**Expo Design: Public Procurement
Service**
Designer: Inyoung Choi

Associative Color Response:
· rich, upward: high-chroma blue
· powerful, classic, futuristic: high-
  chroma blue-violet

Color Scheme: simple analogous

The gradient found within this
logomark amplifies the kinetic
energy and, at the same time,
helps to create a 3-D illusion. Using
gradients within marks is a delicate
matter. If done poorly, the mark will
date quickly and/or look trite; in
this case, however, the gradient is
handled masterfully.

Cat Head
Designer: Art Chantry

Associative Color Response:
· aggression, excitability: high-
  chroma red
· powerful, strong: black

Color Scheme: one hue with neutral

The color scheme of red and black
are well suited for this energetic
mark. When using drop shadows,
make sure to use them in a way that
amplifies the content, otherwise
this technique looks dated and trite.
In the Cat Head mark, the dropped
shadow is masterfully utilized to
amplify the kinetic energy found
within the letterforms.

Kelly's Seafood Shack
Designer: Kelly Thacker
Art Director: John T. Drew

Associative Color Response:
· water, ice, service: high-chroma
  blue
· quality, classic: neutral gray

Color Scheme: one hue with neutral
(tinted)

The Kelly's Seafood Snack logomark
is an excellent example of an ink
rubbing. To create an ink rubbing,
use a spray bottle filled with India
ink. Using the mist setting, spray
down the object, carefully place
butcher's paper on top of the object,
and rub.

In this case, an ink rubbing
is appropriate for the content
(historically, Japanese fishermen
would ink-rub the catch of the day).
This formal technique can yield
interesting marks.

Development Partner Pilot Program
Designer/Art Director: Jun Li
Studio: Juno

Associative Color Response:
powerful, strong: black
quality, classic: neutral gray

Color Scheme: one hue with neutral
(tinted)

The Development Partner Pilot
Program logotype is a fine example
of a modular system. Constructed
from only two shapes (a square
and a triangle), this mark reads the
same either right-side-up or upside-
down. Color is used to delineate
between the "D" and "P"—a great
example of the practical use of color.

hgc
Designer: Julie J. Park
Art Director: John T. Drew
Studio: Juno

Associative Color Response:
· producing, growing, strong: high-
  chroma orange
· durable: earth-tone brown

Color Scheme: simple analogous
with shading

In this example, the arts of
substitution and gestalt are
executed to a high level. A ")" is
used from the same font by rotating
it at 90 degrees and substituting
it for the loop of the lowercase
"g." Gestalt is utilized to give the
lowercase "g" just enough visual
clues to determine what it is.

**Expo Design: National Institute of
Korean History**
Designer: Inyoung Choi

Associative Color Response:
· producing, growing, strong: neutral
  gray
· durable: high-chroma blue

Color Scheme: one hue with neutral
(tinted)

Designer Inyoung Choi creates a
magnificent 3-D illusion on a 2-D
plane. This is carried out through
the use of two-point perspective and
color choice.

Expo Design: Ministry of Unification
Designer: Inyoung Choi

Associative Color Response:
· new growth: high-chroma yellow-green
· mature, upward: high-chroma blue

Color Scheme: near incongruous

In silkscreen printing, a split fountain is achieved when more than one ink is placed in the fountain—that is, on the screen. Typically, these are spaced apart so that a cascade of different hues is achieved. Here, designer Inyoung Choi creates the equivalent of a split fountain on the computer to achieve a masterfully created gradient of hues.

IntelliVue Unplugged
Designer: Jun Li

Associative Color Response:
· healing, warm: high-chroma orange
· mature, upward: high-chroma blue

Color Scheme: direct complementary

A direct complementary color palette is best suited for asymmetrical design such as the IntelliVue Unplugged logomark. This color scheme creates simultaneous contrast when used in butt register and in disproportionate amounts. Kinetic energy is induced anytime opposition occurs. Applying harmony to composition is more suited to symmetrical design. With that said, there is a scale to everything. The more formal techniques used to induce kinetic energy, the more likely the composition is to be asymmetrical, and vice versa.

The Frisky Biscuit Bread Company
Designer: Mark Raebel
Studio: Arsenal Design

Associative Color Response:
· elegant, magical: black
· sweet taste: high-chroma red-violet

Color Scheme: one hue with neutral

For practical reasons, any time a continuous-tone image is used for part or all of a mark, it is critical to use a gross screen pattern such as The Frisky Biscuit Bread Company logo. The coarser the screen pattern, the faster the logo will go through a fax machine.

Explorers Incorporated
Designer: Mark Raebel
Studio: Arsenal Design

Associative Color Response:
· powerful, strong: black
· enterprise, drive, goal, powerful: high-chroma yellow-orange

Color Scheme: one hue with neutral

The choice of hues within the Explorers Incorporated logomark suits the subject matter. Yellow-orange and black create a powerfully strong and enterprising color scheme.

Arsenal Design
Designer: Mark Raebel
Studio: Arsenal Design

Associative Color Response:
· quality, classic, timeless: neutral gray
· enterprise, drive, goal, powerful: high-chroma yellow-orange

Color Scheme: one hue with neutral (tinted)

The color palette in the Arsenal Design logomark is well suited to reflect the qualities associated with this coat of arms or family crest. The high-chroma orange is associated with an enterprising company that strives to create quality.

Anemone Makeup
Designer: Mark Raebel
Studio: Arsenal Design

Associative Color Response:
· quality, classic, timeless: neutral gray
· classic: mid-green

Color Scheme: one hue with neutral (tinted)

The color schemes found in the Anemone Makeup logomark is toned down (tinted) to create a subdued message that is timeless and classic. This is a good color strategy to help give the mark a classic and sophisticated appearance.

Hoody Nation 1
Designer: Mark Raebel
Studio: Arsenal Design

Associative Color Response:
· powerful, strong: black
· intense, powerful, aggressive:
  high-chroma red

Color Scheme: one hue with
neutral (tinted)

Often the physicality of form—the
textual basis of line—is what
makes the mark. There is no finer
example than the Hoody Nation
logomark—the splattered line work
draws the audience in and holds
their attention.

Grafika 180
Designer: Mark Raebel
Studio: Arsenal Design

Associative Color Response:
· powerful, strong: black
· intense, powerful, aggressive:
  high-chroma red

Color Scheme: one hue with shading
plus neutral

Classified as a two-color job,
the Grafika 180 logomark uses
overprinting to create an additional
third color. When using overprinting,
there is no extra cost to create
additional hues. This makes it an
excellent way to stretch a budget.

Express Divers
Designer: Mark Raebel
Studio: Arsenal Design

Associative Color Response:
· powerful, strong: black
· intense, powerful, aggressive:
  high-chroma red

Color Scheme: one hue with neutral

When using color in this manner
(mostly black with an accent of red),
the predominant hue dominates the
interpretation. However, the most
interesting part about this mark is
the substitution of the diving flag
for the letterform "X." Furthermore,
a water wave is substituted for the
airline stroke within the letterform
"X." The dive flag is used when
divers are out on the water. The
juxtaposition of the descending diver
underneath the flag puts the activity
in context.

Armadyne Inc. 1
Designer: Mark Raebel
Studio: Arsenal Design

Associative Color Response:
· communication: high-chroma
  orange
· corporate, practical: neutral gray

Color Scheme: one hue with neutral
(tinted)

The high-chroma orange and
neutral gray create a well-balanced
color scheme that is energetic and
that communicates with subtle
sophistication.

Armadyne Inc. 2
Designer: Mark Raebel
Studio: Arsenal Design

Associative Color Response:
· communication, energizing,
  stimulating: high-chroma orange
· corporate, practical: neutral gray

Color Scheme: one hue with neutral
(tinted)

When comparing Armadyne 1 and
Armadyne 2, the role-reversal of
the neutral gray and high-chroma
orange is evident. In Armadyne 1,
the neutral gray plays a predominant
role within the color scheme,
whereas in Armadyne 2 the high-
chroma orange is the predominant
color. Note how the interpretation of
these two marks changes by virtue of
how the hues are implemented.

KLW Group 1
Designer: Mark Raebel
Studio: Arsenal Design

Associative Color Response:
· sweet taste, subtle, creative: high-
  chroma red-violet
· powerful, basic: black

Color Scheme: one hue with neutral
and tinting

In the KLW Group logo, a 3-D illusion
is achieved through warm and cool
colors and scale. To exaggerate this
3-D illusion, the scale of the circles,
from large to small, would need to be
increased, and tinting would need to
be eliminated.

SitOnIt Seating 1
Principal Designer: Yang Kim
Studio: BBK Studio

Associative Color Response:
· inspiring: mid-range orange
· elegant, refined: dark red

Color Scheme: near simple analogous with tinting and shading

In the three versions of SitOnIt Seating, cool and warm colors are used most effectively to create a 3-D illusion on a 2-D plane; the cool colors recede and the warm colors come forth. It is interesting to note that the 3-D illusion flips back and forth from a seat to steps.

SitOnIt Seating 2
Principal Designer: Yang Kim
Studio: BBK Studio

Associative Color Response:
· lively, pleasing: high-chroma blue

Color Scheme: one hue with shading (monochromatic)

Hoody Nation 2
Designer: Mark Raebel
Studio: Arsenal Design

Associative Color Response:
· brilliant, intense, energetic: high-chroma red
· future, young, forward: neutral gray

Color Scheme: one hue with neutral and tinting

When a logotype boils down to the selection of typeface, as in the Hoody Nation mark, it is critical to discern what constitutes good anatomical structure and what does not. Most typefaces that are considered to be of quality have a stroke width-to-height ratio from 1:5 to 1:7.5; a stroke width-to-width ratio of 1:5.25 to 1:7.33; a width-to-height ratio from 0.89:1 to 1:1; and a stroke width-to-counterform ratio of 1:3.25 to 1:5.3. The "Hoody" typeface follows this rule, and is an excellent selection. Script fonts do not necessarily follow the above ratios, and in this case "Nation" does not. What makes this logotype so interesting is the opposition between the two fonts selected.

SitOnIt Seating 3
Principal Designer: Yang Kim
Studio: BBK Studio

Associative Color Response:
· new growth, trendy: high-chroma yellow-green

Color Scheme: one hue with shading (monochromatic)

KLW Group 2
Designer: Mark Raebel
Studio: Arsenal Design

Associative Color Response:
· charming: mid-range red-violet
· quality: neutral gray

Color Scheme: one hue (tinted) plus neutral (tinted)

Separation through the use of color is exploited here to create a visual hierarchy.

No Field 5
Designer: Mark Raebel
Studio: Arsenal Design

Associative Color Response:
· intense, energetic: high-chroma red
· powerful, strong: black

Color Scheme: one hue with neutral

The No Field 5 logomark is an excellent example of juxtaposing a 3-D object against a flat surface to accentuate the 3-D illusion.

GAIN

island sports
Designer: Mark Raebel
Studio: Arsenal Design

Associative Color Response:
· glad, cheery: mid-range orange
· sharp, growth: high-chroma yellow-green

Color Scheme: near incongruous

The island sports logomark is a near incongruous color scheme—a highly kinetic color palette due to its chroma value. When executed properly, these offbeat color schemes tend to be unique, lively, and energetic.

Neighborhood Lawn Care
Designer: Mark Raebel
Studio: Arsenal Design

Associative Color Response:
· glad, cheery: mid-range orange
· natural, trustworthy: dark green

Color Scheme: two points of a triad both secondary hues with shading

Not every logomark requires a high-chroma hue within the master color palette. There is no finer example of this than the Neighborhood Lawn Care mark. As demonstrated in this book, a majority (more than 80%) of logomarks, logotypes, and symbols utilize high-chroma colors within their master color palette. However, one way to help create a unique mark is to find appropriate hues (that help sell or promote) that are not in the high-chroma.

Stark Ceramics Incorporated
Designer/Creative Director: Drew M. Dallet
Studio: Boom Creative

Associative Color Response:
· dynamic, strength: high-chroma red
· powerful, strong: black

Color Scheme: one hue with neutral

The Stark Ceramics Incorporated logo utilizes four formal techniques in a most effective way to create a 3-D illusion: cool and warm colors; weight; placement; and scale. The formal execution of a mark can be likened to grammar. If grammar is used so poorly that one cannot read for content, the concept will either not be revealed, or revealed to an inadequate level. Either way, the mark or design communicates at an illiterate level.

ordernetwork.com
Art Director: Chevonne Woodard
Studio: Chevonne Woodard Design

Associative Color Response:
· growing, communication, intimate: high-chroma orange
· powerful, strong: black

Color Scheme: one hue with tinting plus neutral

The ordernetwork.com logomark is an excellent example of substitution. The indexical reference to a computer's "power on" button is a fine example of using content appropriate to the subject matter.

Gain
Designer: Carol Chu

Associative Color Response:
· growing, energizing: high-chroma orange
· quality: neutral gray

Color Scheme: one hue plus neutral (tinted)

The Gain logomark uses symbols for movement and perspective to create a mark that is highly kinetic. Within this context, an energizing high-chroma orange is used to reinforce the kinetic energy implied within the formal structure.

the tree hook
Designer: Mark Raebel
Studio: Arsenal Design

Associative Color Response:
· lively, honest, strength: high-chroma blue
· refreshing, clean, cool: pastel blue

Color Scheme: monochromatic

the tree hook logo is an excellent example of using a geometric form to unify a mark. The selection and consistency of typeface chosen also aids in this endeavor. Created from one ink, this two-color mark utilizes tinting to create the additional color. White (not counted as a color) is created through a type reversal in which type is knocked out to the color of the substrate.

celine
YALETOWN SALON

hippOloco

Info Grow
Designer/Creative Director: Drew
M. Dallet
Studio: Boom Creative

Associative Color Response:
· energy, health: high-chroma
  yellow-orange
· memorable, thoughtful: high-
  chroma violet

Color Scheme: near complementary

Color offers meaning, depth, and
insight into the way a company
image is formed. The Info Grow
logotype is a fine example of how
color and shape play an important
role in how a corporate image is
constructed. This logo is energetic,
thoughtful (color-based), and
conservative (form-based).

Congregation Shalom
Designer/Creative Director: Drew
M. Dallet
Studio: Boom Creative

Associative Color Response:
· dignity, calm: high-chroma blue
· valuable, prestigious: gold

Color Scheme: near complementary

The Congregation Shalom mark is
a fine example of the psychological
and learned behavioral effects
of color. Creating the mark
through the use of these two hues
visually displays the values of the
organization.

Sweet Tooth for Youth
Designer/Creative Director: Drew
M. Dallet
Studio: Boom Creative

Associative Color Response:
· soft, sweet, tender, cute:
  pastel pink
· warmhearted, welcome, good,
  healthy: earth-tone red

Color Scheme: near complementary

The Sweet Tooth for Youth logomark
is a superb example of practical
color use. The psychological and
learned behavioral effects of these
two hues match the content, context,
and end-user beautifully. The formal
anatomy of the mark also reflects the
target audience—a masterful job.

Hippoloco
Designer: Carol Chu

Associative Color Response:
· flamboyant, subtle: pastel blue-
  violet
· growing, childlike: high-
  chroma orange

Color Scheme: near complementary

The light and airy quality of the
Hippoloco logomark can be directly
contributed to the colors chosen.
A hippopotamus is anything
but lightweight, however; the
psychological effects of the color
reinforce the humorous nature of
the mark.

Celine Yaletown Salon
Designer: Catherine Ng
Creative Director: Carolina Becerra
Studio: Kübe Communication Design

Associative Color Response:
· quality, classic, professional:
  neutral gray
· electric, energetic, pleasing: high-
  chroma blue

Color Scheme: one hue plus
neutral (tinted)

The Celine Yaletown Salon logotype
uses a classic color palette with
compressed lowercase letterforms
to create an energetic mark with a
contemporary feel.

Filarmonica de Acapulco
Designers: Carolina Becerra and
Dean Kujala
Creative Director: Carolina Becerra
Studio: Kübe Communication Design

Associative Color Response:
· powerful, elegant: black
· radiant, valuable: golden-yellow

Color Scheme: one hue with neutral

The Filarmonica de Acapulco logo is
an excellent example of color choice
coupled with formal execution. The
golden hue (in this book it is built
from CMYK) captures the radiating
essence found within this mark.

FIREFLY

Firefly
Designers: Justin Ahrens and
Kerri Liu
Art Director: Justin Ahrens

Associative Color Response:
· powerful, elegant: black
· hot, fire, heat: high-chroma red

Color Scheme: one hue plus neutral

The physicality of form in the Firefly
mark harmonizes with the color and
typography to create a logomark
that is unsurpassed by many
contemporary logos.

E-Court
Designer: Erik Chrestensen
Studio: Chrestensen Designworks

Associative Color Response:
· powerful, elegant: black
· hot, fire, heat: high-chroma red

Color Scheme: one hue plus neutral

The E-Court logo is a fine example of
hand-rendered typography and line
work to create an energetic mark.

Kikuya
Designer: Erik Chrestensen
Studio: Chrestensen Designworks

Associative Color Response:
· authoritative, confident, strong:
  blue-violet
· lively, strength: high-chroma blue

Color Scheme: simple analogous

The Kikuya logotype uses hand-
rendered typography coupled with
perspective to create a highly kinetic
mark. Reversing the letterforms
out of the blue-violet background
makes the typography pop (warm
colors come forth and cool colors
recede). In this case, the substrate
in which this image is printed on is
critical. Placing the logo on top of
a cool background will reduce the
kinetic energy.

Map Strategies
Designer/Creative Director: Drew
M. Dallet
Studio: Boom Creative

Associative Color Response:
· basic, strong: black
· inviting, cheery: mid-range orange

Color Scheme: one hue plus neutral

The Map Strategies mark is an
excellent example of learned color
response. The mark is designed
after the United States Department
of Motor Vehicles signage system
that includes, in part, this color
scheme and the shape of the sign.
The letterform "S" with two arrows
pointing in different directions
conceptually symbolize the intent
of the mark.

Blu Synthetic
Designer: Dean Kujala and Carolina
Becerra
Creative Director: Dean Kujala
Studio: Kübe Communication Design

Associative Color Response:
· quality, classic, corporate: neutral
  gray
· lively, pleasing, rich: high-chroma
  blue

Color Scheme: one hue plus neutral
(tinted)

The Blu Synthetic logotype uses
a color combination that results
in a successful mark that has a
corporate feel. This is brought about
through the typographic relationship
between "Blu" and "Synthetic,"
consistency of line weight, and the
choice of sans-serif fonts.

BiTiNiT
Designers: Carolina Becerra and
Dean Kujala
Creative Director: Dean Kujala
Studio: Kübe Communication Design

Associative Color Response:
· drive, aggressive, powerful: high-
  chroma yellow-orange
· strength, work: high-chroma blue

Color Scheme: near complementary

The art of substitution is alive and
well in the BiTiNiT logomark—a
lively and energetic mark that uses
a near complementary color palette
to help express the activity in which
this product is used (bits for a screw
gun). A near complementary high-
chroma color palette induces
simultaneous contrast and heightens
stimulation within the eye (the
photoreceptor cells responsible for
detecting blue and yellow-orange fire
with force, creating more stimulation).

PUNK MARKETING™

Monarch Design & Construction
Designer/Art Director: Justin Ahrens

Associative Color Response:
· elegant, prestigious: black
· refined, taste: dark red

Color Scheme: one hue with shading plus neutral

The red-brick hue combined with black creates an impressive color palette suitable for the content. In this case, the red in "monarch" is an indexical reference to the way that many houses and buildings are constructed. The black hue reinforces the quality of the mark by adding power.

Tollar Metal Works
Designer: John R. Kieinpeter
Art Director: John T. Drew

Associative Color Response:
· powerful, classic: high-chroma blue-violet
· strong, taste: dark red

Color Scheme: near incongruous or two points of a tetrad

Tollar Metal Works is a company that designs metal chairs that are used outdoors at bus and subway stops. The mark was designed to reference the three-dimensionality of the chairs and their durability. This is done through the use of two-point perspective, line weight, and cool and warm colors.

Lighthouse
Designer: Justin Deister
Studio: Uppercase Design

Associative Color Response:
· inviting: high-chroma orange
· powerful: black

Color Scheme: one hue with tinting plus neutral

The Lighthouse logomark is an excellent example of substitution and economy of form.

Anglebar Solutions
Designer: Justin Deister
Studio: Uppercase Design

Associative Color Response:
· drive, powerful, energy: high-chroma yellow-orange
· mature, classy: high-chroma blue

Color Scheme: near complementary

The Anglebar Solutions logotype is a highly kinetic color scheme with a binary opposition occurring within the two fonts selected to create visual tension. Eye movement is induced whenever visual tension is created.

Punk Marketing
Studio: 86 The Onions

Associative Color Response:
· aggressive, solid: high-chroma red
· heavy, basic: black

Color Scheme: one hue plus neutral

The Punk Marketing logomark uses consistency of line and simplicity of graphics to create an aesthetically pleasing mark.

Watkins College of Art & Design
Designer: Leslie Haines

Associative Color Response:
· energizing, pride: high-chroma orange
· lively, pleasing: high-chroma blue

Color Scheme: direct complementary

Direct complementary color schemes typically create high-energy marks. This can be attributed to simultaneous contrast, high-chroma color palettes, and a greater stimulation of the photoreceptor cells found within the eye.

KüBE

oh! Oxygen™

nexus°™

 SULING

Kübe
Studio: Kübe Communication Design

Associative Color Response:
· wise, professional: dark gray
· enterprise, drive, goal: high-chroma yellow-orange

Color Scheme: one hue plus neutral (tinted)

Typically when a dark gray is utilized within a logotype, such as Kübe, a professional, corporate feel is induced. This works well with standardized type—typefaces consisting of the proper stroke width-to-width ratio, stroke width-to-height ratio, and stroke width-to-counterform ratio. A high-chroma yellow-orange is used as an accent color to help energize the mark.

Nexus
Studio: Kübe Communication Design

Associative Color Response:
· classic, quality: neutral gray
· power, stimulating: high-chroma red

Color Scheme: one hue plus neutral (tinted)

A neutral gray and high-chroma red color scheme has a classic appearance. This color combination tends to yield a lively yet conservative color palette.

Oh Oxygen
Studio: AdamsMorioka

Associative Color Response:
· classic, quality: neutral gray
· strength, lively: high-chroma blue

Color Scheme: one hue plus neutral (tinted)

Anytime a high-chroma color is utilized as the predominant hue, kinetic energy is induced. In this case, scale plays an important role in creating the lively Oh Oxygen logotype.

Suling
Designer: Suling Pong

Associative Color Response:
· powerful, elegant: black
· mature, serious: dark red

Color Scheme: one hue with shading plus neutral

In the Suling logomark, the line weight of the outer line harmonizes well with the font utilized. A dark red and black color scheme further induces a harmonious relationship, with black added to the red to darken it (shading).

Carley Sparks 1
Studio: Sharp Pixel

Associative Color Response:
· powerful, strong: black
· stimulating, aggressive, exciting: high-chroma pink

Color Scheme: one hue with tinting plus neutral

The Carley Sparks logo is an excellent example of utilizing ingredients in a unique way to induce kinetic energy. In this case, the gradients help to create a 3-D illusion on a 2-D plane that activate the mark.

Carley Sparks 2
Studio: Sharp Pixel

Associative Color Response:
· joyful, active: pastel pink
· subtle, energetic: pastel pink

Color Scheme: monochromatic with tinting and shading

This Carley Sparks logo is a fine example of a subdued mark brought about through tinting and shading. Note the difference between the scheme in Carley Sparks 1 and this color scheme—each induces a different psychological effect on the viewer.

CdLS Foundation
Designer: Laurie Churchman
Studio: Designlore

Associative Color Response:
· tender, classic: blue-purple
· pristine, pure: blue-green

Color Scheme: two points of a split complementary

This logomark is a unique color scheme that helps to communicate the values of the CdLS Foundation. This mark is superbly executed, and is a wonderful example of economy of line.

EVD 4x4
Studio: 86 The Onions

Associative Color Response:
· energizing, hot: high-chroma orange
· quality, passion: neutral gray

Color Scheme: one hue plus neutral (tinted)

The EVD 4x4 logomark utilizes a conservative color scheme with a typeface that has a bold thick-to-thin relationship that helps to induce kinetic energy.

eos Airlines
Studio: Hornall Anderson Design Works

Associative Color Response:
· luxurious, cheery: high-chroma yellow-orange
· clean, calm: pastel blue

Color Scheme: near complementary with shading and tinting

This logotype is an excellent example of understanding typographic anatomy in relationship to motion. The letterforms are extended so that the counterforms are five times wider than the stroke, or a 1:7 stroke width-to-width ratio. The typeface has a moderate thick-to-thin relationship, allowing for excellent legibility at a distance—the thinnest part of the letterforms will disappear first. On the tail section of the airplane, the logotype is reversed out to white through a dark blue-violet, allowing for excellent legibility at a distance in daylight.

clearwire
Studio: Hornall Anderson Design Works

Associative Color Response:
· classic, powerful: high-chroma blue-violet
· strength, sharp: high-chroma yellow-green

Color Scheme: two points of the triad/near incongruous

The color scheme chosen for the Clear Wire logotype reinforces the company's mission statement. Gestalt is used within the lowercase letterform "i," further strengthening the conceptual metaphor.

SunSafe
Studio: AdamsMorioka

Associative Color Response:
· fun, excitement: high-chroma yellow-orange
· lively, energetic: high-chroma blue

Color Scheme: near complementary

In this logotype, both the color palette chosen and the line work surrounding the capital letterform "S" energize the mark.

AdamsMorioka
Studio: AdamsMorioka

Associative Color Response:
· dignity, power: high-chroma red
· elegant, powerful: black

Color Scheme: one hue plus neutral

The AdamsMorioka logotype is a superb example of a conservative color scheme coupled with a classical typeface (stroke width-to-height ratio 1:6.25, stroke width-to-width ratio 1:5.25, width-to-height ratio .84:1, and stroke width-to-counterform ratio 1:3.25). A minimum amount of substitution is used, creating a classically restrained and sophisticated mark.

Insite Works
Studio: Hornall Anderson Design Works

Associative Color Response:
· producing, communication: high-chroma orange
· powerful, expensive: high-chroma blue-violet

Color Scheme: near complementary

The logotype for Insite Works uses a high-chroma, near complementary color scheme to energize a typically staid industry.

Vector
Studio: Hornall Anderson Design Works

Associative Color Response:
· dramatic, electric: high-chroma blue
· powerful, expensive: high-chroma blue-violet

Color Scheme: simple analogous

The Citation Shares Vector logomark uses a simple analogous color palette to counterbalance the highly active formal relationships found within the mark. This type of color palette helps to unify a mark. If this was a direct complementary or near complementary color palette, the mark would appear to be fragmented.

allconnect
Studio: Hornall Anderson Design Works

Associative Color Response:
· warm, durable, secure: earth tone
· strength: high-chroma yellow-green

Color Scheme: two points of a split complementary with shading and tinting

In the allconnect logotype, substitution and separation are used to create a highly effective mark. The "power-on" symbol is substituted for the "o" in "connect" to metaphorically represent the company. Separation is used (a formal technique to clearly distinguish the most meaningful part or parts) by use of cool and warm colors. The yellow-green hue represents not only "power on" (learned behavioral association), but also visually separates the word "on" from "connect."

Mad Chinaman
Designer: Audrey Koh
Studio: Plastic Soldier Factory Pte Ltd

Associative Color Response:
· dramatic, energetic: high-chroma orange
· electric, vibrant: high-chroma blue

Color Scheme: direct complementary

Pronounced simultaneous contrast occurs when there is an imbalance in the proportion of two hues on the opposite side of the color wheel (large to small). Such is the case in this mark design by Audrey Koh. Pronounced simultaneous contrast induces a strobing effect caused by the receptor cells responsible for detecting color.

Sundance Institute
Studio: AdamsMorioka

Associative Color Response:
· dramatic, energetic: high-chroma orange
· powerful, strength: black

Color Scheme: one hue plus neutral

The choice of font, color scheme, and placement of type and color within the Sundance Institute logotype is designed to give the mark stability. The typeface chosen is an expanded face, giving the mark a longer horizon line. This is amplified by the amount of tracking utilized. The black hue is employed, as a foundation, for Sundance to set upon—further adding stability. Finally, the type is arranged symmetrically to further amplify this notion.

KO:KE
Designer: Zeljka Zupanic

Associative Color Response:
· stimulating, cheerful: high-chroma yellow-orange
· powerful, strength: black

Color Scheme: one hue plus neutral

The KO:KE logomark use of one hue with a neutral color is symmetrically balanced to give the mark authority.

Funny Boy Films
Designers: Shaun Webb, James Sakamoto, and Matt Sloane
Art Director: Mark Sackett
Studio: Sackett Design

Associative Color Response:
· stimulating, cheerful: mid-range green
· powerful, strength: black

Color Scheme: one hue plus neutral

The method of separation (i.e., marking out plainly the most meaningful part) is utilized within the Funny Boy Films logotype. Within this method, four formal techniques are utilized to help create a jumping sensation: 3-D illusion; extra fat-to-skinny; flipped-backwards typography; and a tilting letterform off the pre-existing plane. When added up, this logotype constitutes a lively and energetic mark.

communities.com
Designer: Mark Sackett

Associative Color Response:
· classic, powerful: high-chroma blue-violet
· powerful, strength: black

Color Scheme: one hue plus neutral

The communities.com logotype uses similarity of form to harmonize all parts. The dot at the end of "communities" is the exact size of the eye of the lowercase "i." The dot is then enlarged to be utilized as a balloon. Blue-violet is used in the enlarged dot as if it were an inflection in someone's voice.

TerraVida Coffee
Studio: Hornall Anderson Design Works

Associative Color Response:
· tasty, warm: high-chroma orange
· powerful, strength: black

Color Scheme: one hue plus neutral

Texture and substitution is utilized in the TerraVida Coffee logo to create visual appeal. Texture acts as a visual magnet—it draws the viewer in. The modified "A" and "V" in TerraVida use the idea of a leaf or coffee bean to attract visual interest.

Seattle's Convention and Visitors Bureau
Studio: Hornall Anderson Design Works

Associative Color Response:
· classic: mid-range green
· powerful, strength: black

Color Scheme: one hue plus neutral

The color black in the Seattle's Convention and Visitors Bureau mark is primarily used to unify the mark. The mid-range green is used to humanize the symbol.

San Francisco Marriott
Studio: Hornall Anderson Design Works

Associative Color Response:
· flavorsome: dark yellow
· pleasant, harvest, natural: golden-yellow

Color Scheme: one hue with shading (achromatic)

Due to the color palette chosen, the San Francisco Marriott mark is warm, inviting, and restful. The symmetrical balance further amplifies this feel.

virtutech
Studio: Hornall Anderson Design Works

Associative Color Response:
· flavorsome: neutral gray
· pleasant, harvest, natural: high-chroma orange

Color Scheme: one hue plus neutral (tinted)

Any time a warm, high-chroma hue is juxtaposed next to a neutral gray, the color will pop. This is the case with the high-chroma orange in the virtutech logomark—it appears to jump forward.

Full Moon Foods
Designer: Wayne Sakamoto
Art Director: Mark Sackett
Studio: Sackett Design

Associative Color Response:
· dignified: buttery, golden-yellow/
  beige
· regal, classic: high-chroma blue-
  violet

Color Scheme: direct complementary
with tinting and shading

The Full Moon Foods logomark is
an excellent example of using the
right hues for food products. The
golden-yellow hue suggests baked
goods, whereas the blue-violet when
juxtaposed with fruit causes the
warm colors of the fruit to pop.

Screamer
Studio: Hornall Anderson Design
Works

Associative Color Response:
· mature, solid: neutral blue-gray
· harvest, natural: high-chroma
  orange

Color Scheme: one hue plus neutral
(tinted)

The Screamer logomark is a fine
example of utilizing warm and cool
colors to make the mark pop off
the page.

River Place
Studio: Hornall Anderson Design
Works

Associative Color Response:
· natural: olive
· calm, relaxed: high-chroma blue

Color Scheme: one hue plus neutral

The high-chroma, blue-and-olive
color scheme is a fine example
of both learned association and
psychological understanding.

Centraal Museum 2
Studio: Thonik Design

Associative Color Response:
· hope, lively: high-chroma green
· powerful, fantasy: high-chroma
  blue-violet

Color Scheme: two points of a tetrad

This offbeat color combination
harmonizes through the use of cyan.
The mark consists of a bold graphic
shape with a lowercase letterform
"c" stepped and repeated to create a
modular mark.

Centraal Museum: Neo
Studio: Thonik Design

Associative Color Response:
· aggressive, exciting: high-chroma
  pink
· vigorous, youthful: high-chroma
  yellow

Color Scheme: incongruous

The Neo logomark uses a high-
chroma color palette to help create
a highly kinetic mark. Part of a
series (see left), the lowercase
letterform "c" is utilized again
to create visual consistency from
mark to mark, as well as to induce
kinetic energy through placement
and scaling.

Mocha Bees
Designer: Tanya A. Ortega
Art Director: John T. Drew

Associative Color Response:
· wholesome, good, healthy: earth-
  tone red
· harvest, natural: golden yellow

Color Scheme: two points of a
Tetrad

The hues chosen for this mark were
based on learned color identification
(milk chocolate and honey). Tinting
the hue to give it a more favorable
appetite rating toned down the
honey color.

Centenal
Designer: Tanya A. Ortega
Art Director: John T. Drew

Associative Color Response:
· exciting, flamboyant: high-chroma red-violet
· lively, dramatic: high-chroma blue

Color Scheme: two points of a tetrad (near incongruous)

This modular-system logomark utilizes an offbeat color combination to create a vibrant and kinetic mark. High-chroma hues coupled with a directional mark (spinning) allow the typography in the Centenal mark to interlock.

Tega 3
Designer: Tanya A. Ortega
Art Director: John T. Drew

Associative Color Response:
· classic, timeless, practical: neutral gray
· solid, classic: dark gray

Color Scheme: achromatic

This color palette creates a highly professional and subdued logomark for a fishing outfitter. Focusing on quality, a reductive illustration was created utilizing shades of gray to reinforce the idea.

Xilox
Designer: Tanya A. Ortega
Art Director: John T. Drew

Associative Color Response:
· brilliant, energizing: high-chroma red
· powerful, elegant: black

Color Scheme: one hue plus neutral

The Xilox logomark is an excellent example of a modular system—the mark consists of two repeating parts. Red and black make an energetic color scheme that creates a highly kinetic experience in combination with the mark. The mark is placed on an angle to help induce kinetic energy by creating visual tension with the company name—an oppositional technique. This color scheme is highly energetic. A high-chroma red hue is intensely vivid and warm and moves forward to more than most warm colors. The black hue is very cool, in opposition to the red hue.

Stage
Designer: Tanya A. Ortega
Art Director: John T. Drew

Associative Color Response:
· brilliant, energizing: high-chroma red
· powerful, elegant: black

Color Scheme: one hue plus neutral

Red-and-black color schemes work well for inducing kinetic energy or for activating a mark. (See Xilox, left.)

Doree
Designer: Tarun Deep Girdher

Associative Color Response:
· brilliant, energizing: high-chroma red
· lively, pleasing: high-chroma blue

Color Scheme: primary

Within this mark, the high-chroma hues are utilized to energize the logo and make it harmonize with the typographic forms.

 # Yes
Designer: Stefan G. Bucher
Studio: 344

Associative Color Response:
· brilliant, energizing: high-chroma red
· lively, pleasing: high-chroma orange

Color Scheme: two points of the split complementary

The #Yes logomark utilizes a warm color palette in combination with perspective to create an intriguing mark that looks 3-D.

Rockridge 1
Designer: Brenda Spivack
Studio: Red Table

Associative Color Response:
· quality: neutral
· classic: high-chroma blue-violet

Color Scheme: one hue plus neutral (tinted)

The combination of the typeface and color palette here creates a classic and timeless logotype.

Rockridge 2
Designer: Carlo Irgoyen
Art Director: Brenda Spivack
Studio: Red Table

Associative Color Response:
· cool, classic: light gray
· corporate, timeless: neutral gray

Color Scheme: simple achromatic

The Rockridge logotype is a fine example of using gestalt to create an identifiable mark (double R).

Bagirna
Designer/Art Director: Scott Pridgen

Associative Color Response:
· cool, classic: high-chroma red-violet
· corporate, timeless: high-chroma yellow-green

Color Scheme: near/direct complementary

The Bagirna logotype is a superbly executed retro mark that uses substitution in a clever and intriguing way. The direct complementary, high-chroma color palette helps to communicate the psychedelic nature of the mark.

Rockridge 3
Designer/Art Director: Scott Pridgen

Associative Color Response:
· rustic, warm: earth-tone red
· corporate, timeless: neutral gray

Color Scheme: one hue with tinting and shading plus neutral (tinted)

This logo in the Rockridge series uses the font Copperplate coupled with the earth tone and neutral gray color scheme to communicate a rustic feel.

K&G
Designer: Carlo Irgoyen
Art Director: Brenda Spivack
Studio: Red Table

Associative Color Response:
· smooth, quiet: pastel green
· corporate, timeless: warm neutral gray

Color Scheme: one hue plus neutral (tinted)

The form/counterform relationship found within the K&G logotype is superbly executed to create a cohesive whole. The muted color palette softens the capitalized letterforms to create a conservative corporate feel.

hoopnotica
Designer: Carlo Irgoyen
Art Director: Brenda Spivack
Studio: Red Table

Associative Color Response:
· stimulating, exciting: high-chroma pink
· feminine, flamboyant: high-chroma red-violet

Color Scheme: simple analogous

The high-chroma hues used in this logomark create an atmosphere that is highly dynamic and filled with kinetic energy.

City Beverage
Designer/Art Director: Scott Pridgen

Associative Color Response:
· charming, refined: mid-range
  red-purple
· sweet taste, exciting: high-chroma
  red-violet

Color Scheme: monochromatic
with tinting

The City Beverage logotype uses
typographic opposition to create
a visually intriguing mark. The
monochromatic color scheme is
utilized to unify the mark.

Tecnokar
Designer/Art Director: Scott Pridgen

Associative Color Response:
· work, strong: high-chroma blue
· powerful, heavy: black

Color Scheme: one hue plus neutral

The use of the blue hue (cool color)
within the Tecnokar logomark helps
to articulate a 3-D illusion. This is
also achieved through perspective
and opposition with the company
name.

Waiter
Designer/Illustrator/Art Director:
Lanny Sommese
Studio: Sommese Design

Associative Color Response:
· energizing, dramatic: high-chroma
  red
· elegant, night: black

Color Scheme: one hue plus neutral

The master of substitution, designer
and illustrator Lanny Sommese,
illustrates the art of camouflage
and deception within this mark.
The counterform of the center
forearm creates a waiter's face—a
wonderfully executed example of
economy of line.

2004 Pet Extravaganza
Designer/Illustrator/Art Director:
Lanny Sommese
Studio: Sommese Design

Associative Color Response:
· new growth: high-chroma green
· prestigious, spiritual, basic: black

Color Scheme: one hue plus neutral

The 2004 Pet Extravaganza logomark
creates a form/counterform
relationship that unites the two
halves of the mark. The high-chroma
green is utilized, through the
use of learned association, as
representative of grass.

Joel Confer
Designer/Illustrator/Art Director:
Lanny Sommese
Studio: Sommese Design

Associative Color Response:
· stimulating, fun: high-chroma pink
· spiritual, basic: black

Color Scheme: one hue plus neutral

As noted in most of the two-color
logomarks illustrated in this
chapter, the black hue is utilized
with an additional color. This color
is typically on the warm side of the
color wheel, helping to make the
mark pop or stand out. This is the
case with the Joel Confer logo.

Mt
Designer: Mike Paz
Art Director: John T. Drew

Associative Color Response:
· thought, receptive: high-chroma
  orange
· enterprise, powerful: high-chroma
  yellow-orange

Color Scheme: simple analogous

This logotype is a beautiful
combination of color, gestalt, and
economy of line. Note how the stroke
of the capital letterform "M" is
perfectly executed by placing the
counterform at the right distance
away from the "t." The color scheme,
which is simple analogous, perfectly
matches the elegant execution of
this logotype.

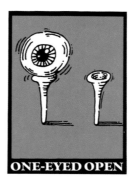

Vyway Market & Brand Strategy
Designer: Renita Breitenbucher
Studio: Nita B. Creative

Associative Color Response:
· lively, pleasing: high-chroma blue
· classic, corporate, timeless: neutral gray

Color Scheme: one hue plus neutral (tinted)

The Vyway Market & Brand Strategy mark demonstrates the simplicity of a well-executed design. The color scheme is well chosen to communicate a professional atmosphere.

Gullifty's
Designer/Art Director: Lanny Sommese
Calligrapher: Bill Kinser
Studio: Sommese Design

Associative Color Response:
· life, fresh: high-chroma green
· dignified, pleasant: golden yellow

Color Scheme: near incongruous

The unusual color palette chosen for the Gullifty's logomark demonstrates the uniqueness of incongruous color schemes. If done well, these types of color palettes can infuse marks with lively interplay.

The Saloon
Designer: Kristin Sommese
Art Directors: Kristin Sommese and Lanny Sommese
Studio: Sommese Design

Associative Color Response:
· agreeable, pleasant, youthful: high-chroma yellow
· powerful, heavy, basic: black

Color Scheme: one hue plus neutral

Often, overlapping objects induce kinetic energy—this is the case with The Saloon logomark. Note how the beer mug is moving into the circle. A large portion of the beer mug is within the circle, while a small part is outside. This causes the beer mug image to move in an inward direction; it is also helped by the way the object is drawn. If a greater part of the image were placed outside of the circle, no matter how the object was drawn, the object would move in an outward direction.

One-Eyed Open
Designer/Illustrator/Art Director: Lanny Sommese
Studio: Sommese Design

Associative Color Response:
· nervous, grass: high-chroma green
· powerful, basic: black

Color Scheme: one hue plus neutral

The One-Eyed Open logomark uses learned color association to help place this mark in context. This humorous mark references the human anatomy, not only the eyeball but also by the placement of the two golf tees.

Safe Chicago
Designer: Michael Gray

Associative Color Response:
· hoping, warm: high-chroma red
· powerful, basic: black

Color Scheme: one hue plus neutral

This mark is an excellent example of economy of line. The red cross is perfectly positioned so that the top section also functions as the front door. The color red is symbolically used to communicate a welcome hope.

Bear's Kitchen
Designer: Minato Ishikawa

Associative Color Response:
· hoping, warm: high-chroma red
· powerful, basic: high-chroma blue

Color Scheme: primary

Here, quality of line work coupled with the primary color palette is superbly geared toward the target audience (children).

Nita B. Creative
Designer: Renita Breitenbucher
Studio: Nita B. Creative

Associative Color Response:
· elegant: black
· dignity, pleasing, mature: high-chroma blue

Color Scheme: simple monochromatic plus neutral

This simple monochromatic study (two steps) with a neutral (black hue) is executed to convey elegance. This is brought about through the color choice, typeface, and geometric forms.

ir 2
Designer: Alex Prompongsatorn
Art Director: John T. Drew

Associative Color Response:
· stimulating, active: high-chroma red
· pleasure, refreshing: pastel blue

Color Scheme: primary with tinting

Here, the economy of line, form/counterform relationship, and outlined letterforms create a highly kinetic logotype. The primary color palette further amplifies the kinetic energy of this mark.

Sommese Posters
Designer/Illustrator/Art Director:
Lanny Sommese
Studio: Sommese Design

Associative Color Response:
· cheerful, youthful: high-chroma yellow
· powerful: black

Color Scheme: one hue plus neutral

The Sommese Posters mark uses a combination of a high-chroma hue (yellow) and type as image to create a human face.

Fisher Girls' Golf Benefit
Designer/Illustrator: Lanny Sommese
Art Directors: Kristin Sommese and Lanny Sommese
Studio: Sommese Design

Associative Color Response:
· cheerful, youthful: high-chroma yellow
· powerful: black

Color Scheme: one hue accent plus neutral

The Fisher Girls' Golf Benefit uses substitution in a most elegant way. Separation is utilized, through the use of color, to highlight the most meaningful part.

Sommese Design
Designer/Illustrator/Art Director:
Lanny Sommese
Studio: Sommese Design

Associative Color Response:
· cheerful, curious: high-chroma red
· provoking, stimulating: dark orange

Color Scheme: simple analogous with tinting and shading

This male/female mark utilizes a simple analogous color palette to help communicate a humorous yet tasteful mark.

NS
Designer: Jessica L. Howard
Art Director: John T. Drew

Associative Color Response:
· cheerful, curious: high-chroma blue-green
· provoking, stimulating: dark blue

Color Scheme: simple analogous with tinting and shading

The blue hue within the NS logotype uses shading to create the darker color and tinting to lighten the hue up a little. This hue is juxtaposed next to the high-chroma blue-green hue to create a dynamic simple analogous (two steps) color palette. These two hues are utilized to create a visual separation between the capital letterforms "N" and "S."

Savannah Hill

love Pollution
Designer: Betty Avila
Art Director: John T. Drew

Associative Color Response:
· love, compassion: high-chroma red
· debase: dark gray

Color Scheme: one hue with neutral
(tinted)

Substitution and color coding
is utilized in the love Pollution
logomark to create a wonderful
masthead. Both the dark gray and
high-chroma red utilizes learned
color association to execute the
concept.

Alex Design
Designer: Alex Prompongsatorn
Art Director: John T. Drew

Associative Color Response:
· lively, strong: pastel blue
· restrained: mid-range pink

Color Scheme: primary with tinting

This modular-system mark uses a
blue dot placed in the center that is
exactly one-half the thickness of the
stroke adjacent to it. This ensures
that the dot harmonizes with the two
adjacent elements.

Savannah Hill
Designer/Illustrator/Art Director:
Lanny Sommese
Studio: Sommese Design

Associative Color Response:
· comfortable, romantic: pastel pink
· paradise, pure: high-chroma blue-
  green

Color Scheme: near complementary
with tinting

The color combination for the
Savannah Hills mark uses learned
color association to communicate
a tropical paradise. This is also
brought about through the form and
silhouette of the object used.

Kenney Yang
Designer: Kenney Yang

Associative Color Response:
· powerful, strong: black
· corporate, quality: neutral gray

Color Scheme: simple achromatic

If done correctly, when using a
modular system to create a logomark,
consistency at all levels of business
operations is implied. In this case,
the choice of color palette
communicates quality.

**Faculty of Arts and Sciences:
Rutgers University Newark**
Designer/Art Director: Ned Drew

Associative Color Response:
· elegant: black
· brilliant: high-chroma red

Color Scheme: one hue with neutral

The economy of line found within the
logotype is superbly executed. Note
how the top spine of the "s" and the
bowl of the lowercase "a" are used
as one element to communicate
both letterforms. The sophistication
of this logotype, coupled with the
red-and-black color combination,
communicates content and context.

The Design Consortium
Designer/Art Director: Ned Drew

Associative Color Response:
· quality: neutral gray
· energizing: high-chroma red

Color Scheme: one hue with neutral

As a student graphic Studio, Rutgers
University (The State University
of New Jersey, Newark) Design
Consortium presents enthusiasm
with a polished finish in their
logomark. The color choice creates a
3-D effect while being mindful of the
studio's well-respected and award-
winning design status.

GraphicInstinct

i-COPACK

Graphic Instinct
Designer: Linda Liejard

Associative Color Response:
· elegant, strong: black
· brilliant: high-chroma red

Color Scheme: one hue with neutral

Economy of line is one of the most effective ways to create a logotype. The Graphic Instinct mark is a fine example of this formal technique.

i-Copack
Designer: Linda Liejard

Associative Color Response:
· active: dark yellow
· energizing, stimulating: high-chroma red-orange

Color Scheme: near incongruous with shading

These types of color palettes are used less often and therefore offer a more unusual color appearance. A near incongruous, or two points of a tetrad, color palette is less likely to clash than a straight-up incongruous color scheme.

Richie H. Eap 1
Designer: Richie H. Eap
Art Director: John T. Drew

Associative Color Response:
· active: high-chroma orange
· energizing, stimulating: high-chroma blue-violet

Color Scheme: near complementary

In the Richie H. Eap personal logotype, note how the top bowl of the lowercase "e" and the arm of the lowercase "r" line to create a unified mark. A complementary color palette is utilized to help activate the composition.

Richie H. Eap 2
Designer: Richie H. Eap
Art Director: John T. Drew

Associative Color Response:
· active: high-chroma yellow-green
· energizing, stimulating: high-chroma violet

Color Scheme: near complementary

An excellent example of substitution, designer Richie H. Eap supplants a lowercase "r" for the stem of the Uppercase "E." He further uses substitution by replacing the arm of the uppercase "E" with a tilde sign found within the same typeface. This ensures visual consistency. A near complementary color scheme is utilized to activate the mark.

APS Corporation
Designer: Linda Liejard

Associative Color Response:
· dignity: high-chroma blue
· friendly: high-chroma orange

Color Scheme: near complementary

By placing the mark on an angle and using a high-chroma near complementary color palette, the mark becomes energized. APS is separated from the rest of the mark by placing it on a horizontal angle (it is broken from the pre-existing plane). This draws the eye toward it and calls forth the most meaningful part of the mark.

Wu Design
Designer: Songlin Wu
Art Director: John T. Drew

Associative Color Response:
· dignified, relaxed: high-chroma blue
· calm, quiet: pastel blue

Color Scheme: simple monochromatic with tinting

The mark produced by Songlin Wu is an excellent example of a modular system. A simple, monochromatic color palette with tinting is utilized to help create a 3-D illusion on a 2-D plane.

Adventure Travel Group
Designer/Art Director: Saied Farisi

Associative Color Response:
· energetic: high-chroma red
· elegant, mysterious: black

Color Scheme: one hue plus neutral

The mark that is displayed
within this logomark is perfectly
symmetrical. To ensure that all
anatomical parts are a mirror to one
another, execute only one half of the
mark, then copy, place, and flip the
mark into position.

**Bureau of Primary Care and Rural
Health Systems 1**
Designer/Art Director: Saied Farisi

Associative Color Response:
· warm, secure: earth-tone red
· elegant: black

Color Scheme: one hue (shaded)
plus neutral

The rectangle utilized in this
logomark references the State in
which this bureau operates; the
flower depicted within the rectangle
is indigenous to the region; and
the color palette is coded to the
landscape (inter-mountain west of
the United States).

Artistry Nails
Designer: Linda Liejard

Associative Color Response:
· bold: high-chroma yellow-green
· stimulating: high-chroma pink

Color Scheme: near complementary
with tinting

Simplicity of line and effective color
use and placement unifies the four
components found within the mark.
A near complementary color palette
is utilized to create a lively color
scheme.

APS Corporation
Designer: Linda Liejard

Associative Color Response:
· active: dark yellow

Color Scheme: simple
monochromatic

The APS mark is a fine example of
the phenomenon that cool colors
recede and warm colors come forth.
A simple monochromatic color study
is utilized to help articulate the 3-D
illusion. Tinting is applied to the two
shapes that appear to be in front. If
this color solution were reversed, the
mark would appear to be flat.

gr
Designer: Songlin Wu
Art Director: John T. Drew

Associative Color Response:
· pleasing, lively: high-chroma blue
· refreshing, dependable: pastel
 blue

Color Scheme: simple
monochromatic with tinting

The similarity of form (five circles)
in the logotype act to unify the mark,
and the simple monochromatic color
palette is utilized to help establish a
visual hierarchy.

Ward Engineering Group
Designer/Art Director: Saied Farisi

Associative Color Response:
· brilliant, energizing: high-chroma
 red
· power, dignified: high-chroma
 blue-violet

Color Scheme: two points of a split
complementary

This highly energetic color
combination infuses vigor into a
mark that already has kinetic energy.
By doing so, a 3-D penetrating effect
is created.

Bureau of Primary Care and Rural Health Systems 2
Designer/Art Director: Saied Farisi

Associative Color Response:
· healing: high-chroma orange
· pure: high-chroma blue-green

Color Scheme: near complementary with shading

Note how the flower is primarily inside of the rectangle, implying that this species of flower is indigenous to the geographical location (intermountain West of the United States).

aspire
Creative Director: David Ferrell

Associative Color Response:
· endearing: dark gray
· quality, passion: neutral gray

Color Scheme: simple monochromatic with tinting

The aspire logotype uses a gradient to metaphorically symbolize the meaning of the word. The font chosen is a very open counterform typeface to help reinforce the concept. The logotype is beautifully simple.

Flux
Designer: Diana Gonzalez
Art Director: Jen Bracy

Associative Color Response:
· energetic: high-chroma red
· powerful, strong: black

Color Scheme: one hue plus neutral

The formal execution and the applied color use is an excellent example of the literal meaning of the word. This superbly executed mark clearly demonstrates how color can be used in the creation of content.

bike u.s.a.
Designer: Andrew Ung
Art Director: John T. Drew

Associative Color Response:
· brilliant, energizing: high-chroma red
· honesty, strength: high-chroma blue

Color Scheme: incongruous

The logotype created for bike u.s.a. is an excellent example of learned color association. Patriotic in its theme, this logotype is an excellent example of type as image.

Chicago Children's Choir
Studio: Essex Two

Associative Color Response:
· energizing: high-chroma red
· strong, basic: black

Color Scheme: one hue plus neutral

Separation and consistency of form help to create this unified mark.

Irox
Designer: April Medina

Associative Color Response:
· energizing: high-chroma red
· strong, basic: black

Color Scheme: one hue plus neutral

When using any color combination, a more dynamic color palette can often be created when there is an imbalance of hues, as shown here.

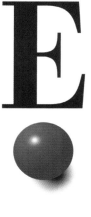

Rhombus Technologies
Designer/Art Director: Saied Farisi

Associative Color Response:
· energizing: high-chroma red
· strong, basic: black

Color Scheme: one hue plus neutral

The practical use of color is often overlooked. The way that the color is placed within this mark creates eye movement in a positive direction.

Hetrick Communications
Studio: Essex Two

Associative Color Response:
· energizing: high-chroma red
· strong, basic: black

Color Scheme: one hue plus neutral

An imbalance in color here helps to create a dynamic logotype. Placing the capital "H" on an angle helps to further induce kinetic energy.

ICIN
Studio: Essex Two

Associative Color Response:
· lively: high-chroma blue
· powerful, strong, basic: black

Color Scheme: one hue plus neutral

This modular system is an excellent example of using separation to create a figure/ground relationship within a mark. The blue modular unit is slightly separated and placed in a different hue that is lighter than the four other units. This gives the impression that this is the top right portion of the mark.

Camp Madron
Studio: Essex Two

Associative Color Response:
· earthy, strong: dark red
· rustic, earthy: earth-tone red

Color Scheme: simple achromatic

The simple achromatic color scheme employed within this mark harmonizes with the aesthetic form. This includes utilizing a dark red and earth-tone red hue.

Equity Residential
Studio: Essex Two

Associative Color Response:
· elegant, refined: dark red
· powerful, strong: black

Color Scheme: one hue plus neutral

Any time a flat object is juxtaposed with an object that looks 3-D, both objects will amplify their corresponding effects.

Burack & Co
Studio: Essex Two

Associative Color Response:
· springtime, life: high-chroma green
· happy, dramatic: high-chroma blue

Color Scheme: two points of a split complementary

A near simple analogous color palette, or two points of a split complementary, this mark utilizes the hue scheme to its fullest potential. The green hue is lighter than the blue, creating a foreground/background relationship.

Intellivue Unplugged

Designer: Jun Li

The logo for Intellivue Unplugged represents a new system of wireless patient monitoring developed by Phillips. Designer Jun Li wanted the mark to convey a sense of free, uninhibited motion, innovation, simplicity, and the benefits of modern technology. Bright colors were chosen to convey a sense of warmth and excitement through the newly realized mobility gained by Intellivue wireless technology. Orange and light blue were used because of their psychological and behavioral effects. (Orange = healing, warm, happy, energizing, friendly, cheerful, exciting, and stimulating. Light blue = pleasurable, quiet, peaceful, refreshing, faithful, and dependable.)

Intellivue Unplugged was launched at a national conference in 2004 via a series of onscreen presentations. In order to ensure legibility within this context, a color investigation of different textural backgrounds was conducted. Later color studies were carried out to make sure that the mark worked not only within an Internet context, but also on the company's off-white monitor devices. Through these color studies, Li found that the logomark projected well on dark textural backgrounds as well as on off-white.

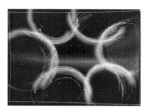

1. Blue circles appear on the screen, from small to big

2. Blue circles fly towards the viewer in perspective view

3. Blue circles turn and face straight towards the viewer, illuminating

4. "Dancing" blue circles

5. Blue circles start to form and suggest the shape of logo

6. Blue circles connect with each other

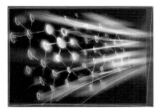

7. Blue circles multiply themselves and form the network, then one circle starts to shine and turns into orange color

8. Zoom in, the rest of the blue circle network fades away

9. The line connector breaks

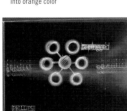

10. "Unplugged" logo forms with type

T Two simple rules need to be followed to make sure that a mark, logomark, or logotype can be seen clearly at great distances. First, the anatomical structure of the mark needs to be created so that at a minimum the counterforms within the mark are equal to or greater than the form. This assures that the counterform/form relationships have the same visual angle, or that the counterform has a greater visual angle, ensuring that the mark does not collapse in on itself at any distance. The above logomark is a great example of this.

The second rule is that the color value differential (CVD) should be set at 20%. This can be verified through the use of the PANTONE Color Cue. When taking color measurements or samples, use the "Y" of the tristimulus values (see Glossary) displayed on the Color Cue. (Note: some color combinations break the 20% rule, but can be seen at their prescribed distance.)

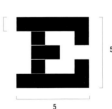

In this case Dr. Snellen's letterform has the same size counterform as the stroke-width of the capital "E," and therefore has the same visual angle.

The Museum of Sex

Designer: Brenda McManus

This experimental noncommissioned work is a highly diverse logomark designed for the Museum of Sex in New York City. Designer Brenda McManus wanted to experiment by making the logomark as flexible and divergent as the subject matter. This unique mark, first designed in black and white, demonstrates the richness of content, appropriateness of color use, and variants/consistency of form (an oxymoron). The logo reflects the variety of content, from a two-color to a three-color, five-color, six-color, seven-color, and eight-color multiformity. The mark is designed to transform itself to fit the subject matter from birth control to homosexual life.

 When dealing with found imagery, several issues need to be considered so that the job prints in the manner expected. (Found imagery for the Web, motion graphics, and broadcast purposes are nonissues.)

Original Images

(photographs/negatives)

With old photographs or negatives, the concern for quality reproduction should be ascertained by inspecting sharpness, deterioration, fading, and discoloration. If the photograph or negative is deemed to be in good shape, a drum scan would capture the highest amount of information and quality. Do not go below a flatbed scanner in quality. Scan the image in at 300dpi, CMYK mode, Tagged Image File Format (TIFF) formatting, and at 100% of size. If the image is a slide, use a drum scan, or have the image developed into the largest photograph possible while still keeping the image in focus. Once the image is developed, a flatbed scanner can be used. If the image is going to be used larger than 100% of size, add twice the amount of dpi for twice the size of the image (see diagram).

Found Objects

If possible, use a flatbed scanner for found objects. Spray-paint the inside of a shoebox with a flat black to create a quality scan. Take the flatbed scanner lid off, and place the shoebox over the object. This does two things. First, it creates a solid black background around the scanned image. Often, a quick mask can be created quite easily with this type of background. Second, by creating a black box, a flatbed scanner is able to create a larger depth of field—more of a 3-D object will be in focus by using a black box. Scan the object in using the same settings as above.

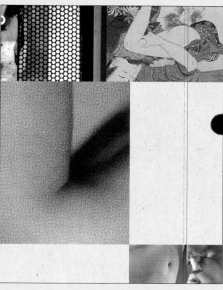

Found Images

(commercially printed)

Found images that have been commercially printed most often have a halftone dot (although there are some exceptions). The best way to determine whether a found image has a pre-existing dot pattern is by using a loop. A loop is basically a magnifying glass. Sheet-fed offset printing is typically run at 150 lines per inch; web-offset printing has a dot pattern of 133 lines per inch; silkscreen is 75 to 65 lines per inch; and a typical black-and-white newspaper is 55 lines, or dots, per inch (this is called frequency). Scanning in any commercially printed image that has a halftone dot will most often cause a moiré pattern. A moiré pattern is an undesirable pattern caused by an incorrect screen angle(s) of halftone dots. In four-color process printing, each channel or plate has

a different screen angle assigned for each continuous-tone color (cyan, magenta, yellow, and black). When a commercially printed image is placed on a flatbed scanner, more often than not an incorrect screen angle will be created in the scan, thus causing a moiré pattern. To help guard against this, place the image on the flatbed scanner at an angle of 20 degrees. The image may have to be scanned in several times in order to find the exact angle that will prevent the least amount of moiré pattern.

There are two ways to eliminate the moiré pattern entirely. First, go to Pixelate, under Filter in the main menu of Photoshop, and select Color halftone. This filter applies a crude halftone dot to the found image (less than newspaper). Second, a color halftone dot can be hand-built by selecting, copying, and pasting each of the channels (cyan, magenta, yellow, and black) into its own

grayscale document. (Make sure to name the grayscale documents "Cyan," "Magenta," "Yellow," and "Black" so that there is no confusion.) After each channel is placed into its own grayscale document, convert the document to bitmap. The Cyan document should have a screen angle of 108 degrees; the Magenta document an angle of 162 degrees; the Yellow document an angle of 90 degrees; and the Black document 45 degrees. The resolution output should still be 300dpi. There are four default screen patterns and an option to create a custom pattern. Experiment with all of them to achieve the best result. Three other options exist: the halftone screen pattern, the shape of the halftone (round, diamond, ellipse, line, square, and cross), and its frequency. Again, experimentation is needed for optimal results. With each method used, a noticeable halftone pattern will occur.

Found Illustrations

(100% of color)

With illustrations, flat pattern and printed at 100% of color, moiré patterns will not occur. If the illustration is in good shape, the image will scan in well on a flatbed scanner—follow the directions above for Original Images.

Three Colors

A true three-color logomark, using three inks, is rare in comparison with all other marks. Not quite four colors, a three-color mark offers little budgetary gain, and is far more expensive than a one- or two-color mark. Therefore, stretching two colors to make them look like three is often a better solution. Many of the logos found within this chapter stretch two colors to make them look like three, or they use a four-color process to build a three-hue color combination.

Many of the traditional color schemes that have been empirically tested by generations use three hues. Primary, secondary, tertiary, triadic, split complementary, and an analogous color scheme use three hues to construct the palette. However, many of the traditional color palettes that utilize two hues can be easily altered to create a complex color scheme. Within this chapter there are excellent examples of color use and color management. From budgetary concerns to legibility issues, color ultimately controls the effectiveness of the end product.

Polar bear

Lion

HRT
Designer: Boris Ljubicic

Associative Color Response:
· brilliant: high-chroma red
· dignity: high-chroma blue
· quality: neutral gray

Color Scheme: two hues of a triad plus neutral tint

This logo reveals the acronym of the Croatian broadcasting corporation and includes a color representation of each arm—blue for television, red for radio, and white for joint services. The logo incorporates two red squares from the Croatian coat of arms that can be manipulated equally well on all static and motion collateral. This gives the designer ultimate control of the visual imagery while maintaining a consistent graphic standard.

Dash
Studio: Bremmer & Goris Communications

Associative Color Response:
· agreeable: high-chroma yellow
· lively: high-chroma blue
· motion: high-chroma green

Color Scheme: random/primaries and secondary hues

The negative white lines of this logomark build layers of information from foreground to background through variable thicknesses. The lines become thick and bolder in the foreground and diminish to a thin horizon line. This basic design concept is strengthened through the use of pure colors that activate the eye and reinforce the directional quality inherent in the mark.

Envent, Inc. (ent) 1
Designer: Francisco Ortiz
Art Director: John T. Drew

Associative Color Response:
· valuable: gold
· dignity: high-chroma blue
· quality: neutral gray

Color Scheme: incongruous plus neutral (tinted)

The planes of color build letter recognition from left to right. The prominent white "e" serves as a wayfinding tool that defines the starting point, further reiterated in the thin line that unifies the mark and connotes the minimal characteristics of each letter.

In the examples shown here, the foreground, background, and the movement between these areas are created through the change of line quality in both of these marks. What makes each of them distinctive is the subtle connotations implied by the quality of the line (organic versus inorganic).

Lion
Designer: Chihiro Katoh

Associative Color Response:
· healing, growing, happy: high-chroma red-orange
· exhilarating, inspiring, stimulating: dark orange
· restrained, soft, quiet: mid-range pink

Color Scheme: near analogous plus tint

Polar bear
Designer: Chihiro Katoh

Associative Color Response:
· charming, refined: high-chroma blue-violet
· serene, credible, devoted: dark blue
· elegant: mid-range blue-violet

Color Scheme: monochromatic (plus tint and shade)

ENOUGH
Studio: Bremmer & Goris Communications

Associative Color Response:
· brilliant, intense, energizing: high-chroma red
· powerful, basic: black
· excitement, stimulating, fun: high-chroma yellow-orange

Color Scheme: near incongruous plus neutral

The three colors that make up this logotype have each been paired as a background and foreground color for two letters (black on red, red on yellow-orange, and yellow-orange on black). Stated in this order, it is easy to see the algorithmic pattern defined by the designer. The overlap of colors, to create a depth of field in a narrow space, is one of the details that make this mark interesting.

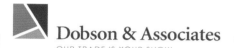

Alligator

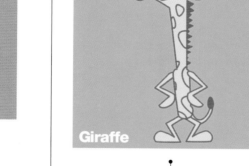

Giraffe

unplugged

Dobson & Associates
Studio: Bremmer & Goris
Communications

Associative Color Response:
· classic: mid-range green
· serene, credible, devoted: dark blue

Color Scheme: near incongruous plus neutral with tinting

Adding white to the blue diminishes the intensity of the hue and fools the eye into believing that a pure gray color is included. Although only the transparency or volume of ink laid down in the halftone pattern has been manipulated, this method is an excellent way of creating a three-color design using only two inks. Different inks may yield highly unexpected results depending on the purity or build of the hue.

Envent, Inc. (ent) 2
Designer: Francisco Ortiz
Art Director: John T. Drew

Associative Color Response:
· valuable: gold
· dignity: high-chroma blue
· quality: neutral gray

Color Scheme: incongruous plus neutral (tinted)

Envent, Inc. (ent) 3
Designer: Francisco Ortiz
Art Director: John T. Drew

Associative Color Response:
· valuable: gold
· dignity: high-chroma blue
· quality: neutral gray

Color Scheme: incongruous plus neutral (tinted)

Giraffe
Designer: Chihiro Katoh

Associative Color Response:
· healing, growing, happy: high-chroma orange
· exhilarating, inspiring, stimulating: dark orange
· gentle: pastel orange

Color Scheme: monochromatic (plus tint and shade)

Alligator
Designer: Chihiro Katoh

Associative Color Response:
· life, motion, growth: high-chroma green
· natural, growth, restful: dark green
· classic: pastel green

Color Scheme: monochromatic (plus tint and shade)

These four marks are unified through the use of an overriding tetrad color scheme (red, blue, orange, green). Each mark uses its primary color as a point of departure to define additional analogous or monochromatic hues. In this way, the designer achieves unity within each mark and creates an overall playful identity that would work well for children.

Phillips Intellivue unplugged 1
Designer/Art Director: Jun Li
Studio: Juno Studio

Associative Color Response:
· brilliant, intense, energizing: high-chroma red
· powerful, basic: black
· quality: neutral gray

Color Scheme: hue plus neutral tints

This logomark for a wireless patient-monitoring system highlights the freedom and mobility patients gained from wireless technology through a disconnected circle that is projected in bright and cheery colors. The gray communicates a level of competency expected from the medical field, and the thickness of each stroke implies equality in the services provided. Together, these colors build a complex picture of cutting-edge technology delivered with warmth and excitement.

TermeTuhelj

THE dub HOUSE

encode

unplugged

TermeTuhelj
Designer: Izvorka Serdarevic
Studio: Tridvajedan

Associative Color Response:
· lively, pleasant: high-chroma blue
· new growth, sharp: high-chroma yellow-green
· powerful, basic: black

Color Scheme: near incongruous

The Terme Tuhelj logomark was designed for a natural-spring spa in the inner part of Croatia (Zagorje). The blue and yellow-green hues symbolically reference water and the natural surroundings of the spa.

Sen Nen Bi
Designer: Hiroyuki Matsuishi

Associative Color Response:
· dignified, lively, pleasant: high-chroma blue
· life, motion, growth: high-chroma green
· brilliant, intense, energizing: high-chroma red

Color Scheme: direct complementary plus blue-violet

This logotype possesses one secondary and two primary hues. Visual consistency is brought about through the equal proportion of color application and font to create a dynamic mark.

The Dub House
Designer: Kiley Del Valle
Creative Director: Jonathan Gouthier
Studio: Gouthier Design

Associative Color Response:
· pleasant, peaceful, happy: pastel blue
· quality: neutral gray
· powerful, basic: black

Color Scheme: one hue with neutrals (tinted)

The gray hue is used as a shadow to help build the mark dimension. The pastel blue is used to separate out the most meaningful part to help brand the mark long-term.

encode
Designer: Holly Gressley
Interactive Designer: Doug Lloyd
Art Director: Petter Ringbom
Studio: Flat

Associative Color Response:
· dignified, lively, pleasant: high-chroma blue
· power: dark violet
· powerful: black

Color Scheme: incongruous

This incongruous color palette is made from two inks: blue (cyan) and red (magenta). These two inks are then overprinted to create a third additional color—black. This is an excellent way to stretch color on press to generate more hues than what is loaded in the inkwells.

Phillips Intellivue unplugged 2
Designer/Art Director: Jun Li
Studio: Juno Studio

Associative Color Response:
· new growth, sharp: high-chroma yellow-green
· powerful, basic: black
· quality: neutral gray

Color Scheme: hue plus neutral tints

Tomophase 2
Designer/Art Director: Jun Li
Studio: Juno Studio

Associative Color Response:
· dignified: high-chroma blue
· charming: high-chroma blue-violet
· powerful, basic: black

Color Scheme: simple analogous
plus black

Tomophase 1
Designer/Art Director: Jun Li
Studio: Juno Studio

Associative Color Response:
· taste: dark red
· dignified: high-chroma blue
· powerful, basic: black

Color Scheme: incongruous plus
neutral

Tomophase Corporation is a young
high-tech company that specializes
in developing innovative solutions
for Minimally Invasive Diagnostics
(MID). This optical technology offers
new ways of diagnosing diseases
and performing operations. The
Tomophase logo had to convey the
innovation and technology of these
novel optical devices, and their
association with the medical field.
Therefore, different shades of blue
were used to connect the product
to its working environment. Prior
studies included the use of red with
black or blue to draw attention to the
first two syllables of the logotype.

Jazz Life
Designer: Hiroyuki Matsuishi

Associative Color Response:
· brilliant, intense, energizing: high-
chroma red
· powerful, basic: black
· restrained, soft, quiet: mid-range
pink

Color Scheme: one hue with tinting
plus neutral

The Jazz Life logomark is an excellent
example of effectively using a
gradient to generate motion within a
mark. The organic typeface utilized
within this design is partially layered
(breaking out) on top of the red
rectangle to also convey movement,
and the free style of jazz.

Focus Finance, LLC
Designer/Art Director: Jonathan
Gouthier
Studio: Gouthier Design

Associative Color Response:
· dignified, lively, pleasant: high-
chroma blue
· pleasant, peaceful, happy: pastel
blue
· quality: neutral gray

Color Scheme: monochromatic plus
neutral (tinted)

The pragmatic use of color within
the focus logomark is superbly done.
In this case, hue is implemented to
create stress points and inflections
within the mark.

2005: The Year of The Rooster
Designer: Chen Wang

Associative Color Response:
· energetic, glow: mid-range yellow-
orange
· brilliant, intense, energizing: high-
chroma red

Color Scheme: near incongruous
plus neutral

This is an outstanding example of
type as image. Red and black are
used for their cultural significance
within the Chinese-American
community.

Collectible Creations
Designer: Mark Raebel
Studio: Arsenal Design

Associative Color Response:
· valuable, radiant: gold
· new, pristine, pure: high-chroma blue-green
· mellow: pastel blue-green

Color Scheme: incongruous with tinting

The way in which the mark is cropped (square) in correspondence to the pragmatic color use creates a foreground, middle ground, and background. The typography is centered underneath the mark so the logo remains the focal point.

Aerobloks
Designer: Mark Raebel
Studio: Arsenal Design

Associative Color Response:
· dignified, lively, pleasant: high-chroma blue
· stimulating, aggressive, exciting: high-chroma pink
· memories, power, import: high-chroma violet

Color Scheme: incongruous with overprinting

This incongruous color palette is made from two inks. A third color is created by overprinting the high-chroma pink (magenta) on top of the high-chroma blue (cyan).

Expo Design: Hwacheon-gun
Designer: Inyoung Choi

Associative Color Response:
· dignified, lively, pleasant: high-chroma blue
· healing, growing, happy: high-chroma orange
· new growth, sharp: high-chroma yellow-green

Color Scheme: near split complementary with yellow-green

This highly unusual color palette is superbly executed. When trying to build unique color palettes, try using a traditional scheme that is slightly off. The uniqueness of the mark will be further helped by this approach.

Expo Design: National Maritime Police Agency
Designer: Inyoung Choi

Associative Color Response:
· brilliant, intense, energizing: high-chroma red
· dignified, lively, pleasant: high-chroma blue
· charming, elegant, refined: high-chroma blue-violet

Color Scheme: incongruous with blue-violet

Again, designer Inyoung Choi uses a traditional color palette that is slightly off by adding an additional hue—blue-violet.

KLW Group 2
Designer: Mark Raebel
Studio: Arsenal Design

Associative Color Response:
· flamboyant, elegant: high-chroma red-violet
· quality: neutral gray
· sensual, unique: mid-range red-violet

Color Scheme: monochromatic with tinting

In this logo the hues are tinted and then overprinted to create additional hues. The "*" marks placed around the typography, along with the overprinting and block shapes, help to generate kinetic energy.

Via 101
Studio: AdamsMorioka

Associative Color Response:
· new growth, sharp: high-chroma
  yellow-green
· brilliant, intense, energizing: high-
  chroma red
· pleasant, peaceful, happy: pastel
  blue

Color Scheme: near split
complementary

The simplicity of this mark coupled
with the high-chroma hues creates
a highly vivid logotype that is also
stable. Again, a slightly off split
complementary color palette is
utilized to help create a unique
color palette.

Dr Paley Inc
Designer/Creative Director: Drew
M. Dallet
Studio: Boom Creative

Associative Color Response:
· dignified, lively, pleasant: high-
  chroma blue
· quality: neutral gray
· powerful, basic: black

Color Scheme: one hue with
neutrals (tinted)

The black hue in this logomark
creates a third additional hue. This
hue (neutral gray) is used to create
a shadow for the blue mark as well
as a visual tangent to connect the
mark and typography. Conceptually,
the neutral gray form references
the MRIs and X-rays provided by Dr.
Paley's services.

**Expo Design: Ministry of
Government**
Designer: Inyoung Choi

Associative Color Response:
· pleasant, peaceful, happy: pastel
  blue
· charming, elegant, refined: high-
  chroma blue-violet
· new growth, sharp: high-chroma
  yellow-green

Color Scheme: near incongruous
with tinting

This incongruous color scheme is
superbly utilized, helping to create
a unique mark. A gross halftone
screen pattern is added in pastel
blue and yellow-green to help create
kinetic energy.

**Expo Design: Korea-Japan Super
Expo**
Designer: Inyoung Choi

Associative Color Response:
· elegant, refined, taste: dark red
· dignified, lively, pleasant: high-
  chroma blue
· charming, elegant, refined: high-
  chroma blue-violet

Color Scheme: near complementary

This double near complementary
color palette helps to create a
3-D illusion on a 2-D plane. This is
brought about through perspective
and color gradients to make the
"top" believable.

Caliente Mexican Restaurant
Designer: Justina Wang

Associative Color Response:
· life, motion, growth: high-chroma
  green
· brilliant, intense, energizing: high-
  chroma red
· healing, growing, happy: high-
  chroma orange

Color Scheme: direct complementary
with accent orange

When creating a dominant hue
within the parent color scheme,
utilizing an accent color that is
proportionately relative (the way
in which the color is built) to the
predominant hue will create a stress
point or focal point.

SmartEd
Designer/Creative Director: Drew M. Dallet
Studio: Boom Creative

Associative Color Response:
· powerful, basic: black
· flamboyant, elegant: high-chroma red-violet
· welcome, warm-hearted: earth-tone yellow-orange

Color Scheme: incongruous plus neutral

Within the parent color scheme—incongruous plus neutral—red-violet is utilized to unite the logomark. Warm colors come forth and cool colors recede, making the red-violet act as a catalyst within the mark.

The Tipperary Inn: 12 years of mighty craic!
Designer: Mark Raebel
Studio: Arsenal Design

Associative Color Response:
· powerful, basic: black
· life, motion, growth: high-chroma green
· quality: neutral gray

Color Scheme: one hue with neutrals (tinted)

The black and green hues found within this logomark are symbolically used to reference Irish heritage and dark ale (Guinness). Additional content is added through pragmatic color use.

St. Paddy's Day
Designer: Mark Raebel
Studio: Arsenal Design

Associative Color Response:
· flavorsome, active: dark yellow
· natural, growth, restful: dark green
· life, motion, growth: high-chroma green

Color Scheme: near simple analogous with shading

The signifiers embedded in this logomark are quite humorous. The "*" marks, tilted but full beer glass, three-leaf clover, and the use of two shades of green add up to one hell of a night!

Island Genuine Sports
Designer: Mark Raebel
Studio: Arsenal Design

Associative Color Response:
· new growth, sharp: high-chroma yellow-green
· new, pristine, pure: high-chroma blue-green
· powerful, basic: black

Color Scheme: near simple analogous plus neutral

The Island Sports logomark is symmetrically balanced, creating a secure and stable composition. High-chroma yellow-green and blue-green are utilized to engender activity, making the mark more lively and appropriate to the content—an excellent color choice.

The Joe Ski Club
Designer/Creative Director: Drew M. Dallet
Studio: Boom Creative

Associative Color Response:
· natural, growth, restful: dark green
· memories, power, import: high-chroma violet
· powerful, basic: black

Color Scheme: incongruous plus neutral

The typography used for "The Joe Ski Clue" gives the mark dimension and depth.

Center *for* Justice, Tolerance, *and* Community
University of California, Santa Cruz

the dorrance group

a m a n g a h

Center for Justice, Tolerance, and Community, University of California, Santa Cruz
Designer: Carol Chu

Associative Color Response:
· charming, elegant, refined: high-chroma blue-violet
· elegant: pastel blue-violet
· dignified, lively, pleasant: high-chroma blue
· pleasant, peaceful, happy: pastel blue

Color Scheme: simple analogous with tinting

If done correctly, any time a 3-D illusion can be achieved within a logomark, the mark will inherently have redeeming attributes. The four bands representing justice, tolerance, community, and university are conceived in such a way as to give this mark unity and depth.

amangah
Designer: Azin Ghazinia

Associative Color Response:
· powerful, basic: black
· brilliant, intense, energizing: high-chroma red
· excitement, stimulating, fun: high-chroma yellow-orange

Color Scheme: primary plus neutral

The economy of line found within this logotype is remarkable. The two letterforms, lowercase "a" and "g," not only act as initials for "amangah" but also operate as a face. The red and yellow dots reference human eyes, and the ascender and descender represent hair and the silhouette of a jaw line respectively.

The Tipperary Inn: Aids Arms Life Walk
Designer: Mark Raebel
Studio: Arsenal Design

Associative Color Response:
· empathy, complete, smooth: pastel yellow-green
· new growth: mid-range yellow-green
· brilliant, intense, energizing: high-chroma red

Color Scheme: near complementary with tinting

The two hues utilized within this mark are conveyed in a symbolic manner appropriate to the content. "A picture is worth a thousand words," as the old saying goes, and in this case the message is conveyed through the use of color.

Let's Go To Work
Designer: Mark Raebel
Studio: Arsenal Design

Associative Color Response:
· excitement, stimulating, fun: high-chroma yellow-orange
· pleasant, peaceful, happy: pastel blue
· dignified, lively, pleasant: high-chroma blue

Color Scheme: direct complementary with tinting

As shown here, a gross screen pattern and high-contrast image is best when it is utilized within a mark. In this way, the mark can be used in all media with no significant loss of quality.

The Dorrance Group
Designer: Mark Raebel
Studio: Arsenal Design

Associative Color Response:
· comfortable: mid-range yellow-orange
· mellow: mid-range blue-green
· quality: neutral gray

Color Scheme: incongruous plus neutral (tinted)

The Dorrance Group mark is constructed in a symmetrical manner. However, the mid-range yellow-orange and blue-green are added to energize the mark. The "dg" is tilted in an upward 45-degree angle, amplifying the positive kinetic energy found within this color scheme.

CBPTV
Designer: Greg Friedrick

Associative Color Response:
· pleasant, peaceful, happy: pastel blue
· dignified, lively, pleasant: high-chroma blue
· excitement, stimulating, fun: high-chroma yellow-orange

Color Scheme: near complementary with tinting

The color scheme utilized within this logotype operates in a manner that clarifies how the acronym should be pronounced.

Har-Vest
Designer/Creative Director: Drew M. Dallet
Studio: Boom Creative

Associative Color Response:
· dignified, lively, pleasant: high-chroma blue
· quality: neutral gray
· powerful, basic: black

Color Scheme: one hue with neutrals (tinted)

The black hue operates to define the silhouette of the mark, and is very legible from a distance. The high-chroma blue functions to define details within, while the neutral gray conveys highlights and softens the harshness of the mark.

Delta Chi International Convention
Designer/Creative Director: Drew M. Dallet
Studio: Boom Creative

Associative Color Response:
· powerful, basic: black
· excitement, stimulating, fun: high-chroma yellow-orange
· brilliant, intense, energizing: high-chroma red

Color Scheme: near incongruous plus neutral

The two warm, high-chroma hues are juxtaposed next to the cool, bold black forms to create a mark that pops from within.

Bumbershoot Forge
Designer/Creative Director: Drew M. Dallet
Studio: Boom Creative

Associative Color Response:
· excitement, stimulating, fun: high-chroma yellow-orange
· flamboyant, elegant: high-chroma red-violet
· powerful, basic: black

Color Scheme: incongruous plus black

This beautifully executed color scheme harmonizes well with the script typeface, giving the mark a look of elegance.

David Ellis Photography
Designer/Creative Director: Drew M. Dallet
Studio: Boom Creative

Associative Color Response:
· quality: neutral gray
· professional: dark gray
· powerful, basic: black
· brilliant, intense, energizing: high-chroma red

Color Scheme: one hue with neutrals (tinted)

The method of separation is utilized within this logotype to pull out the most meaningful content. This is done through the use of color (red). Note that "photography," in red, is typeset much smaller than the rest of the mark. There are many technical ways to create separation (to mark out plainly the most meaningful part), and one of these is to be understated—this technique is superbly done here.

Hughes Holdings
Designer/Creative Director: Drew M. Dallet
Studio: Boom Creative

Associative Color Response:
· warm-hearted, welcome, good: earth-tone red
· serene, credible, devoted: dark blue
· clean, cool, innocent: white

Color Scheme: near incongruous with white

The white hue is achieved through type reversal. Many times an additional hue can be achieved by reversing out the type to the color of the substrate. However, if the paper is something other than white, the colors within the hue scheme will be tinted the hue of the substrate.

Tirestore.com
Designer/Creative Director: Drew M. Dallet
Studio: Boom Creative

Associative Color Response:
· powerful, basic: black
· flamboyant, elegant: high-chroma red-violet
· friendly: high-chroma red-orange

Color Scheme: near simple analogous plus neutral

In this logomark, black is utilized to ground the mark while red-orange and red-violet are used to create a lively color combination that helps to create kinetic energy and make the mark memorable.

Prescriptions Plus
Designer/Creative Director: Drew M. Dallet
Studio: Boom Creative

Associative Color Response:
· service, clear, security: high-chroma blue
· new, pristine, pure: high-chroma blue-green
· powerful, basic: black

Color Scheme: simple analogous plus neutral

Choosing the right color scheme for the right job or subject matter can sometimes make a critical difference. In this case, designer Drew M. Dallet selected two hues that match the safety and health aspects concerning the delivery of prescription drugs.

Velo
Designer/Creative Director: Drew M. Dallet
Studio: Boom Creative

Associative Color Response:
· warm-hearted, welcome, good: earth-tone red
· flamboyant, elegant: high-chroma red-violet
· powerful, basic: black

Color Scheme: simple analogous plus neutral

This simple analogous color palette helps to convey the client's intent by creating a mark that appears to be both global and radiating out from the center. This is brought about through the use of warm and cool colors.

Chelsea Title Agency
Designer/Creative Director: Drew M. Dallet
Studio: Boom Creative

Associative Color Response:
· valuable, radiant: gold
· powerful, basic: black
· brilliant, intense, energizing: high-chroma red

Color Scheme: near incongruous plus neutral

The Chelsea Title Agency crest is an excellent example of using the correct color combination to create a visual impression. In this case, gold, red, and black combine to help create a mark of prestige.

Note, when dealing with metallic inks, create a sidebar electronic mechanical that runs on the wastepaper surface of the printed job. Overprint the metallic inks, in different tints, with the other hues. Most printers, so long as there is no trim work, will print the sidebar with no additional cost. This will yield tremendous insight into how to use metallic inks more effectively and uniquely. This can be done with all hues.

First Nation Supply
Designer/Creative Director: Drew M. Dallet
Studio: Boom Creative

Associative Color Response:
· excitement, stimulating, fun: high-chroma yellow-orange
· brilliant, intense, energizing: high-chroma red
· powerful, basic: black

Color Scheme: near incongruous plus neutral

The mark and color scheme for First National Supply is a Native American symbol, Dreamcatcher, and reflects the sensibilities of the owner's and client's cultural sensibilities.

InSight
Designer/Creative Director: Drew M. Dallet
Studio: Boom Creative

Associative Color Response:
· charming, elegant, refined: high-chroma blue-violet
· classic: mid-range blue-violet
· elegant: pastel blue-violet

Color Scheme: monochromatic with tinting

This simple monochromatic color study with tinting effectively creates movement from right to left. Emphasis is placed on "In" to create a stress point for proper pronunciation and inflection.

Yujin Ono 1
Designer: Yujin Ono
Art Director: John T. Drew

Associative Color Response:
· quality, basic: muddy gray
· quality: neutral gray
· professional: dark gray
· powerful, basic: black

Color Scheme: achromatic

An achromatic color palette is utilized here to create a mark that is conservative and professional. The two circles are added to help create a counterbalance and infuse the mark with a minimal amount of kinetic energy.

Myogenix
Designer: James Sakamoto
Art Director: Mark Sackett
Studio: Sackett Design

Associative Color Response:
· brilliant, intense, energizing: high-chroma red
· dignified, lively, pleasant: high-chroma blue
· powerful, basic: black

Color Scheme: primary plus neutral

The two primary hues within this color palette are used to indicate the way in which "Myogenix" is pronounced.

Sporty Joe Consultancy
Studio: Plastic Soldier Factory Pte Ltd

Associative Color Response:
· quality: neutral gray
· new, pristine, pure: high-chroma blue-green
· healing, growing, happy: high-chroma orange

Color Scheme: near complementary plus neutral (tinted)

Substitution, warm and cool hues, and color value play an important role in the success of this mark. The blue-green hue harmonizes more appropriately with the neutral gray than the orange. (Both the blue-green and the neutral gray are cool colors and the eye makes an easier transition back and forth between these two components.) Orange is utilized as a shadow form and the human figure is placed in different positions to symbolize a multitude of sporting activities. All three hues have a near-same color value, thereby uniting the mark.

Chabadum Jewish Student Central 1
Designer: Marc Rabinowitz

Associative Color Response:
· excitement, stimulating, fun: high-chroma yellow-orange
· new growth, sharp: high-chroma yellow-green
· quality, basic: muddy gray

Color Scheme: near analogous utilizing tertiary hues plus neutral (tinted)

Chabadum Jewish Student Central 2
Designer: Marc Rabinowitz

Associative Color Response:
· excitement, stimulating, fun: high-chroma yellow-orange
· new growth, sharp: high-chroma yellow-green
· quality, basic: muddy gray

Color Scheme: near analogous utilizing tertiary hues plus neutral (tinted)

The color combination utilized here creates a lively and energetic mark for the Jewish Student Central. Substitution is applied within the stroke of the "u" and "m" for recognition and cultural identity.

The Rebel Connection
Designer: Ken Kelleher

Associative Color Response:
· brilliant, intense, energizing: high-chroma red
· quality: neutral gray
· powerful, basic: black

Color Scheme: one hue with neutrals (tinted)

The red hue is utilized in a symbolic reference, whereas the swooping line work conceptually conveys the idea of connection.

Yujin Ono 2
Designer: Yujin Ono
Art Director: John T. Drew

Associative Color Response:
· powerful, basic: black
· classic: mid-range blue-violet
· brilliant, intense, energizing: high-chroma red

Color Scheme: near simple analogous plus neutral

The red hue is strategically placed to make the "Y" of Yujin pop. The mark is perfectly symmetrical, creating one centralized focal point, "Y."

Glenshore

Nth°

Nth Degree Consulting

HETHE
BESTE
VAN OF
WIM T.
SCHIP
PERS

HARRY RUHÉ

Sova Architecture
Studio: Hornall Anderson Design Works

Associative Color Response:
· healing, growing, happy: high-chroma orange
· quality: neutral gray
· professional: dark gray

Color Scheme: one hue with neutrals (tinted)

Separation is utilized to make a clear delineation between "Sova" and "Architecture." The "o" is further embellished to create a stress and focal point.

Ax Mill
Designer: Tanya Ortega
Art Director: John T. Drew

Associative Color Response:
· dignified, lively, pleasant: high-chroma blue
· pleasant, peaceful, happy: mid-range blue
· healing, growing, happy: high-chroma orange

Color Scheme: direct complementary with tinting

Along with the form of the logomark, tinting is utilized to help create a 3-D illusion on a 2-D plane.

Glenshore 1
Designer: Nate Burgos

Associative Color Response:
· pleasant, peaceful, happy: pastel blue
· classic: pastel green
· classic: mid-range green

Color Scheme: near analogous with tinting

The combination of hues utilized and the form create a mark that looks very natural.

Nth Degree Consulting
Designers: Clifford Boobyer and Andrew Philip
Studio: Firedog Design

Associative Color Response:
· excitement, stimulating, fun: high-chroma yellow-orange
· comfortable: pastel yellow-orange
· powerful, basic: black

Color Scheme: monochromatic with tinting plus neutral

The tinting and gradients applied within this logotype help to create a 3-D illusion. The size of "Nth Degree Consulting" is scaled down so that "Nth°" floats above and forward.

He The Best Evan Of Wim T. Schippers
Designer/Art Director: Ragna Hom
Studio: Thonik Design

Associative Color Response:
· brilliant, intense, energizing: high-chroma red
· life, motion, growth: high-chroma green
· powerful, basic: black

Color Scheme: direct complementary plus neutral

Separation is applied in order to help speed up recognition and to create visual interest.

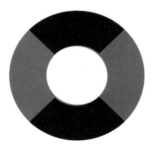

Less + More
Designer/Art Director: Ragna Hom
Studio: Thonik Design

Associative Color Response:
· brilliant, intense, energizing: high-chroma red
· powerful, basic: black
· dignified, lively, pleasant: high-chroma blue

Color Scheme: incongruous made from primaries plus neutral

Fracture is utilized to help draw attention to the mark and create visual interest. (Fracture: to knock off the pre-existing plane content that is most relevant by rotating, flipping, chopping, cropping, and subtraction.)

Gent Gand 1
Designer/Art Director: Ragna Hom
Studio: Thonik Design

Associative Color Response:
· brilliant, intense, energizing: high-chroma red
· dignified, lively, pleasant: high-chroma blue

Color Scheme: incongruous made from primaries plus neutral

Fracture, first described by Professor Ben Day of Virginia Commonwealth University, is an excellent visual technique to draw attention. In this case, this visual technique is utilized for a campaign of marks (shown here and on page 93).

Centraal kidds
Designer/Art Director: Ragna Hom
Studio: Thonik Design

Associative Color Response:
· powerful, basic: black
· brilliant, intense, energizing: high-chroma red
· life, motion, growth: high-chroma green

Color Scheme: direct complementary plus neutral

The high-chroma, direct complementary color palette used for the Centraal Museum is an excellent color choice to attract kids of any age. The "c" of the main Centraal Museum logo is used throughout the campaign to create brand recognition—an excellent example of substitution.

Thrillz hungry for xcitement
Designer: Tarun Deep Girdher

Associative Color Response:
· energizing: high-chroma red-orange
· excitement, stimulating, fun: high-chroma yellow-orange
· dignified, lively, pleasant: high-chroma blue

Color Scheme: split complementary

A highly active color scheme coupled with exhilarating line work creates an exciting and energetic mark. Note how the line work utilized for this mark harmonizes with the color scheme chosen.

Gent Gand 2
Designer/Art Director: Ragna Hom
Studio: Thonik Design

Associative Color Response:
· brilliant, intense, energizing: high-chroma red
· dignified, lively, pleasant: high-chroma blue

Color Scheme: incongruous made from primaries plus neutral

Gent Gand 3
Designer/Art Director: Ragna Hom
Studio: Thonik Design

Associative Color Response:
· brilliant, intense, energizing: high-
  chroma red
· dignified, lively, pleasant: high-
  chroma blue

Color Scheme: incongruous made
from primaries plus neutral

Centraal Museum 3
Designer/Art Director: Ragna Hom
Studio: Thonik Design

Associative Color Response:
· healing, growing, happy: high-
  chroma orange
· clean, cool, innocent: white
· powerful, basic: black

Color Scheme: one hue with neutral
and white

Once again, the lowercase "c" for
the Centraal Museum is incorporated
into the design to create a mark that
will appeal to young and old alike.

Centraal Museum 4
Designer/Art Director: Ragna Hom
Studio: Thonik Design

Associative Color Response:
· powerful, basic: black
· brilliant, intense, energizing: high-
  chroma red
· life, motion, growth: high-chroma
  green

Color Scheme: direct complementary
plus neutral

The high-chroma, direct
complementary color palette used for
the Centraal Museum is an excellent
color choice to attract kids of any
age. The "c" of the Centraal Museum
is used throughout the campaign
to create brand recognition—an
excellent example of substitution.

**State of Qatar: The Planning
Council and The General
Secretariat**
Designer: Manar Al-Muftah

Associative Color Response:
· comfortable: pastel yellow-orange
· pleasant, peaceful, happy: pastel
  blue
· warm-hearted, welcome, good:
  dark red

Color Scheme: near triad

The color palette applied within
these marks is both symbolic and
indexical. The dark red/maroon hue
is the state color, while pastel blue,
and pastel yellow-orange reference
the two halves of the landscape (the
desert and the sky).

State of Qatar
The Planning Council
The General Secretariat

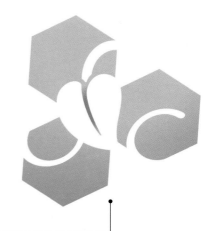

State of Qatar: The Planning Council and The General Secretariat
Designer: Manar Al-Muftah

Associative Color Response:
· comfortable: pastel yellow-orange
· pleasant, peaceful, happy: pastel blue
· warm-hearted, welcome, good: dark red

Color Scheme: near triad

The color palette applied within these marks is both symbolic and indexical. The dark red/maroon hue is the state color, while pastel blue, and pastel yellow-orange reference the two halves of the landscape (the desert and the sky).

Miracle Reach
Designer: Brenda Spivack
Studio: Red Table

Associative Color Response:
· new growth, sharp: high-chroma yellow-green
· dignified, lively, pleasant: high-chroma blue
· quality: neutral gray

Color Scheme: near incongruous plus neutral (tinted)

The high-chroma blue and high-chroma yellow-green is realized in such a way as to create a halo affect—most appropriate for the content.

aqualung
Designer: Savio Alphonso

Associative Color Response:
· charming, elegant, refined: high-chroma blue-violet
· dignified, lively, pleasant: high-chroma blue
· pleasant, peaceful, happy: pastel blue

Color Scheme: simple analogous with tinting

The aqualung mark is an excellent example of a simple analogous color scheme. Designer Savio Alphonso creates a third additional hue by tinting the high-chroma blue-violet to denote imperfection within the lungs.

HOH
Designer: Nophadonh Phongsav
Art Director: John T. Drew

Associative Color Response:
· dignified, lively, pleasant: high-chroma blue
· charming, elegant, refined: high-chroma blue-violet
· new growth: mid-range yellow-green

Color Scheme: simple analogous plus dark yellow-green tinted

Gestalt is used most effectively in the HOH logotype. Note how the form/counterform relationships are brought about through economy of line.

Sagent
Designer: Brenda Spivack
Studio: Red Table

Associative Color Response:
· healing, growing, happy: high-chroma orange
· gentle, enticing, good spirit: mid-range orange
· excitement, stimulating, fun: high-chroma yellow-orange
· new growth, sharp: high-chroma yellow-green
· new growth: mid-range yellow-green
· smooth: pastel yellow-green

Color Scheme: simple analogous

In both marks, color gradients are utilized to help create kinetic movement. To further create activity within the mark the logo is placed at an angle, and white activity lines (reversed out) are incorporated to allow the viewing audience to move freely in and out of the mark.

Cures Now: Finding Cures Now for A Bright Future
Designer: Rendi Kusnadi Suzana

Associative Color Response:
· powerful, basic: black
· quality: neutral gray
· peaceful, happy: pastel blue-violet

Color Scheme: one hue with shading and tinting plus neutral

Note how the interlocking elements of the heart are woven in such a way that the mark becomes 2-D. This helps to emphasize and unite the mark into a holistic symbol.

absecon
Designer: Scott W. Santoro
Studio: Worksight

Associative Color Response:
· dignified: golden yellow
· powerful, basic: black
· classic: pastel green

Color Scheme: near analogous with tinting plus neutral

Repetition is used within the absecon mark to create continuity and activity. A golden-yellow and pastel green are toned back to create a thoughtful visual hierarchy within a complex mark.

Heart Bra
Studio: Essex Two

Associative Color Response:
· stimulating, aggressive, exciting: high-chroma pink
· soft, sweet, tender, comfortable: pastel pink
· restrained, soft, quiet: mid-range pink

Color Scheme: monochromatic with tinting

If used inappropriately, culturally identifiable symbols can become trite quickly. In this case, repetition of form and color tinting are applied so that the mark takes on a more unique shape.

Neverous Construction
Studio: Essex Two

Associative Color Response:
· powerful, basic: black
· quality, basic: muddy gray
· quality: neutral gray

Color Scheme: achromatic

The Neverous Construction logo was created for a building contractor. In this case, the 3-D shape of the mark and the overall mass conceptually relate to the subject matter. An achromatic color palette is applied to make the mark appear even more massive.

Ronald McDonald Children's Charities
Studio: Essex Two

Associative Color Response:
· agreeable, pleasant, welcome, youthful: high-chroma yellow
· brilliant, intense, energizing: high-chroma red
· powerful, basic: black

Color Scheme: incongruous plus neutral

The Ronald McDonald Children's Charities mark is an excellent example of empathy carried out through the execution of form and pragmatic color use.

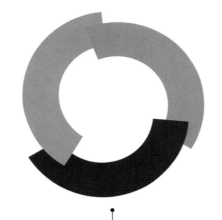

State Of Mind Gallery
Designer: April Medina

Associative Color Response:
· powerful, basic: black
· healing, growing, happy: high-chroma orange
· new growth, sharp: high-chroma yellow-green

Color Scheme: near incongruous plus neutral with tinting

The physicality of form and pragmatic color use create a composition that reflects the state of mind of the gallery.

3W
Designer: Steven Gonsowski
Art Director: John T. Drew

Associative Color Response:
· quality, basic: muddy gray
· healing, growing, happy: high-chroma orange
· charming, elegant, refined: high-chroma blue-violet

Color Scheme: near complementary plus muddy neutral (tinted)

The high-chroma orange and blue-violet create a masterfully energetic logotype. The muddy gray is utilized to tone down the mark and give it a more professional feel. Note in this case that background color studies were created (for example, muddy gray), to determine choice of paper.

Sommese Design
Designers: Kristin Sommese and Lanny Sommese
Studio: Sommese Design

Associative Color Response:
· new growth: mid-range yellow-green
· restrained, soft, quiet: mid-range pink
· powerful, basic: black

Color Scheme: near complementary plus neutral

The mark was created for Sommese Design, a graphic design studio where the two principals are a husband-and-wife team. This logo is a wonderful example of representing this design studio. Note that the mark is made up of signifiers that denote both male and female, including color.

Zone Defense
Studio: Essex Two

Associative Color Response:
· powerful, basic: black
· dignified, lively, pleasant: high-chroma blue
· brilliant, intense, energizing: high-chroma red

Color Scheme: primary plus neutral

This modular-system mark symbolizes a collaboration of several communication firms. The two primary hues, red and blue, together with black are used to denote this collaboration.

360° Living
Designer/Art Director: David Ferrell
Studio: HMA

Associative Color Response:
· natural, growth, restful: dark green
· new, pristine, pure: high-chroma blue-green
· new growth, sharp: high-chroma yellow-green

Color Scheme: analogous with shading

The combination of a color scheme applied and the shapes and line work found within the mark create a highly energetic logo that conceptually fits the content.

Identity: The Branding Specialists
Designer: Steve Gonsowski
Art Director: John T. Drew

Associative Color Response:
· dignified, lively, pleasant: high-chroma blue
· healing, growing, happy: high-chroma orange
· powerful, basic: black

Color Scheme: direct complementary plus neutral

The use of a thumbprint to form the "d" in "Identity" suggests a human touch to the company's workings.

Qatar
Designer: Tarek Atrissi

Associative Color Response:

· new, pristine, pure: high-chroma
  blue-green
· healing, growing, happy: high-
  chroma orange
· brilliant, intense, energizing: high-
  chroma red

Color Scheme: split complementary

This wonderfully elegant mark is
beautifully executed both in the
physicality of form and in the color
palette applied.

Dagger
Designer: Manar Al-Muftah
Art Director: John T. Drew

Associative Color Response:

· provoking: high-chroma muddy
  orange
· inspiring: mid-range muddy
  orange
· sound: pastel muddy orange

Color Scheme: monochromatic
with tinting

This dagger mark is beautifully
executed. Substitution is applied
within the handle of the dagger
(Arabic typography that is part of
the national anthem for the state
of Qatar).

Dr. Paley Inc.

Designer: Drew M. Dallet

Designer Drew M. Dallet chose colors for the Dr. Paley Inc. logo to convey a strong sense of expertise and professionalism. The metallic silver, deep blue, and black color combination communicates an invaluable service in a traditionally conservative and sober market. The legibility of the mark was of great concern when choosing colors. Playing off the concept of an MRI scan or X-ray, the legibility of the mark was accomplished through the use of bold colors that contrasted well with white. The hue scheme has a color value differential (CVD) greater than 30% in juxtaposition with white.

Dallet used the computer to develop the mark from start to finish, including thumbnail sketches. In his words, "I find that jumping into Illustrator really helps me to explore the potential of any mark. There are certainly lots of Post-its and notepads lying around on which I do sketches while on the phone or thinking through a mark." With a strong initial concept—the depiction of a human head and images generated by an MRI or X-ray machine—using the computer as a medium to generate multiple directions and variations was quite easy. The computer work included color studies that allowed Dallet to find the optimal scheme for his client. Once the mark and color scheme were worked out, the branding of the stationery system could take place. A strong color palette was necessary to make his business card and stationery system unique and memorable. Dr. Paley's stationery is set apart from competitors through the use of an effective color palette.

The Quilts of Gee's Bend in Context

Designer: Kelly Bryant

This logo was created for the exhibition "The Quilts of Gee's Bend in Context," highlighting the life of the women of Gee's Bend, Alabama, their quilts, and the historical significance and context of their work. The design of the logomark needed to meet three major objectives: to be feminine and reflect an African-American color sensibility; for the "quilt" to be seen as art; and to give a sense of context. Furthermore, designer Kelly Bryant felt it was imperative to capture the essence of this quilting style without creating a direct representation—to create a design vernacular that was more holistic and less iconographic in its approach.

After the basic logomark was completed, color studies were conducted by sampling the actual work. The unique color palettes found within this style of quilting led to vibrant color studies (high-chroma hues counterbalanced by blacks and grays). Kelly Bryant's final color study captures the spirit of the African-American women of Gee's Bend, and the physicality of their quilts. The red and violet shapes found within the mark are meant as brackets to showcase the quilt, whereas the white vertical lines are both symbolic and iconic of the stitch work found within this style. The three-color logo is truly a superb analogous with neutral gray color scheme.

Typesetting the lines on an angle other than horizontal is an excellent example of fracture. The method of fracture is used to emphasize content by knocking it off its pre-existing plane. In this case, the plane is horizontal. Additionally, visual and conceptual content is added to the stationery system by indirectly referencing the stitch work and quilt work found in the Gee's Bend style.

A simple example of typographic fracture. The subhead is knocked-off the dominant plane.

Four Colors

With the globalization of printing, coupled with interactive and motion design, the cost of adding additional colors to a logo has changed dramatically. No longer are corporations always limited to creating a mark with a restrictive color palette. However, this relatively new phenomenon can make designing logos more complex and harder to control. Today we are not only faced with understanding print production, we are also charged with understanding the Web, its interactivity, motion design, and, in many cases, environmental graphic design, packaging, textiles, and product design. Managing color has never been so complex, both in its technical application and conceptual direction. In this chapter, some of the world's most inspiring four-color logomarks are showcased to help us understand how these issues have been addressed by utilizing hue to its fullest potential.

From large corporations to small fashion houses, from building facilities to advertising, marks and their colorful use engulf our environment and influence our consumption. Understanding how, when, and why colors should be used in a given circumstance is the mainstay of hue application.

S.P. SHAUGHNESSEY
& COMPANY

CAMPUS LASIK

ask me! *about* UNLV

Team CdLS
Designer: Laurie Churchman
Studio: Designiore

Associative Color Response:
· good spirits, inviting: mid-orange
· dignity, pleasing: high-chroma blue
· surging, brilliant: red
· new growth, hope: green

Color Scheme: split complementaries plus one hue (tetrad)

This logomark uses a tetrad color arrangement (a contrast of four or more colors on the color wheel) for emphasis. The equally weighted blue, green, and negative white line encompass the colors and create unity within the arrangement.

S. P. Shaughnessey & Company
Designer/Art Director: Drew M. Dallet
Studio: Boom Creative

Associative Color Response:
· brimming with life, thinking: green
· quality, practical: gray
· strong, prestigious: black

Color Scheme: monochromatic plus neutral (tinted)

The equal line weight of the inverted white type creates a "C" and "P" individually and a broken "S" as a whole. In addition, the counterform defines a contiguous green "S" that is unified with the white stroke through proportion. The white stroke is half the weight of the green stroke.

Campus Lasik
Designer/Art Director: Drew M. Dallet
Studio: Boom Creative

Associative Color Response:
· clear, thinking: green
· quality, practical: gray
· service, professional: blue
· school, prestigious: black

Color Scheme: analogous plus neutral (tinted)

The font choice connotes a university emblem, while the thick-and-thin line quality unifies the mark in a way similar to the stitching used to attach a badge to a college leather jacket. The blue fields seem to indicate the circular form of the iris.

Ask Me! About UNLV
Designer: Ken Kelleher

Associative Color Response:
· cheerful, warm: orange
· passion, practical: gray
· school, prestigious: black
· brilliant, extrovert: red

Color Scheme: two hue plus achromatic tints

The sans-serif type adds to the quick read, and the orange exclamation point emphasizes the passion and energy with which questions will be answered. Hierarchy in the statement is determined by the tints and hues of each word, with "about" being the least important. The change from sans serif to serif in addition to the red color emphasizes "UNLV."

techSource
SOLUTIONS, LLC

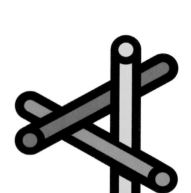

Firedog
Designers: Clifford Boobyer and
Andrew Philip
Studio: Firedog Design

Associative Color Response:
· dynamic, provocative: red
· professional, solid: gray
· powerful, basic: black

Color Scheme: one hue with tinting
and shading

The subtle shift from shadow to
highlight creates dimensionality to
the button. Although the dog sits
on a narrow depth of field, adding
black to the red prevents the tint
from turning pink and reinforces the
dog's vigor.

WeB·X Internet Solutions
Designer/Art Director: Drew M. Dallet
Studio: Boom Creative

Associative Color Response:
· dynamic, provocative: red
· professional, solid: gray
· strong, invulnerable: black

Color Scheme: one hue plus
achromatic tints

The white "x" seems to radiate out
from the red dot at the center of
the logomark. This is enhanced by
the smooth transition from thick to
thin line, the elliptical gray shapes
in the background, and subtle
simultaneous contrast of the gray
and red triangles. These qualities
are mirrored in the type choice and
placement.

tech Source Solutions LLC
Designer/Art Director: Drew M. Dallet
Studio: Boom Creative

Associative Color Response:
· develop, experience: dark red
· versatility, trustworthy: green
· basic, invulnerable: black

Color Scheme: complementary tints
plus neutral

The shadow produced by the gear
belies the flat appearance of the
wheel. The lack of dimension
is created through the equal
line weights and shades of
complementary color (red and
green), while the tint of black in the
shadow defines depth.

St. Patrick's Massacre
Designer: Mark Raebel
Studio: Arsenal Design

Associative Color Response:
· St. Patrick's Day, springtime: green
· new growth, fruity: high-chroma
  green-yellow
· wheat, cheerful: yellow
· basic, neutral: black

Color Scheme: analogous plus
neutral

Overlapping of imagery
communicates depth, and in this
logomark creates the illusion that
the knife is spearing the shamrock.
Yellow is used in both the foreground
of the knife and the background
field. This helps to unify the
composition but does not detract
from the implied depth.

Saint Pat's at the Tip
Designer: Mark Raebel
Studio: Arsenal Design

Associative Color Response:
· St. Patrick's Day, refreshing: green
· tasty, friendly: orange
· heavy, basic: black

Color Scheme: two points of a triad
with tinting plus neutral

The orange calls attention to the
predominant hierarchy and helps
to slow the reader's eye, which
is essential for this typeface. In
addition, the bold white line around
the distressed black type helps to
clarify the readability and unifies
"Saint Pat's" with the secondary
type.

Pediatric Palliative Care
Studio: Essex Two

Associative Color Response:
· stimulating, fun: red
· happy, pleasing: blue
· energetic, warmth: yellow
· school, spatial: black

Color Scheme: additive primaries
plus neutral

Not only are the primary colors
equally spaced from each other on
the color wheel, they are also equally
spaced within this logomark. This
helps to reinforce the building-block
effect of the interlinking structure
without diminishing the significance
of the mark as too childish.

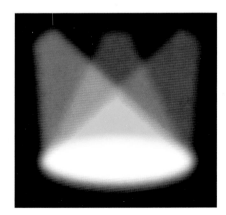

SpotLight Projects
Studio: Essex Two

Associative Color Response:
· anticipation, welcome: yellow
· spatial, mysterious: black

Color Scheme: one hue plus neutral with tints and shades

The subtlety with which the spotlights are trained is achieved through the definition of each tint. This effect can only be accomplished through controlled overprinting of one gradation over another and a precise halftone dot that gradually reveals the foreground of the stage.

Microsoft Office Licensing Products.com
Designer: Ann M. Simon

Associative Color Response:
· producing, vital: orange
· strength, work: blue
· use, hope: green
· active, vital: yellow

Color Scheme: complementary (orange, blue) plus diad (yellow, green)

The shift from equally weighted sans-serif typefaces in the background to a serif typeface in the foreground increases the depth in this narrow field. The thick and thin stroke of the "O" calls attention to the triangles created within the blue field.

Eternal Health & Wellness
Designer: Carlo Irigoyen
Art Director: Brenda Spivack
Studio: Red Table

Associative Color Response:
· luxuriance, energy: yellow-orange
· life, warm: brown

Color Scheme: two hues with tints

The equal line weight of the mark is in stark contrast to the thick and thin strokes of the typography. The juxtaposition of contrasting line weight allows both the logomark and the logotype to work independently of each other. Together the logo is unified through the binary opposition as yin/yang and the commonality of the color.

Grachten Festival
Designer/Art Director: Ragna Hom
Studio: Thonik Design

Associative Color Response:
· brilliant, dynamic: red
· spaciousness, upward: blue
· thought, atmospheric: purple

Color Scheme: three hues plus tints and neutralizing

The soft tints of blue give an airy quality to this mark, making the thick red type appear as if it is floating on the blue background. This counterintuitive approach works well—even where the background violates the red type, the readability is uncompromised.

urban visions
Studio: Hornall Anderson Design Works

Associative Color Response:
· classy, reposed: high-chroma blue
· pristine, tranquillity: blue-green
· biology, strength: high-chroma yellow-green
· new growth, lemony: high-chroma green-yellow

Color Scheme: near complex analogous

The analogous color scheme unifies the logomark so completely that upon initial viewing it is easy to notice only the footprint and overlook the leaf and water droplet. To complete the synchronization of elements throughout the logomark and logotype, the water droplet is used in substitution for the dot on the letter "i."

Fullerton Arboretum
Designer: Jay Pilar
Art Director: John Drew

Associative Color Response:
· healing, growing: orange
· welcome, noble: yellow
· neutral, life: black

Color Scheme: analogous tints plus neutral

The layered hands are an excellent example of metaphor. In substitution of a flower, they clearly communicate the stewardship of an arboretum.

Adventure
Travel Group

Parkkarte

Marta Herford

revalesio

friends of
LAGUNA BEACH
DOG PARK

island
sports

Adventure Travel Group
Designer/Art Director: Saied Farisi

Associative Color Response:
· life, motion: green

Color Scheme: monochromatic tints

The sharp points of the logomark reference many things. Most obvious is the reference to a tree, but, like a needle on a compass, the tangents also indicate that there are many paths to take. Referencing words in the dictionary also provides insight for the designer. Among the many words listed are "promontory," "spit," and "bluff."

eSoy
Studio: Sommese Design
Designer: Lanny Sommese

Associative Color Response:
· youthful, energy: yellow
· healing, tasty: red-orange
· pristine, consistent: blue-green
· powerful, life: black

Color Scheme: direct complementary with tinting and accent hue plus neutral

This logotype for an online distributor of soy-based products is crisp and bright. The designer intentionally utilized a color palette that would be in keeping with the perception of soy as a healthy product. The short name and vibrant colors create an easily identifiable and memorable logotype.

MARTa Herford: Parkkarte
Designer/Art Director: Ragna Hom
Studio: Thonik Design

Associative Color Response:
· pleasing, unique: cyan
· exciting, promising: magenta
· quality, passion: gray
· noble, expensive: black

Color Scheme: subtractive primaries plus neutral with tinting

This logo and identity system for a museum designed by world-renowned architect Frank Gehry in Herford, Germany, consists of three stripes of color used in multiple combinations with a standardized black logotype stating "MARTa Herford." The stripes are used to develop a display face that adapts depending upon the situation and yet references each department within the museum: design, art, and architecture. In this case, color is used to communicate remarkable diversity with precision.

Laguna Beach Dog Park
Designer: Tricia Diaz
Studio: Cherrybomb

Associative Color Response:
· vibrant, summer: blue
· grass, life: green

Color Scheme: simple near analogous with tints

The setting of the park among the hills is established in the green background tints and also serves as a metaphorical reference to the love that owners feel toward their pets. Also, this heart shape is subtly referenced in the sitting position of the dog and literally revealed in the dog's tags.

Revalesio
Studio: Hornall Anderson Design Works

Associative Color Response:
· cool, relaxed: blue
· strength, sunlight: yellow-green
· pristine, consistent: blue-green
· life, strong: black

Color Scheme: near analogous plus neutral

Overprinting the high-chroma yellow-green and the pure blue results in a saturated blue-green. A painterly quality is revealed by the imprecise fit of the color mixture to the black outline. This helps to bring a hand-crafted feel to the logo that implies a loving and one-on-one attention. If the type did not reinforce the concept through a hand-drawn logotype, the concept would be negated.

island sports
Designer: Mark Raebel
Studio: Arsenal Design

Associative Color Response:
· sky, wet: blue
· sunlight, trendy: yellow-green
· pleasant, vigorous: yellow
· fun, exciting: yellow-orange

Color Scheme: near complementary with analogous

The stroke weight of the typeface is the base proportion of the entire logomark and helps to create unity. For example, the thickness of each orange, yellow, and green stripe is 3 times the thickness of the font. The space between each stripe is 1.5 times the thickness, and the blue border is 5 times the thickness. This use of prime number proportionality (1, 3, 5, 7) can be seen throughout the mark and is a common method of creating intuitively pleasing compositions.

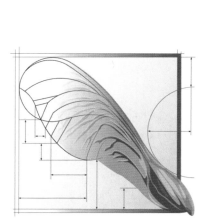

National Research Institute of Cultural Properties
Designer: Inyoung Choi

Associative Color Response:
· dignity, unique: blue
· strength, sharp: yellow-green
· folksy, sheltering: brown

Color Scheme: two points of a tetra plus neutral tinting

The horizon line created by the overlapping fields of green and blue attract the eye and create a perception of depth. However, a psychological shift in color takes place as the brain tries to make sense of the white field. According to atmospheric conditions, light colors come forward and dark colors recede. In this composition, interest is held by the inverse of that principle. Where the mind believes depth will occur, a light color (white) is placed.

adria resorts
Creative/Art Directors: Davor Bruketa and Nikola Zinic

Associative Color Response:
· water, sky: blue
· basic, elegant: black

Color Scheme: monochromatic plus nuetral

This logomark for a consortium of resorts along Croatia's coast accurately depicts the brilliant color and light of the area. The overlapping circles communicate unity and the nature of the water to change the appearance of form through reflection.

ireland
Designer: Mark Raebel
Studio: Arsenal Design

Associative Color Response:
· Irish, brimming with life: green

Color Scheme: analogous with tinting

The two overlapping green tints produce a more pure color. This is a result of increased saturation as the white is eliminated from the hue. This can often be a negative effect when trapping two pastel colors around type or image. However, this logomark uses the effect in a positive way to generate a green that is near, but not the same as, the outline of the shamrock.

Befu Eye Clinic
Designer: Hiroyuki Matsuishi

Associative Color Response:
· healing, whimsical: orange
· service, security: blue

Color Scheme: direct complementary with tinting

The counterforms of the type create a dynamic composition as the mind's eye switches from foreground to background to create the bird or read the name of the company. For example, the wing and eye of the bird create the counters of the "B." In contrast, the overlapping of the "e" and "f" switch from letterform to foot and leg respectively. By lessening the recognition of the letterforms as the word progresses, the designer is able to keep the audience's interest by forcing them to solve the puzzle.

attenex
Studio: Hornall Anderson Design Works

Associative Color Response:
· spaciousness, levels: blue

Color Scheme: monochromatic plus neutral

This logo seems to undulate in space like a cloud in the sky. The soft overlaying of color, the tilt of the letterforms, and the shift in size create a boiling effect that attracts the viewer's attention to the logotype.

Seed (Sustainable Energy Efficient Design)
Illustrator/Art Director: Scott A. Gunderson

Associative Color Response:
· sheltering, durable: earth-tone red-brown
· calm, natural: pastel green
· spatial, invulnerable: black

Color Scheme: complementary tints/shades plus neutral

Traditionally, red and green are learned signifiers for Christmas. This color association can be negated through the tints and shades of each hue as well as a disproportionate usage of one color over another. The designer has used these techniques to emphasize the development and construction of energy-efficient homes.

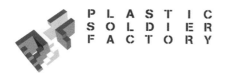

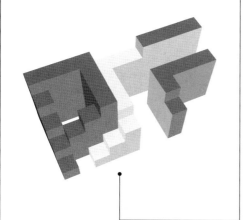

Glenshore 2
Designer: Nate Burgos
Studio: Nate Burgos, Inc.

Associative Color Response:
· spacious, security: blue
· foliage, lakes: green
· expensive, prestigious: black

Color Scheme: near analogous tints
plus neutral

Blue is the common hue running
through the background and
leaf pattern that symbolically
represents the shore and unifies the
composition. The syllabification of
the type through placement on the
background acknowledges the color
selection without being overt.

Plastic Soldier Factory
Studio: Plastic Soldier Factory
Pte Ltd

Associative Color Response:
· passion, professional: gray
· spatial, strong: black

Color Scheme: achromatic

This logomark has excellent depth
achieved through minute variation in
value. Multiple colors and fields can
be implied through a commanding
usage of tints and shades. The
layers build to create an acronym
that is revealed when the full name
is placed on the uppermost plane.
The equally spaced letters of the full
name create a horizontal alignment
that runs strictly perpendicular
to the crossbar in the "F" of the
acronym.

upshot
Designer: Nicolas Ammann
Studio: 86 The Onions

Associative Color Response:
· energetic, happy: cyan
· stimulating, high-energy: high-
  chroma pink
· powerful, strong: black
· enduring, solid: gray
· delicious, rich: brown

Color Scheme: monochromatic
plus neutral

The colors of this concentrated
energy drink reflect its flavors,
while the inverted arrow implies
how quickly the drink should be
consumed and will take effect. The
type choice in combination with the
color allows the packaging to look at
home in a gas station or a hip club.

拉拔克華人協會
LUBBOCK CHINESE AMERICAN ASSOCIATION

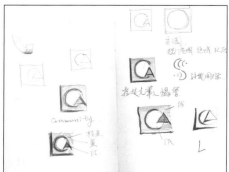

Lubbock Chinese American Association
Designer: Chen Wang

The Lubbock Chinese American Association (LCAA) was founded in 1990 to facilitate communication within the Chinese community and to promote cultural exchange and awareness within mainstream America. The LCAA hosts three major events annually: the Duan Wu Festival; the Mid-autumn Festival; and Chinese New Year. For each event, the LCAA wanted a mark to represent their association within the Chinese American community, and to broadcast, in part through their mark, the positive virtues of this community within mainstream America. To meet these goals, this logotype featured an "L," "C," and "A" combined to brand the association.

The challenge in designing this mark was keeping the typographic hierarchy. The client wanted the initials of the association to be readable. Designer Chen Wang chose for the logotype bright colors that were uplifting, energetic, cheerful, agreeable, pleasant, and welcoming. In Wang's words, "Additionally, I chose yellow to represent the Chinese community." The square shape of the overall mark symbolically represents the settlement of an established and peaceful community. The letterforms of "L" and "C" represent the integration of the Chinese community into mainstream America and its contribution to cultural diversity.

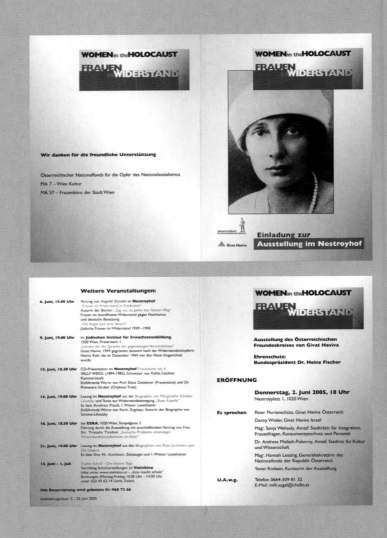

Faces of Resistance:
Women in the Holocaust
Designer: Zev Harari

Here, the word "women," isolated in red, conveys a powerful statement of femininity, respect, and dignity. The words making up the logotype, "Faces of Resistance," are placed over the gradient background, a part of the design and branding of the identity system. The women's resistance groups (Moreshet) were comprised of partisans who resisted the Nazis. Designer Zev Harari felt it was imperative to create a design that introduced the integration of two historically dominant colors (red and black) with purple and ochre. In doing so, the full context of the subject matter could be revealed and displayed in a macro-/micro-relationship that represents the tragic and heroic events.

The mark was the primary element, including its color scheme, that would fuse and brand the collateral materials and environmental graphics. The Faces of Resistance logotype implies the various women's resistance groups, their activities, and geographical locations. Therefore, it was essential that the mark be clearly legible. Color studies were implemented to make sure the right hue of red was chosen that would ensure maximum legibility.

Zev Harari used the computer as a medium to generate his process. He wanted each part of the logotype to create its own statement. When designing the environmental graphics, black lines were used, as a graphic armature, to help the viewer navigate and absorb both the written and visual content. Background gradients were designed to connect the title of the exhibit to the content. Tests were conducted to make sure that there was no massive color shifting when the mark was applied to a Web-based medium.

Faces of Resistance is a comprehensive project that includes seminars, educational kits for instructors and students, an anthology of female Holocaust resistance fighters, films of testimonies, and online content via the Internet. The traveling exhibit encapsulates a variety of women's stories, providing inspiration and new insight into the role that women played during the Holocaust.

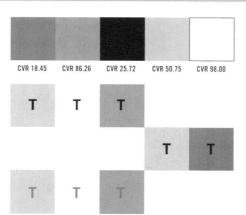

When creating a mark for the Web that has a gradient, Joint Photographic Experts Group (JPEG) formatting is recommended, as it is designed to capture continuous tone.

The color value rating (CVR) is also known as the Y tristimulus value. In conducting legibility studies make sure to visually verify the type and color combinations. To ensure that a color combination works have, at minimum, 20% contrast value differential (CVD). Some color combinations work with less than 20%, as shown on this diagram.

CVR 18.45   CVR 86.26   CVR 25.72   CVR 50.75   CVR 98.00

Five Colors

Most, if not all, five-color marks are created with four inks or fewer—not many logos are created with five-spot hues. With the globalization of printing and the Internet, many companies are now opting for multicolored logomarks, which was unheard of just a decade ago. Corporations and small businesses that primarily utilize the Internet, multimedia, broadcast television, and/or motion graphics to advertise, display collateral material, and sell their goods and services are becoming more aware of the impact that color has on their patrons. With the low cost and high quality of personal printers, many businesses, large and small, can now print in-house on demand with no significant loss of quality. This is truly a color revolution that equalizes the budgetary playing field of large and small businesses.

With that said, understanding color theory, including subtractive, additive, and 3-D, along with empirically tested color schemes, will dramatically improve the quality of color use within the marketplace. Just because a mark has multiple color use does not mean it is good. In fact, the chances of a mark being perceived as out-of-kilter increases as complexity increases. Even the best five-color marks demonstrate a level of constraint.

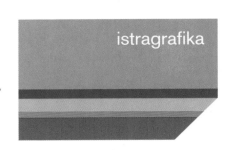

Storyteller: Diane Macklin
Studio: Conceptual Geniuses

Associative Color Response:
· exhilarating, provoking: dark orange
· warm, communication: high-chroma orange

Color Scheme: complex analogous with tinting and shading

This five-color logomark, including tints and shades, is an excellent example of successfully limiting the range of hues to keep the mark intact. In doing so, the squiggly lines, stars, sun, heart, human figure, and bird (representing thought) easily become one with the human face and typography. Most successful marks having this number of hues limit the palette in some way to harmonize the mark. In this case, the palette is a complex analogous color scheme.

International Cricket Council
Studio: Minale Bryce Design Strategy

Associative Color Response:
· motion: high-chroma green
· lively, upward: high-chroma blue
· intense, energizing: high-chroma red
· powerful: black

Color Scheme: near split complementary with tinting plus neutral

Control and restraint is utilized within this color scheme to create a superbly executed mark. A near split complementary plus black is utilized in an effective manner. The red dot, used as an accent color in the word "Cricket," is just large enough so that the viewer's eye is pulled down into the typography. The black typography acts as a ground and is flat. This allows the earthlike ball to explode three-dimensionally off the page. Tinting is utilized to help create this 3-D illusion.

Island Sports
Designer: Mark Raebel
Studio: Arsenal Design

Associative Color Response:
· quality: neutral gray
· trustworthy: pastel green
· pleasant: pastel yellow-green
· exhilarating: pastel of dark yellow-orange
· welcome: pastel earth-tone orange

Color Scheme: near complex analogous with tinting and shading

This near complex analogous color scheme utilizes both tinting and shading to control the value and harmonize the mark. This allows all five components of the logo to act as one.

anemone
Designer: Mark Raebel
Studio: Arsenal Design

Associative Color Response:
· good spirits: pastel mid-range orange
· charming, elegant: pastel mid-range red-violet
· comfortable: pastel pink
· friendly: pastel of red-orange

Color Scheme: complex analogous with tinting and shading

The color value of the mark is controlled through tinting and shading to harmonize it into a cohesive whole. In addition to the typeface chosen, the complex analogous color palette limits the intricacy of hues and harmonizes the mark.

istragrafika
Creative/Art Directors: Davor Bruketa and Nikola Zinic

Associative Color Response:
· lively: high-chroma blue
· exhilarating: dark orange
· happy: high-chroma orange
· lively, motion: high-chroma green
· brilliant, exhilarating: high-chroma red

Color Scheme: complex tetrad

The istragrafika logomark utilizes numerous color techniques to create an extremely interesting mark. So that the high-chroma blue and orange do not create simultaneous contrast and create a clashing of color, the dark orange is placed in between to harmonize the two hues. The orange is neutralized by adding a percentage of blue to create the dark orange. The orange and red are left intact and juxtaposed with the green to create pronounced simultaneous contrast. Using a small proportion of hue as an accent, in comparison to the blue field, pronounced simultaneous contrast is induced, creating a lively interplay within the complex tetrad.

Sales
Designer: Chihiro Katoh

Associative Color Response:
· innocent: white
· powerful, school: black
· joy: high-chroma yellow-orange
· exhilarating: dark orange
· childlike: high-chroma orange

Color Scheme: simple analogous with shading plus black and white

To control the complexity of this mark, a simple analogous color palette is utilized. The color palette chosen harmonizes well with the childlike illustration. The hues of black and white are utilized to give the mark depth, as well as a major focal point that pops.

Rodan + Fields Dermatologists
Designer: Chihiro Katoh

Associative Color Response:
· pleasant, healthy: high-chroma yellow-orange
· powerful: black
· strength: high-chroma yellow-green
· trustworthy: dark green
· vibrant: high-chroma blue

Color Scheme: random—using one primary, one secondary, and two tertiary hues

It is important when using a random color palette to constrain the outcome in some formal manner. In this case, scale (primarily) and the consistency of form is utilized to constrain the color scheme so that it does not look chaotic.

Yotin Foundation
Designer: Triesta Hall
Studio: Blu Art & Design

Associative Color Response:
· elegant: burgundy
· enterprise, energy: high-chroma yellow-orange
· dignity, lively: high-chroma blue-violet
· important: high-chroma violet
· classic, powerful: pastel blue-violet

Color Scheme: direct/near complementary with tinting plus a burgundy accent

A disproportionate use of color (blue-violet) unites the Yotin Foundation logotype and at the same time constrains the color scheme. The other four hues are used as accent colors to create an upbeat color palette.

The Tipperary Inn
Designer: Mark Raebel
Studio: Arsenal Design

Associative Color Response:
· powerful, elegant: black
· tasty: high-chroma orange
· inviting: mid-range orange
· Irish: high-chroma green

Color Scheme: two points of a tetrad with tinting plus black

Constraining the color palette helps to simplify the complexity of the logomark, and at the same time creates a color palette that is uniquely suited for the content. The high-chroma orange is tinted to create three distinct hues that are utilized to create the 3-D effect found in "The Tip."

Autumn Techology
Studio: Bremmer & Goris Communications

Associative Color Response:
· powerful, elegant: high-chroma blue-violet
· growing, communication: high-chroma orange
· inviting: mid-range orange
· stimulating, provoking: dark orange

Color Scheme: near complementary with tinting

This two-spot color logomark possesses five hues through the use of tinting—a superb example of stretching the color palette (with no additional cost to the client) to create greater intrigue. Note how all the leaves are uniformed (modular) and are rotated to create the mark.

Enviro Pro
Designer: Irene Marx
Studio: a+morph

Associative Color Response:
· powerful, elegant: black
· quality: neutral gray
· exhilarating, inspiring: dark orange
· wet: high-chroma blue
· springtime, wilderness: high-chroma green

Color Scheme: two points of a split complementary with an accent plus neutral with tinting

This complex color palette helps to create a wonderful mark that represents the environment we live in. The color palette is divided into two halves: green and blue are utilized to represent the earth, and black, gray, and orange-brown are utilized to denote humans. The three figures are holding hands to create the earth—an excellent color strategy that helps to reveal the overall concept.

Nickelodeon: Nick Jr
Studio: AdamsMorioka

Associative Color Response:
· growing, happy: high-chroma orange
· sweet, inviting: mid-range orange
· stimulating: dark orange
· thought-provoking: high-chroma blue
· service: dark blue

Color Scheme: direct complementary with tinting and neutralizing

In the Nick Jr marks, the color technique of neutralizing is used to create multiple hues. Neutralizing occurs when black—or, in this case, its complementary color—is used to create additional hues. This would also be considered overprinting.

World of Water
Designer: Erin Wright

Associative Color Response:
· quality, classic: muddy gray
· wet: high-chroma blue
· new: pastel blue-green
· liquid: mid-range blue-green
· ocean: high-chroma blue-green

Color Scheme: simple analogous with tinting, shading, and overprinting

The continents found within the logomark use a combination of tinting, shading, and overprinting. The tinting is to add white with the aid of a screened percentage. In this case, blue and blue-green are added together at 100% of color with a percentage of black to create the dark hues found within the mark.

Enclave At Sunrise
Designer/Art Director: Erik Chrestensen
Studio: Chrestensen Designworks

Associative Color Response:
· warm-hearted, wholesome: earth-tone red
· healing, warm: high-chroma orange
· inviting: mid-range yellow-orange
· gentle: mid-range orange
· stimulating: high-chroma yellow-orange

Color Scheme: simple analogous with tinting and shading

This simplistic color palette is an excellent associative match for the subject matter. Elegant in its approach, the symmetrical execution befits a sunrise.

oh! Oxygen
Studio: AdamsMorioka

Associative Color Response:
· powerful, elegant: black
· quality: neutral gray
· exciting, flamboyant: high-chroma red-violet
· refined: pastel red-violet
· charming: mid-range red-violet

oh! Oxygen
Studio: AdamsMorioka

Associative Color Response:
· powerful, elegant: black
· quality: neutral gray
· sweet: pastel pink
· restrain: mid-range pink
· brilliant: high-chroma red

oh! Oxygen
Studio: AdamsMorioka

Associative Color Response:
· powerful, elegant: black
· quality: neutral gray
· credible: dark blue
· dignified, lively: high-chroma blue
· pleasure: pastel blue

Color Scheme: monochromatic with tinting plus neutral with tinting

A simplistic color palette is created in each of these color studies. As indicated in the associative responses, black and neutral gray act as the governor between each study presented. The high-chroma hue (blue, red-violet, red, red-orange, yellow-green, and yellow-orange) is tinted to create movement from left to right. Each color combination creates a different associative response.

oh! Oxygen
Studio: AdamsMorioka

Associative Color Response:
· powerful, elegant: black
· quality: neutral gray
· gentle: pastel red-orange
· inviting: mid-range red-orange
· brilliant, intense: high-chroma red-orange

oh! Oxygen
Studio: AdamsMorioka

Associative Color Response:
· powerful, elegant: black
· quality: neutral gray
· tart: pastel yellow-green
· strength: mid-range yellow-green
· sharp, bold: high-chroma yellow-green

oh! Oxygen
Studio: AdamsMorioka

Associative Color Response:
· powerful, elegant: black
· quality: neutral gray
· pleasant: pastel yellow-orange
· warmth: mid-range yellow-orange
· powerful, energy: high-chroma yellow-orange

Color Scheme: monochromatic with tinting plus neutral with tinting

A simplistic color palette is created in each of these color studies. As indicated in the associative responses, black and neutral gray act as the governor between each study presented. The high-chroma hue (blue, red-violet, red, red-orange, yellow-green, and yellow-orange) is tinted to create movement from left to right. Each color combination creates a different associative response.

The 9th Annual Serious Moonlight Rio Style
Designer/Creative Director: Francheska Guerrero
Studio: Conversant Studios

Associative Color Response:
· agreeable, welcomed: high-chroma yellow
· energetic, joyful: pastel pink
· sentimental: mid-range pink
· stimulating: high-chroma pink
· energizing: high-chroma red

Color Scheme: two points of a triad with tinting

Harking back to the psychedelic past, this retro-style logomark utilizes a high-chroma color scheme coupled with font selection to help create visual tension and kinetic energy.

podravina
Designer/Art Director: Toni Adamic
Studio: Elevator

Associative Color Response:
· refreshing: mid-range blue
· honesty, strength: high-chroma blue
· credible: dark blue
· expensive, regal: high-chroma blue-violet

Color Scheme: simple analogous with tinting and shading

The podravina logomark is a refreshing example of a simplistic color palette that is wonderfully executed. The way in which the colors are formally laid out within the mark creates a rotating progression of color that energizes the mark and gives it kinetic energy.

TreVida
Designer: Celeste Parrish

Associative Color Response:
· pleasant, refreshing: pastel blue
· strength: high-chroma yellow-green
· sentimental: mid-range pink
· inviting: high-chroma orange
· elegant, refined: dark red

Color Scheme: near tetrad with tinting

The harmony of high-chroma colors coupled with consistency of typeface chosen creates a logotype that is both lively and inviting.

Discovery Day Care
Studio: Essex Two

Associative Color Response:
· basic: black
· lively, happy: high-chroma blue
· stimulating, fun: high-chroma red
· joy, stimulating: high-chroma yellow-orange
· infancy, lively: high-chroma green

Color Scheme: near tetrad plus neutral

The high-chroma primary, secondary, and tertiary colors found within this mark are well suited for the content. Most children of daycare age tend to gravitate toward these types of color schemes, and in this scenario it is learned behavior.

TravelPORT

SYDNEY 2000

sharp■pixel

Baby Basics
Studio: Essex Two

Associative Color Response:
· basic: black
· lively, happy: high-chroma blue
· stimulating, fun: high-chroma red
· joy, stimulating: high-chroma
  yellow-orange
· infancy, lively: high-chroma green

Color Scheme: near tetrad plus
neutral

The Baby Basics logotype is well
suited for this kind of color scheme.
Muddy and dirty colors are not
favored by children of this age.

Beast of The East.Net
Designers: Kristin Sommese and
Lanny Sommese
Studio: Sommese Design

Associative Color Response:
· powerful: black
· quality, passion: neutral gray
· lively, strength: high-chroma blue
· brilliant, aggressive: high-chroma
  red
· strength: high-chroma yellow-
  green

Color Scheme: random plus neutral
with tinting

Beast of The East.Net is an excellent
example of a logomark that does not
follow a standardized color scheme.
However, this mark does follow
learned color association—red for
tongue, white for teeth, black for
dog, and blue for the environment.

Brent Pong Photography
Designer: Suling Pong

Associative Color Response:
· exhilarating: dark orange
· lively: high-chroma blue
· active: dark yellow
· elegant: high-chroma red-violet
· motion: high-chroma green

Color Scheme: random with shading

The logotype is an excellent example
of using shading to tone down the
chroma level of the hues used. Not
every mark created requires hues
that use the highest level of chroma
within their respective families.

Sydney 2000 Olympics
Designers: Michael Bryce and Ron
Hurley
Creative Director: Michael Bryce
Studio: Minale Bryce Design Strategy

Associative Color Response:
· lively, mature: high-chroma blue
· welcome: high-chroma yellow
· elegant, powerful: black
· motion, hope: high-chroma green
· energizing: high-chroma red

Color Scheme: primary, secondary,
plus neutral

Indexical references to a geographic
location are an excellent way to
create a symbol-based mark.
Inspired by the Sydney Opera House
and Aboriginal art, the Sydney 2000
Olympics mark captures the spirit
of a nation.

Travel Port
Studio: Hornall Anderson Design
Works

Associative Color Response:
· energizing, active: high-chroma
  red
· excitement: high-chroma yellow-
  orange
· quality, passion: neutral gray
· honesty, pleasant: high-chroma
  blue
· spring: high-chroma green

Color Scheme: near tetrad plus
neutral (tinted)

Opposition is an excellent way to
create visual tension within a mark.
The duality found between "Travel,"
in neutral gray, and "Port," in
high-chroma primaries and tertiary
hues, creates a counterbalance that
allows one half to play off the other.
Note how "Port" jumps off the page
and "Travel" settles back, creating a
visual foundation.

sharp pixel
Studio: Sharp Pixel

Associative Color Response:
· energizing, active: high-chroma
  red
· stimulating: high-chroma pink
· delicate, energetic: pastel pink
· powerful, basic, elegant: black

Color Scheme: monochromatic
plus neutral

The sharp pixel logomark is a
showcase of restraint. Using both
a monochromatic color study and
a modular system induces visual
consistency that represents a
corporate feel. The typeface chosen
harmonizes with the anatomical
structure of the mark, visually
creating an overall masterpiece.

French Leave Resort
Designers: Kristin Sommese and
Lanny Sommese
Studio: Sommese Design

Associative Color Response:
· pleasure, peaceful, quiet: pastel
  blue
· calm, natural: pastel yellow-green
· comfortable, cozy: pastel pink
· pleasant: pastel yellow-orange
· powerful, basic, elegant: black

Color Scheme: near tetrad using
primaries and tertiary with shading

This beautifully constructed
mark, utilizing substitution, was
created for a resort on the island
of Eleuthera in the Bahamas.
Indexically referencing the beauty
of the insect life found on the
island, and the cultural center the
resort represents to tourists and
indigenous people alike, this mark
symbolizes the atmosphere of the
resort. A near tetrad using primary
and tertiary pastel hues adds to the
colorful nature of the mark.

**ICC Cricket World Cup: West
Indies 2007**
Designers: Dean Power and Michail
Kowal
Creative Director: Michael Bryce
Studio: Minale Bryce Design Strategy

Associative Color Response:
· strength: high-chroma blue
· drive: high-chroma yellow-orange
· intense: high-chroma red
· powerful, basic, elegant: black

Color Scheme: primaries and
tertiary hues plus neutral

This highly energetic mark is
beautifully conceived through the
high-chroma colors chosen and the
agitation of line work.

Cross Conditioning Systems
Designer: Justin Deister
Studio: Uppercase Design

Associative Color Response:
· exciting: high-chroma red-violet
· growing: high-chroma yellow-
  orange
· pristine, pure: high-chroma blue-
  green
· energizing: high-chroma red
· powerful, basic, elegant: black

Color Scheme: triad with red plus
neutral

The directional flow of a mark is as
important as any other formal and
conceptual aspects. A mark that
has a downward or backward flow
will create a negative impact on
the viewer.

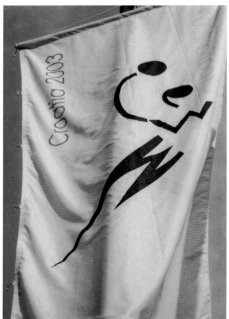

XVIth Women's World Handball Championship

Designer: Boris Ljubcic

The Olympic Games inspired the color palette for the XVIth Women's World Handball Championship (WWHC). Each color (red, orange, green, blue, and black) represents a continent. The logotype is constructed from the letterforms "W," "W," "C," part of a character (the dot of the lowercase "i"), and a punctuation mark (the comma). The logotype is designed to represent both the WWHC and a handball player with a ball. The legibility of the mark was critical in its development. The logotype needed to be legible on almost any imaginable surface—textiles, wood, metal, paper—and through any electronic means, incuding the Web or broadcast television. The logotype in its original color palette was designed so that the background color used a high color value rating, in the 90s (yellow/white), but also so that the color palette could be simplified to accommodate different materials and painted surfaces. In the case of the gold, silver, and bronze medals, the mark was debossed (etched) and laminated with different colors. Athletes are emotional about the medals they have won, and by debossing the surface the medals could be appreciated through the sense of touch.

T When creating a logotype that represents any kind of human interaction, constructing letterforms so that they reflect the action, interaction, motion, iconic representation, or content is a means for unique solutions.

When devising a color palette for a mark that is going to be used on multiple surfaces and materials, make sure to color sample each specimen to determine the color value rating, or Y tristimulus value. This helps to determine the legibility and the distance at which the mark can be seen. The PANTONE Color Cue will shoot almost any material and provide the corresponding Y tristimulus values. Even if the Color Cue is for ink-matching systems, the Y tristimulus values provided will be accurate enough to determine whether the color combination, for example, metal and printing ink, are legible. Remember that a CVD of 20% is needed.

Sydney 2000 Olympic Games

Studio: Minale Bryce Design Strategy

The Sydney 2000 Olympic Games logomark
is beautifully conceived—a rendering of the
Sydney Opera House inspired by Aboriginal art.
The five-ringed Olympics symbol represents
the five continents, and was first proposed by
Pierre de Coubertin in 1914. The crude nature
of the Sydney 2000 Olympics logomark and the
positioning of the colors create a mechanical
that can be easily reproduced in almost any
medium—trapping is not an issue. Blue and
black when trapped create black, black and red
when trapped create black, red and yellow when
trapped create red, and yellow and green when
trapped create green—an invisible trap.

 To understand whether certain hues, when overprinted, create a visible trap, use the Multiply feature in Photoshop. For example, create a color study consisting of five hues. In a Photoshop document, make each hue 1-inch squared, and place each hue on its own layer. Once this is done, use the Multiply feature in the layer dialog box to visually verify how the hues will overprint. Each hue can be visually activated or not by clicking on and off the "eye symbol" in the layer dialog box. This will allow for visual verification of two-color, three-color, four-color, and five-color overprinting.

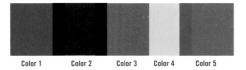

Color 1   Color 2   Color 3   Color 4   Color 5

This diagram depicts which hue combinations will create a visible trap. For more information on this subject, see Chapter 7.

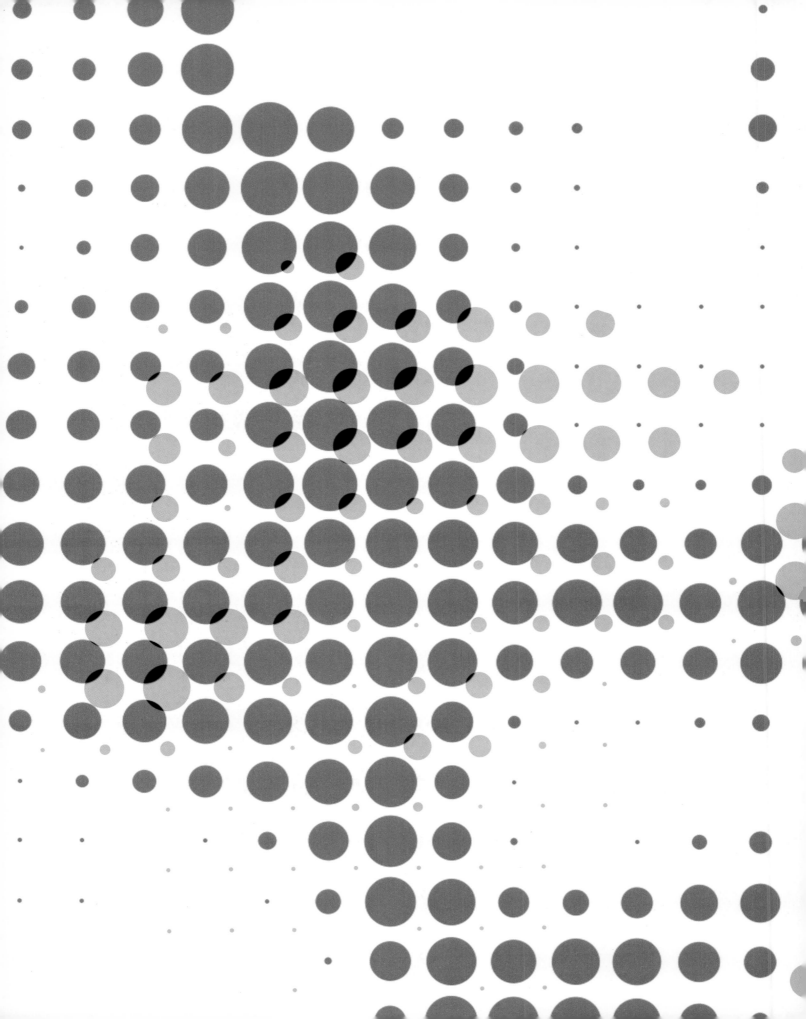

Six+ Colors

Six+ color marks are relatively new, and were most often seen in the past in the television and film industries. That is not the case today. From "mom and pop" businesses to large corporations, multicolored marks are influencing how graphic designers create logos and how consumers interact with businesses. No longer constrained by astronomical commercial printing costs, a new color vernacular is taking hold. This is reshaping the way in which designers think about the creation of a mark by the context in which it is used and the influence it has.

No longer are businesses, including the business of graphic design, confined to a geographical location and local or regional vendors. A graphic designer may have a closer working relationship with a printer on the other side of the world than the printer next door. The ability to communicate, interact, and purchase 24/7 worldwide has led to dramatic price reductions in printing and to more companies doing a larger share of their business over the Internet, both of which have influenced the amount of color found within a typical mark. A mark may still be designed first in one or two colors, but if a designer is worth his or her salt, the logo will also incorporate multiple colors for every kind of scenario, including the medium in which it is used.

Second Annual World Military Games
Designer: Boris Ljubicic

Associative Color Response:
· motion: high-chroma green
· lively, upward: high-chroma blue
· intense, energizing: high-chroma red
· welcome: high-chroma yellow
· powerful: black
· purity: white

Color Scheme: primary and secondary hues plus neutral and white

The Second Annual World Military Games are similar in spirit and content to the Olympics. As a point of departure and inspiration, five interlocking rings were chosen as the basic geometric shape. In contrast to the Olympics design, these rings were tightly grouped and rendered three-dimensionally into the shape of an open flower—an oxymoron of strong and delicate. Each color (red, blue, yellow, green, and black) on the ring signifies the continents, while the red squares signify the geographical location of the games—in this case, Croatia.

Johnson County Library Foundation
Designer: Eric Looney
Art Directors: Eric Looney and Margaret Bowker
Studio: GouldEvans

Associative Color Response:
· curiosity, communication: high-chroma orange
· stimulating: high-chroma yellow-orange
· inviting: mid-range orange, pastel orange
· quality: neutral gray
· bright: white

Color Scheme: simple analogous with tinting plus neutral (tinted)

The color palette utilized for this logomark is an excellent example of practical color use—stretching the palette. In reality, this logomark could be produced with two inks and a type reversal.

Wasserman Media Group
Studio: AdamsMorioka

Associative Color Response:
· curiosity, communication: high-chroma orange
· energy: high-chroma yellow
· strength: high-chroma yellow-green
· motion: high-chroma green
· lively: high-chroma blue
· forward: high-chroma blue-green
· power: high-chroma violet
· earthy: earth-tone red
· exhilarating: dark orange
· nature: dark green
· quality: neutral gray

Color Scheme: random—primary, secondary, and tertiary hues with tinting and shading plus neutral

This colorful logomark is gloriously vivid. The high-intensity hues coupled with dark and pastel colors create a complex hue hierarchy that is truly amazing. If all the hues used within the color palette were of a high-chroma color scheme, the palette would not work. This is an excellent example of creating a counterbalance between high-chroma, pastel, and dark hues.

DLU: don't let up
Art Director: Chevonne Woodard
Studio: Chevonne Woodard Design

Associative Color Response:
· brilliant: high-chroma red
· strong: dark red
· powerful: black
· classic: dark gray
· quality: neutral gray

Color Scheme: one hue with shading
plus neutral with tinting

The DLU mark is an excellent
example of creating numerous hues
using two inks.

Wasserman Media Group
Studio: AdamsMorioka

Associative Color Response:
· curiosity, communication: high-
chroma orange
· energy: high-chroma yellow
· strength: high-chroma yellow-
green
· motion: high-chroma green
· lively: high-chroma blue
· forward: high-chroma blue-green
· power: high-chroma violet
· earthy: earth-tone red
· exhilarating: dark orange
· nature: dark green
· quality: neutral gray

Color Scheme: random—primary,
secondary, and tertiary hues with
tinting and shading plus neutral

This colorful logomark is gloriously
vivid. The high-intensity hues
coupled with dark and pastel colors
create a complex hue hierarchy that
is truly amazing. If all the hues
used within the color palette were
of a high-chroma color scheme,
the palette would not work. This is
an excellent example of creating
a counterbalance between high-
chroma, pastel, and dark hues.

SMS Foods
Designer: Boris Ljubicic

Associative Color Response:
· classic: mid-range green
· natural: dark green
· quality: neutral gray
· expensive: dark gray
· energizing: high-chroma red
· healing: high-chroma orange

Color Scheme: primary and
secondary hues plus neutral (tinted)

The Slogan for SMS Foods is
"A Message from Nature"—a
gastronomic delight that uses
only natural products (fish, olives,
vegetables, and fruits) from the
Adriatic coastal region of Dalmatia.
The color use in the SMS logotype is
both symbolic and iconic. The two
gray and two green hues reference
fish scales and olive leaves, whereas
the red and orange symbolically
represent edible foods. Both the
high-chroma red and orange have
an excellent appetite rating, with an
associative taste of very sweet.

Mljet
Designer: Boris Ljubicic

Associative Color Response:
· life: high-chroma green
· brilliant: high-chroma red
· pristine, pure: high-chroma blue-
green
· lively: high-chroma blue
· natural: dark blue-green
· quality: neutral gray

Color Scheme: complex analogous
color palette with red accent, tints,
and shades plus neutral

This logotype captures the
Mediterranean feel of Croatia's
coastline. A combination of high-
chroma, dark, and natural hues
is used in an indexical manner to
reference the landscape.

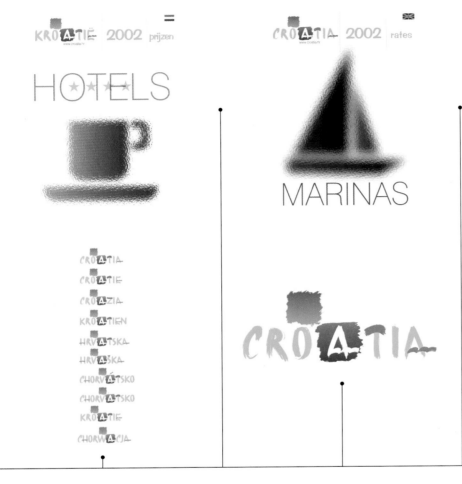

Croatian National Tourist Board
Designer: Boris Ljubicic

Associative Color Response:
· stimulating: high-chroma red
· energizing: high-chroma red-
  orange
· healing: high-chroma orange
· relaxed: high-chroma blue
· memories: high-chroma violet
· strength: high-chroma yellow-
  green

Color Scheme: direct/near/split
complementary

The color palette chosen for the
logotype is quite intense. Designer
Boris Ljubicic wanted to convey
a Mediterranean paradise where
people around the world could relax
and enjoy themselves. The hand-
lettered typography found within the
logotype helps to create a cohesive
whole, no matter what the mark is
juxtaposed with.

Worldcentric Media
Designer: Jessica Flores

Associative Color Response:
· power, dignified: high-chroma
  violet
· pristine: high-chroma blue-green
· excitement: high-chroma yellow-
  orange
· sharp: high-chroma yellow-green
· brilliant: high-chroma red
· exhilarating: dark orange
· motion: high-chroma green
· active: dark yellow
· powerful: high-chroma blue-violet
· strong: black

Color Scheme: hyper-complex near
analogous color palette

Through the use of scale, this
modular logomark creates an
(unusual) active symmetrical
composition. Most symmetrical
compositions are created to make
the viewer's eye rest. This mark,
however, utilizes high-chroma hues
coupled with scale and placement to
create an energetic mark.

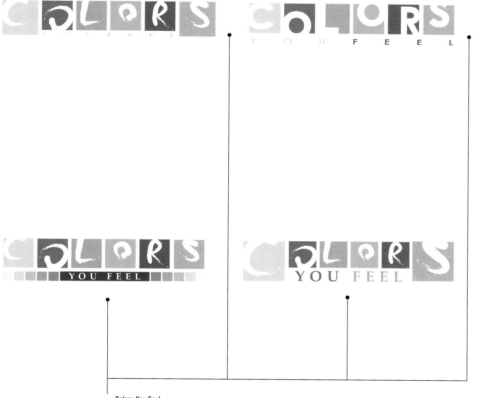

Colors You Feel
Studio: Sharp Pixel

Associative Color Response:
· stimulating: dark yellow
· relaxed: high-chroma blue
· active: dark yellow
· healing: high-chroma orange
· exhilarating: dark orange
· refreshing: pastel blue
· elegant: black
· quality: neutral gray
· wise, solid: dark gray

Color Scheme: direct
complementary with yellow accent
plus neutral and tinting

These modular-system logomarks
are a fine example of utilizing
a complex complementary color
palette within a sequence of 2, 2,
2 (two yellows, two oranges, and
two blues)—not including black
and its tints. The circular logomark
is not complementary but random,
and is also modular, utilizing
cropping, scaling, overprinting, hue
replacement, and sequencing (2, 2,
2) to create a highly kinetic mark.
This is evident in both the black and
white mark as well as the color.

Millennium Foods
Designer: Erik Potter
Creative Directors: Laura Titzer and
Andrew Salyer
Studio: Fahrenheit Design

Associative Color Response:
· bold: high-chroma yellow-green
· enterprise: high-chroma yellow-
orange
· cleanliness: high-chroma orange
· stirring: high-chroma dark orange
· earthy: earth-tone red
· quality: neutral gray

Color Scheme: complex analogous
with green accent plus neutral
and tinting

The Millennium Foods logomark is
a superb example of choosing a
color palette that has an excellent
appetite rating. This complex
analogous color palette is made up
primarily of high-chroma (sweet to
very sweet) orange hues. Choosing
the appropriate color palette for
marks that represent food should
be the first course of action when
developing the mark.

circle of love
Designer/Art Director: Handy Atmali
Studio: HA Design

Associative Color Response:
· pleasure: pastel blue
· powerful: high-chroma yellow-orange
· happy: high-chroma orange
· new growth: high-chroma yellow-green
· exciting: high-chroma red-violet
· quality: black

Color Scheme: tetrad with yellow-orange accent plus neutral

The physicality of the composition and color choice create a highly kinetic mark that encapsulates the subject matter. The light, airy typography harmonizes well with the scaled circular forms and high-chroma hues evoking the feelings of first love.

RebelMail
Designer: Ken Kelleher

Associative Color Response:
· professional: dark gray
· quality: neutral gray
· classic: light gray
· mature: dark red
· growing: high-chroma orange
· inviting: pastel orange

Color Scheme: one hue with tinting and shading plus neutral (tinted)

The mail delivery mark utilizes two inks to create a multitude of colors. Speed lines and drop shadows are used to help create a 3-D allusion on a 2-D plane.

naiva
Studio: Boris Ljubicic

Associative Color Response:
· lively: high-chroma blue
· stimulating: high-chroma yellow-orange
· active, cheer: high-chroma red
· powerful: high-chroma blue-violet
· happy: pastel blue-violet
· fresh: high-chroma blue-green

Color Scheme: random high-chroma hues with pastel accent

This modular-system logotype uses similarity of form, rotation, placement, and high-chroma hues to create continuity within the mark.

Powi
Designer: George White
Art Director: Mark Sackett
Studio: Sackett Design

Associative Color Response:
· classic: mid-range blue-violet
· credible: dark blue
· exhilarating: dark orange
· sound: earth-tone orange
· mature: dark red
· exciting: dark red-violet

Color Scheme: complementary warm and cool colors with overprinting

The Powi logotype is an outstanding use of overprinting to stretch the hues to make them look as though more ink is being utilized. Note where the inks overprint to create additional hues.

Pace International
Studio: Hornall Anderson Design Works

Associative Color Response:
· life, motion: green
· lemony, fruity: green-yellow
· vigorous, inspiring: yellow
· drive, goal: yellow-orange
· healing, tasty: orange
· energizing, powerful: red

Color Scheme: complementary (red and green) plus near analogous

The Pace International logomark is highly kinetic in a circular upward motion. This is brought to bear through the choice of high-chroma hues and scale.

Sun Shine: dick lee's project
Designer: Audrey Koh
Studio: Plastic Soldier Factory Pte Ltd

Associative Color Response:
· good spirits: mid-range yellow-orange
· cheerfulness: high-chroma orange
· stimulating: high-chroma pink
· energetic: pastel pink
· flamboyant: mid-range red-violet
· nostalgic: mid-range violet
· young: high-chroma blue-green
· bold: high-chroma yellow-green

Color Scheme: random

This retro psychedelic-style logomark is superbly crafted through the use of color, shape, and typographic specimen. A visual consistency is achieved through using the hues specified at the same or nearly the same chroma value.

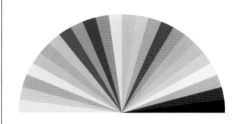

Youn
Designer/Art Director: Kyeong-Wan Youn
Studio: Youn Graphics & Interactive Design

Associative Color Response:
· cheerfulness: high-chroma orange
· bold: high-chroma yellow-green
· lively: high-chroma blue
· intense: high-chroma red
· professional: dark gray
· quality: neutral gray
· powerful: black

Color Scheme: near tetrad plus neutral with tinting

The Youn logomark is an excellent example of utilizing cool and warm colors. Within this mark, designer Kyeong-Wan Youn sets up a binary opposition utilizing the two extremes: black (the coolest color) and high-chroma warm hues (red, orange, and yellow-green). This makes the logomark pop.

Community Unity
Designer: Erik Chrestensen
Studio: Chrestensen Design Works

Associative Color Response:
· classic: dark blue-violet
· cool: pastel blue-violet
· sound: earth-tone red
· stirring: dark orange
· quality: neutral gray

Color Scheme: near complementary with tinting and shading

This logomark is a superb example of stretching color, through the use of gradients, and tinting, to make it seem as though there are numerous hues.

Deerfoot Meadows
Designer: Erik Chrestensen
Studio: Chrestensen Design Works

Associative Color Response:
· dignified: high-chroma red
· refined: dark red
· rustic: earth-tone red
· luxurious: high-chroma yellow-orange
· pleasant: pastel yellow-orange
· powerful: black

Color Scheme: two points of a tetrad with tinting and shading plus neutral

The Deerfoot logotype is a wonderful example of utilizing the appropriate colors and typefaces with the content to achieve the desired visual correspondence.

anchorball
Designer: Ken Kelleher

Associative Color Response:
· pristine: high-chroma blue-green
· bold: high-chroma yellow-green
· drive: high-chroma yellow-orange
· firm: pastel blue-green
· charming: mid-range blue-violet
· elegant: pastel blue-violet

Color Scheme: random with sequential pattern

Although this may seem like a random color palette, there is a logic to the hues chosen. Yellow-orange is two steps away from yellow-green, which is two steps away from blue-green, which is two steps away from blue-violet. When dealing with this kind of color complexity, utilizing other aspects in 2-D design and applying them to practical color use is a prudent measure.

Glenshore 3
Designer: Nate Burgos

Associative Color Response:
· bold: high-chroma yellow-green
· life: high-chroma green
· stirring: dark orange
· growing: high-chroma orange
· pleasing: high-chroma blue
· elegant: black

Color Scheme: random with high-chroma hues plus neutral

Within this logomark, harmony is achieved through primarily a high-chroma-hue color palette. Black and dark orange are implemented to achieve an accent counterbalance.

Color Palette: Sundial of Colors
Studio: AdamsMorioka

Associative Color Response:
· noble: high-chroma yellow
· active: dark yellow
· new growth: dark yellow-green
· sharp: pastel yellow-green
· calm: pastel green
· cool: high-chroma blue-green
· young: dark blue-green
· lively: high-chroma blue
· credible: dark blue
· pure: pastel blue-green
· charming: pastel red-violet
· tender: pastel pink
· excitement: high-chroma pink
· brilliant: high-chroma red
· exhilarating: dark orange
· tasty: high-chroma orange
· joy: high-chroma yellow-orange
· gentle: pastel orange
· warm: pastel earth-tone red
· wholesome: earth-tone red
· powerful: earth-tone black

Color Scheme: hyper complex random with tinting and shading

This modular-system logomark has 24 units. Each unit is in the shape of a wedge and has its own specified hue. The typography is purposely simplified to counterbalance the complexity of the mark.

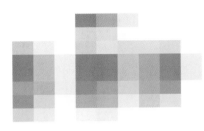

So-net
Designer: Massaaki Omura

Associative Color Response:
· energy: high-chroma yellow
· active: dark yellow
· stimulating: dark yellow-orange
· moving: dark orange
· life: high-chroma green
· growth: dark green
· powerful: black

Color Scheme: near complex analogous with shading plus neutral

Note the opposition occurring within the logomark. The typography acts as a flat 2-D surface to counterbalance the 3-D mark. The hues found within the 3-D mark are warm, whereas the black hue is cool.

San-Gi Kyo Star
Designer: Massaaki Omura

Associative Color Response:
· pristine: high-chroma blue-green
· pure: pastel blue-green

Color Scheme: monochromatic with tinting

Within this mark, one ink is utilized with tinting to create an array of colors.

Medical Channel
Designer: Massaaki Omura

Associative Color Response:
· stimulating: high-chroma pink
· energetic: pastel pink
· growing: high-chroma orange
· exhilarating, inspiring: dark orange
· hope: high-chroma red-orange
· serious: dark red-orange

Color Scheme: simple analogous with tinting

In this digitally rendered mark, the abstract form is made up from a modular system (squares) to create a contemporary mark that references high-definition broadcasting.

Umehachi
Designer: Minato Ishikawa

Associative Color Response:
· exciting: high-chroma red-violet
· select: pastel red-violet
· healing: high-chroma orange
· stimulating: dark orange
· enticing: pastel orange
· warm-hearted: earth-tone red
· powerful: black

Color Scheme: near complex analogous with tinting and shading plus neutral

This modular-system logomark is more organic than most. The round circular shapes are varied in form from one another and placed asymmetrically. This creates a more natural mark.

Sagent 1
Designer: Carlo Irigoyen
Art Director: Brenda Spivack
Studio: Red Table

Associative Color Response:
· agreeable: high-chroma yellow
· stimulating: high-chroma yellow-orange
· healing: high-chroma orange
· active: high-chroma red-orange
· intense: high-chroma red
· new growth: high-chroma yellow-green
· life: high-chroma green
· elegant: black

Color Scheme: complex analogous plus neutral

In this beautifully constructed color palette, the Sagent mark uses size and placement to harmonize the mark with the typography.

Fozzy
Designer: Stefan G. Bucher
Studio: 344

Associative Color Response:
· expensive, warm: gold
· valuable: silver
· powerful: black

Color Scheme: random plus neutral

This unusual logotype is designed to have the look and feel of a hood ornament. This is accomplished primarily through the choice of hues.

Harvest-Drive
Designer: Massaaki Omura

Associative Color Response:
· excitement, stimulating, fun: high-chroma yellow-orange
· healing, growing, happy: high-chroma orange
· energizing: high-chroma red-orange
· exciting: high-chroma pink/red

Color Scheme: complex analogous

Although this may not seem to be a six-color mark (utilizing only two inks) the gradient/split fountain found within the logo design creates a multitude of hues. This is an excellent example of stretching colors to help create movement within a mark.

Aperios
Designer: Massaaki Omura

Associative Color Response:
· refreshing: pastel blue
· lively, electric: high-chroma blue
· elegant: high-chroma blue-violet
· powerful: black

Color Scheme: complex analogous plus neutral

This complex analogous color palette utilizes tinting and shading (through the use of gradients) to create a 3-D illusion on a 2-D plane. The 3-D illusion is minimized by the choice of cool hues.

Liquid Fuxion
Designer: Michael Gray

Associative Color Response:
· quality: light gray
· wise: dark gray
· powerful: black

Color Scheme: achromatic

The line work found in this logomark coupled with the typography creates a contemporary design that symbolizes the digital age. The achromatic color palette helps to simplify and counterbalance this highly complex design.

sagent 2
Designer: Brenda Spivack
Studio: Red Table

Associative Color Response:
· growth: dark green
· active: dark yellow
· sunshine: pastel yellow
· energy: mid-range yellow-orange
· inspiring: dark yellow-orange

Color Scheme: near analogous with shading

The flat-pattern illustration found within this logomark is an excellent example of substitution—the flower is substituted in place of the bowl in the lowercase "g."

Creative Environments of Hollywood
Designer: Brenda Spivack
Studio: Red Table

Associative Color Response:
· dignity: high-chroma blue
· life: mid-range blue
· service: dark blue
· professional: dark gray
· classic: neutral gray
· strong: black

Color Scheme: one hue with tinting and shading plus neutral (tinted)

A 3-D illusion is established through two-point perspective, lighting, and hue control to create a very dynamic mark. The 3-D illusion is intensified by juxtaposing it with a flat object (the company name).

Archilab 2004
Studio: Thonik Design

Associative Color Response:
· warm: high-chroma orange
· soft: mid-range pink
· elegant: mid-range red-violet
· taste: dark red
· powerful: black
· professional: dark gray
· quality: neutral gray

Color Scheme: near analogous with tinting and shading plus neutral (tinted)

This mark was designed for a group of architects exhibiting their work in 2004. The design of the modular-system mark was carried out by the use of proportionate panels throughout the exhibit. Thonik Design wanted to create a strong identity that united all the members who were participating. In the final exhibit, 80 panels were used, each with its own hue.

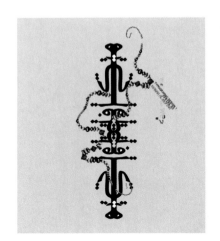

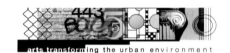

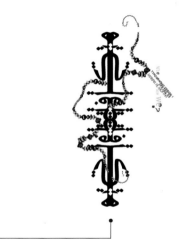

Lighting Council: Australia
Designer: Raymond Koo
Creative Director: Michael Bryce
Studio: Minale Bryce Design Strategy

Associative Color Response:
· refined: mid-range red-violet
· brilliant: high-chroma red
· loud: high-chroma orange
· excitement: high-chroma yellow-
  orange
· sunlight: high-chroma yellow-
  green
· pleasure: pastel blue
· lively: high-chroma blue
· powerful: black

Color Scheme: double direct/near
complementary

The spectrum of colors and
physicality of form created for this
mark is well suited to the content.
Scale and hue are used within this
system to create radiating outward
movement.

em picnic
Studio: Essex Two

Associative Color Response:
· brilliant: high-chroma red
· elegant: dark red
· exciting: high-chroma pink
· fruity: high-chroma yellow-green
· growth: high-chroma green
· nature: dark green
· powerful: black

Color Scheme: direct complementary
plus neutral

Anytime a continuous-tone image
is used to create a logomark for
print-based design, a coarse screen
pattern should be used. In this case,
the mark is design for Web and
motion graphics. If this mark were to
be used in print, it would need to be
printed using four-color process.

Kid Bits
Studio: Essex Two

Associative Color Response:
· brilliant: high-chroma red
· general: mid-range orange
· exhilarating: dark orange
· new growth: high-chroma yellow-
  green
· charming: mid-range blue-violet
· clean: pastel blue
· delicate: pastel blue-violet
· happy: high-chroma blue

Color Scheme: direct complementary
with yellow-green and red accent,
tinting and shading

The physicality of form and color
hues chosen creates a highly kinetic
mark that metaphorically represents
the atmosphere associated with a
daycare center. This is a wonderful
mark that illustrates how color can
add content.

Arts Transforming The Urban
Environment Conference
Designers: Ned Drew, Brenda
McManus, and Dale Garcia
Creative Director: Ned Drew

Associative Color Response:
· healing: high-chroma orange
· enticing, inviting: mid-range
  orange
· stimulating: dark orange
· soft: mid-range pink
· develop: dark red
· quality: neutral gray
· cultured: dark gray
· powerful: black

Color Scheme: complex analogous
plus neutral (tinted)

In the Arts Transforming The Urban
Environment logo, color is injected
into the mark through a slow
transition from left to right. This
treatment symbolizes how the arts
can help revitalize a depressed area.

Who Are We
Designer: Manar Al-Muftah
Art Director: Peter Martin

Associative Color Response:
· pleasant: pastel yellow-orange
· gentle: mid-range orange
· refined, taste: dark red
· quiet: pastel blue
· calm: pastel blue-green
· pure: mid-range blue-green
· new, pristine: high-chroma blue-
  green
· elegant: black

Color Scheme: direct/near
complementary with shading plus
neutral (tinted)

This Arabic logotype is meant to look
like a shisha or hubbly-bubbly water
pipe, and is used here as a cultural
identifier. It has been superbly
executed. In the top version, the
tan hue is meant to reference the
landscape found in this region (the
Arabian Peninsula).

Indianapolis Zoo
Studio: Essex Two

Associative Color Response:
- new growth: high-chroma yellow-green
- outdoorsy: high-chroma green
- happy: pastel blue
- honesty: high-chroma blue
- tender: high-chroma blue-violet
- life: dark red-violet
- pristine: high-chroma blue-green
- earthy: earth-tone red
- enduring: dark gray
- quality: neutral gray
- elegant: black

Color Scheme: hypercomplex, near analogous color palette

When using photographs within logomarks, a coarse screen pattern or high-contrast image is advised. However, if the client is using the mark for Web, or is only going to print, for example, the stationery on a personal color printer, then it is perfectly fine. In an attempt to save money, many institutions are converting to self-publishing and printing via inkjet printers and the like.

Disney's Fantasia Shop
Designer/Art Director: David Ferrell
Creative Director: David Riley
Studio: DR+A

Associative Color Response:
- stimulating: high-chroma yellow-orange
- happy: high-chroma orange
- fun: high-chroma red
- exciting: high-chroma red-violet
- classic: high-chroma blue-violet
- exhilarating: dark orange
- powerful: black

Color Scheme: hypercomplex, near analogous color palette

The Disney's Fantasia Shop mark is a superb example of matching hues with subject matter. Masterfully created, the high-chroma hues fuse in a kinetic liveliness unsurpassed by many other marks.

Pieces
Designer: Inyoung Choi

Associative Color Response:
- rustic: earth-tone red
- rooted: earth tone
- exhilarating: dark orange
- autumn: high-chroma orange
- inviting: mid-range orange
- energy: high-chroma yellow-orange
- powerful: black

Color Scheme: near analogous with tinting and shading plus black

This unusual logotype is created through continuous-tone images. Harmony is achieved by creating a consistent color palette by using shading throughout the logotype.

Sony Life
Designer: Massaaki Omura

Associative Color Response:
- pristine: high-chroma blue-green
- pure: mid-range blue-green
- lively: pastel blue-green
- powerful: high-chroma blue-violet
- refined: mid-range blue-violet
- select: pastel blue-violet
- professional: dark gray

Color Scheme: two points of the split complementary or near analogous plus neutral

In the Sony Life logomark, gradients are used most effectively to create kinetic energy or movement within the mark.

Sony Eco Plaza
Designer: Massaaki Omura

Associative Color Response:
- pristine: high-chroma blue-green
- lively: pastel blue
- powerful: high-chroma blue-violet
- quality: neutral gray

Color Scheme: analogous with tinting plus neutral (tinted)

The layered information found within this logomark is laid out to create an asymmetrical composition within the circle. This creates an intense amount of movement within the mark. The reversed letterform (white, in this case) is utilized as a navigational device to pull the eye in and through the mark.

Anemone Makeup
Designer: Mark Raebel
Studio: Arsenal Design

Associative Color Response:
· refined: pastel red-violet
· classic: pastel gray
· fantasy: pastel blue-violet
· soft: pastel dark pink
· cute: pastel pink
· elegant: black

Color Scheme: near analogous

Harmony of form is achieved through a similarity of line work and pastel color use. By using soft pastel hues, the mark does not become heavy-handed and achieves a sophisticated appearance.

AeroBloks, Tinker Minds, Inc.
Designer: Mark Raebel
Studio: Arsenal Design

Associative Color Response:
· aggressive: high-chroma pink
· brilliant: high-chroma red
· fun: high-chroma yellow-orange
· strength: high-chroma yellow-green
· lively: high-chroma green
· warm: earth-tone red
· exciting: high-chroma red-violet
· quality: neutral gray

Color Scheme: complementary with accent plus neutral

Both of these marks are superb examples of overprinting. When utilizing overprinting, set up color matrixes in Photoshop and apply Multiply in the layers dialog box. This allows for visual verification of the overprinting hues—by doing so, no surprises will occur on press.

Living Well with Cancer
Studio: Bremmer & Goris Communications

Associative Color Response:
· life: high-chroma green
· healthy: high-chroma yellow-orange
· energizing: high-chroma red
· dignity: high-chroma blue
· empathy: pastel green
· powerful: black

Color scheme: direct/near complementary/tertiary with tinting plus neutral

A superb color palette—the symbiotic relationship between the color palette, script typeface, and overall shape create a lively and energetic mark that is most appropriate to the subject matter.

ExpoDesign: Korea-Japan Friendship Year 2005
Designer: Inyoung Choi

Associative Color Response:
· fantasy: high-chroma blue-violet
· pleasing: high-chroma blue
· glory: mid-range blue
· charming: high-chroma red
· excitement: high-chroma red-orange
· childlike: high-chroma orange
· joy: high-chroma yellow-orange
· basic: black

Color Scheme: complementary with tinting plus neutral

This superbly executed mark is cleverly conjoined to create a joyful atmosphere. Gradient hues are utilized to create an innocent, glowing, and loving mood.

ExpoDesign: Visit Gyeonggi-Korea 2005
Designer: Inyoung Choi

Associative Color Response:
· fantasy: high-chroma blue-violet
· pleasing: high-chroma blue
· charming: high-chroma red
· joy: high-chroma yellow-orange
· quality: neutral gray
· powerful: black

Color Scheme: random plus neutral with tinting

The high-chroma hues counterbalanced with white, black, and gray create a unique color combination that is highly kinetic.

books@vba.org
Designer: Caroline Cardwell

Associative Color Response:
· develop: high-chroma dark red
· pleasure: high-chroma blue-violet
· lively: high-chroma green
· fun: high-chroma yellow-orange
· powerful: high-chroma blue
· brilliant: high-chroma red
· creative: high-chroma red-violet
· new growth: high-chroma yellow-green
· welcome: earth-tone orange
· growing: high-chroma orange
· credible: dark blue-violet
· stimulating: high-chroma pink
· classic: mid-range green
· new: high-chroma blue-green

Color Scheme: hyper-complex analogous with orange and orange-yellow complementary

If color sells a product then there is no finer example then this mark. A smorgasbord of high-chroma hues is used to portray a somewhat dry subject, creating a lively atmosphere. When using an array of colors within a design, it is best to start with traditional color palettes and then expand their hue base.

Nuclear Lemonade
Designer: Caroline Cardwell

Associative Color Response:
· agreeable: high-chroma yellow
· exciting: high-chroma yellow-orange
· exhilarating: dark orange
· happy: pastel blue
· young: pastel blue-green
· powerful: black

Color Scheme: near complementary/ tertiary

The primary colors for this logomark are yellow, yellow-orange, and dark orange. Each of these hues has an excellent appetite rating, with a taste association of sweet. The mark was designed for a bar in the San Francisco Bay area. The bar (Nuclear Lemonade) prides itself on using the latest liquor sensations and mixology, embracing creativity from their bartenders to create a hip and playful atmosphere.

Powi

Designer: Mark Sackett

This seven-color logotype not only demonstrates a superior use of color, it is also an excellent example of overprinting. The logotype, in concert with the collateral material, is a true masterpiece and a colorful feast for the eye. Using broad, expansive color-fields that are high-chroma, combined with unconventional color schemes, creates a unique body of work (complex-incongruous, a simple analogous with complementary/near-complementary, and an incongruous/near-incongruous color scheme). This logotype is a great example of how color can sell a product.

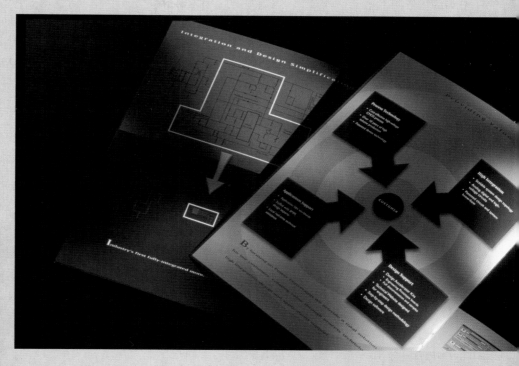

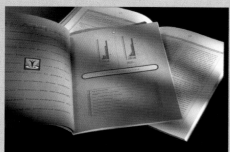

When printing text type on broad, expansive color-fields, the three basic rules, listed below and illustrated right, need to be followed. (*Color Management: A Comprehensive Guide for Graphic Designers* includes visual resources demonstrating this phenomenon.)

1 / Any warm pure or semipure hue can be used at 100% of color with black text type. A pure or semipure color does not have any portion of black in the base ink.

2 / When using high-chroma cool colors, it is best to reverse the type out to white.

3 / Any color that is tinted no greater than 20% will be legible with black text type. This strategy works well for cool colors.

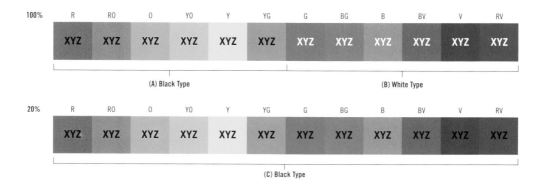

100%	R	RO	O	YO	Y	YG	G	BG	B	BV	V	RV
	XYZ	XYZ	XYZ	XYZ	XYZ	XYZ	XYZ	XYZ	XYZ	XYZ	XYZ	XYZ

(A) Black Type   (B) White Type

20%	R	RO	O	YO	Y	YG	G	BG	B	BV	V	RV
	XYZ	XYZ	XYZ	XYZ	XYZ	XYZ	XYZ	XYZ	XYZ	XYZ	XYZ	XYZ

(C) Black Type

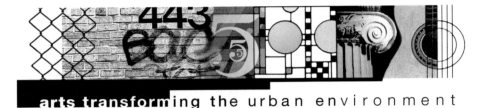

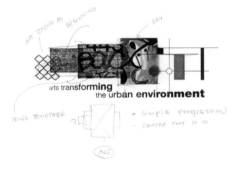

Arts Transforming the Urban Environment Conference

Designers: Brenda McManus, Dale Garcia, and Ned Drew
Creative Director: Ned Drew

The design team was interested in creating, via color, a visual metaphor that expressed change and progression. "We wanted to create a logomark that could represent the grittiness of the urban environment, and, at the same time, convey the progressive nature of the arts." The team wanted to use a color combination that would portray a rough, forbidding state of decline, but also represent an evolution toward a bright, creative, and positive future.

The design team worked with two color combinations to define the different areas within the mark and to activate it, thereby helping to deliver the message. Within the

mark, red was mixed with black to create a sense of the "rough" and "urban." Yellow was mixed with red to create a sense of "illumination" and "richness."

The logomark, developed for a conference held at Rutgers University in 2001, was given a lengthy academic title to reflect the complex issues and objectives involved. Some of the conference's goals were to bring together artists, architects, city planners, politicians, and educators to understand and create awareness about the role artists play in revitalizing depressed urban environments. By highlighting successful situations where the

arts and local governments created partnerships that turned depressed city areas around, all parties involved gained a better understanding of the dynamics.

The design team knew that logo legibility would be a concern in that the audience was going to be groups and/or individuals interested in visual urban culture and arts. The team felt that some latitude should be given with regard to readability. The designers imagined the audience as visually literate and therefore appreciative of a more complex message. "We wanted the title and type to be clear, but we felt the images could be more complex.

We felt confident that it was appropriate to ask our viewers to be more active in the interpretation and communication process." Color plays a subtle but important role in helping with this interpretation, helping to provide visual clues that aid in identifying the various environments.

With the lengthy name of the conference established, Ned Drew encouraged the design team to see this as a challenge—as the essential component in establishing the parameter of the mark. What seemed to be visually too much, too long, turned into an opportunity to create an interesting logomark

that functioned as a history—a linear narrative. Ned Drew felt it was important to have as much visual reference material as possible. "I wanted our team to look, gather, and then manipulate what it found."

The first stage in the process was to generate a word list from free association, with the conceptual primers being the "urban environment" and "arts." "During this process we started with the obvious, the cliché, and worked our way from there through to more interesting and unique associations. From this free-association list we created an image list of possible visuals to be acquired so we could

photograph, collage, and/or draw them." Ned Drew initially sent the designers out in two directions, asking them to first photograph the urban environment and then focus on the arts. After several of these investigations, the design team had a large library of images. These images were to form the basis for all further investigations. "We would and could add to this library, but establishing a solid base was critical before we could move to the next step."

As part of the development of the logomark, Ned Drew created a unique visual exercise for each member of the design team. "I asked the design team to create a series of formal

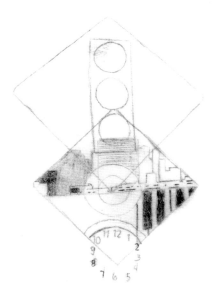

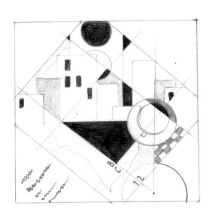

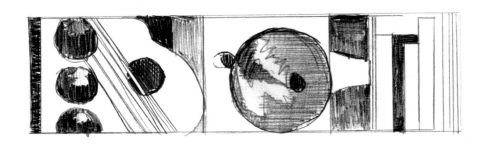

(syntactic) and conceptual (semantic) connections between the images gathered—to create several horizontal/linear narratives. The only constraint I placed on the team was that each connection between images needed to be formal, conceptual, or both. The goal was to generate as many narratives as possible, not allowing for comprehensive evaluations to slow or limit our productivity. Each member of the team worked separately and then in pairs, ensuring a sense of both collaboration and individual accomplishment."

This narrative exercise delivered beneficial results. The team identified a number of key images that would help communicate the goals and objectives of the conference. The team also realized it was easier to make formal connections and harder to find conceptual connections that were interesting and appropriate. Once the key images had been identified, Ned Drew asked

each team member to investigate ways in which to create tighter visual connections. "I wanted them to create, collage, and manipulate these images into a comprehensive message of change, of revitalization of the urban environment through design and the arts."

After several investigations, the design team decided that a horizontal logomark would be most desirable to work with the long title as well as to articulate a long story.

When deciphering this rather long horizontal logomark, the designers wanted to create a visual and temporal interpretation of the title—A Transformation. Reading from left to right, the logo starts with urban images of barriers, fences, walls, and bricks depicted in harsh, black-and-white photography. Color is slowly added (red) to help give the images more dimension and facilitate a visual change. Graffiti, street addresses, and the structure

of the bricks begin to blend with a simplified version of Charles Demuth's famous 1928 painting *I Saw The Figure 5 in Gold*. This simplification is important because it helps build a visual bridge, with several formal connections, between the urban typography of the street and the Frank Lloyd Wright-inspired stained-glass window. Circular shapes are repeated as well, helping to emphasize the formal connections within the mark, art, and found typography, and the images of typography created in our mind's eye.

The logomark was branded on all collateral material used for the conference. These materials included a stationery system, poster, postcards, tote bags, banners, brochure and program events, and badges.

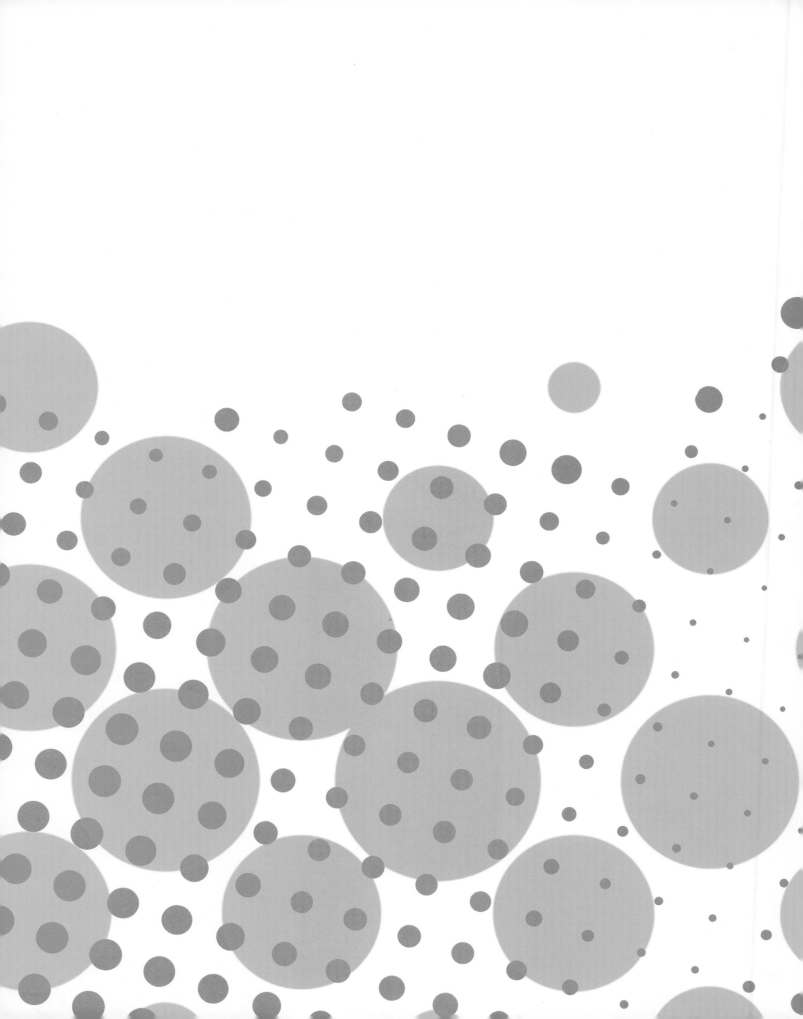

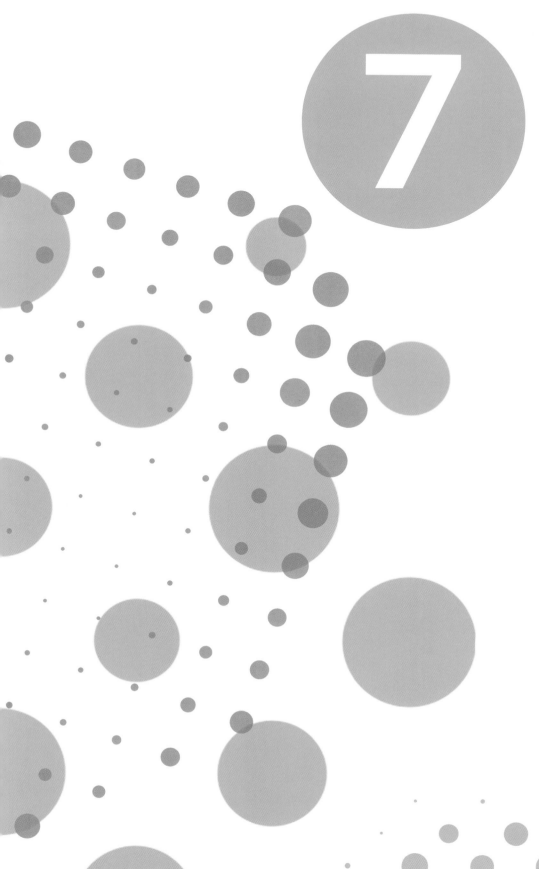

Color Management for Print

In the past, many prepress issues were tasked out to different departments and special-effect houses. Today designers are responsible for more and thus need to possess a broader and more in-depth understanding of color management for print. These issues can have a profound effect on the way we create design and communicate messages. A thorough understanding of prepress and printing issues will give designers tremendous flexibility in their use of color on a day-to-day basis.

Overprinting

Many clients have budgetary constraints in the development of their logo and corporate identity, and color is most often one of them. If used correctly, overprinting can be an excellent way of expanding the color palette by selecting the appropriate hues for the right color effect with no additional cost. Choosing the right colors for the right effect is an easy task so long as the designer understands the basic principles:

· Pure hues will create the largest variety of color range, both in additional hues and in the amounts of chroma. In print-based graphics, a pure hue is made from one ink.

· Pure hues overprinted with semipure hues will create a large variety of color range, both in additional hues and in the amounts of chroma. However, the chroma value will not be as great as mixing pure hues. In print-based graphics, semipure ink is considered to be a hue with no more than three inks (one of which is a small percentage of one of the hues) and with no portion of black or white.

· Semipure hues when overprinting will create a wide variety of colors in additional hues, but the chroma of the colors will be reduced. When overprinting two semipure hues, typically a wide variety of earth tones are created.

· Muddy/dirty hues overprinted with muddy/dirty colors create a spectrum of muddy colors. Muddy/dirty hues are colors made up of three or more inks, one of which is black.

· Pure hues overprinted with muddy/dirty colors create a broad color spectrum that ranges from light to dark, but such hues typically do not create a wide variety of stand-alone hues. These colors tend to have a muddy/dirty shade running throughout.

· Semipure hues overprinted with muddy/dirty colors create a color spectrum from light to dark, but they typically create a spectrum only of muddy/dirty hues.

· In print-based graphics, white can be an ink that is applied to an individual hue or it can be applied as a stand-alone color. When white ink is mixed or overprinted using any of the above scenarios, low chroma (pastel) colors will be created.

Pace International
Design Studio: Hornall Anderson
Design Works

Associative Color Response:
· life, motion: green
· lemony, fruity: green-yellow
· vigorous, inspiring: yellow
· drive, goal: yellow-orange
· healing, tasty: orange
· energizing, powerful: red

Color Scheme:
complementary (red and green) plus near analogous

This primary, secondary, and tertiary color palette creates a wonderful cascade of colors. The logo is made up from six distinct hues that work progressively from green to red, creating a positive movement within the mark (a circular motion that ends by moving to the right and up). The stationery system, package design, and racing apparel incorporate either part or all hues found within the mark; these are

well suited for the content and context. The green hues have an excellent appetite rating for fruit and vegetables; the yellow/slightly yellow-orange has a good appetite rating; and the orange and red have an excellent appetite rating. These six hues imply energy, good health, good taste, excitement, stimulation, fruity flavor, and nature—a superb subliminal message.

T When creating asymmetrical marks, logomarks, or logotypes, a positive directional flow within the mark is advised. This directional movement is likened to charts that show the current trend of a financially sound company. For example, a mark that has a downward movement may subliminally transmit the message that the company is financially unsound. Likewise, if a mark has a directional flow that moves to the left, the company may be perceived as lacking foresight. Any signifier, subliminal or obvious, that can be built anatomically into a mark, through shape, texture, tonality, or color, adds content where there was none.

Diagram 1 This is a composite
two-color matrix that demonstrates
a monochromatic study of both hue
one and two, and the additional
overprinted colors created by these
screen percentages.

Diagram 2 (a and b) This diagram
demonstrates how to create each
layer in Photoshop. Once the two
layers are created use the Multiply
feature to verify overprinted hues.

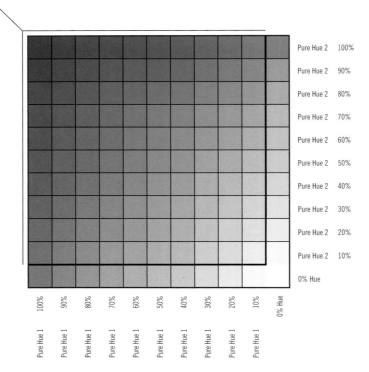

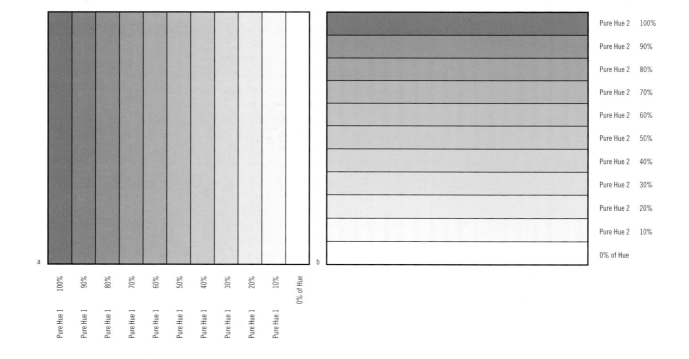

Diagram 3 Pure hues will create the greatest color range, both in additional hues, and in the amounts of chroma. In print-based graphics a pure hue is made from one ink.

Diagram 4 Pure hues overprinted with semipure hues will create a broad color range both in additional hues, and in the amounts of chroma. However, the chroma value will not be as great as that created mixing pure hues. In print-based graphics, a hue with no more than three inks (one of which is a small percentage of one of the hues), and with no portion of black or white, is considered a semipure ink.

Diagram 5 When overprinting, semipure hues will create a wide variety of colors in additional hues, but the chroma of the colors will be reduced. Overprinting two semipure hues generally creates a wide variety of earth tones.

Color Calibration

Designers are responsible for understanding how subtractive, additive, and 3-D color theories are used within the field and in practical applications. Contemporary design requires that designers work both on and off the computer. In doing so, we are moving back and forth from subtractive, additive, and 3-D color space. In most cases, this requires a set process to create a controlled outcome. The mechanics of each color theory are different, but they are interrelated to create a cohesive whole. Hue is likely to shift appearance from one color model to another. For example, when a hue moves from an additive environment to a subtractive one, the color is likely to shift. This can create frustration for a designer.

There are several ways to color calibrate a mark depending upon how the logo or simple symbol is constructed. Four-color process can match over 60% of the PANTONE MATCHING SYSTEM® Colors. The majority of logomarks and logo-types use spot colors from a standardized ink-matching system such as PANTONE® because most designers limit the color palette. In other words, the logo uses fewer than four plates when printing, keeping budgetary constraints down. (The more printing plates, or color, used the more expensive the job is to print—each plate is capable of printing one hue.)

If color accuracy is critical and budgetary constraints are pressing, choosing spot colors that fall inside the CMYK color spectrum is prudent. This decision allows the color palette to be reproduced on almost any four-color-process ink-jet printer, whether low- or high-end. With this said, choosing paper that has the highest brightness rating (98%), or printing on the actual paper stock specified for the job, is critical for accurate color appearance. In this way, color calibration between the hue chosen, computer monitor used, comprehensive printer, and commercial printer for press can be easily achieved with minimal cost.

To verify whether a spot color falls in or out of the CMYK color spectrum, use the Color Picker and Custom Colors under Set Foreground Color in the toolbox in Photoshop. In the Color Picker dialog box, on the right-hand side, click with the mouse on Custom. This will bring up the Custom Colors dialog box. For example, choose the PANTONE color by clicking on it with the mouse. The chosen hue will appear in the swatch window. If the hue chosen falls outside of the CMYK color spectrum an "!" appears to the right of the swatch. For example, for PANTONE 7488 U, the CMYK color spectrum is incapable of matching this hue, and trying to create this color on a comprehensive four-color-process printer is fruitless. A higher-end and more expensive printer or printout is required.

SitOnIt Seating
Design Studio: BBK Studio
Designer: Yang Kim

Associative Color Response:
· calm, relaxed: blue
· charm, energizing: red
· cheerfulness, vital: orange
· classic, life: green
· new growth, fruity: green-yellow

Color Scheme: monochromatic and near analogous

BBK Studio demonstrates a superb use of color within this two-color logomark. A simple and direct monochromatic color palette helps to create the illusion of a 3-D chair. The 3-D illusion is carried out not only through the mark's shape, but also by the placement of the warmest hue on the flat surface to indicate direct sunlight. The seat back and leg are shaded with 39% black to create the shadow areas of the mark. Through the use of color and shape the mark forms an

interesting optical illusion—it can be viewed from two perspectives. At first glance, the mark is viewed as if seen from the front. Staring at the color combination creates conal fatigue, causing the mark to be viewed from an upward-back perspective. This is a very interactive mark, and one that is outstanding for the subject matter.

As shown in the color studies and the collateral material, the choice of hues for the mark was derived from the company's products. This is one of the most successful ways of coming up with color combinations that harmonize the company's identity system to the products they produce and sell. Used literally or as a point of departure to create the corporate hues, color sampling is a very practical form of color

management and branding. For example, sample three hues in a photograph in Photoshop. These three hues can be used as the corporate colors, or as the basis for multiple color studies. Each color sample can be used as a point of departure to create a primary, secondary, tertiary, monochromatic, achromatic complementary, split complementary, analogous, neutral, or incongruous color palette with the various tints and shades.

The designer can see what the CMYK hue looks like in comparison with PANTONE 7488 U by clicking with the mouse back on the Picker setting. Click on the little square below the "!" and the CMYK facsimile (C62%, M0%, Y85%, and K0%) will appear above the PANTONE 7488 U hue—in this case, a dramatic shift in color appearance. By adjusting to a higher percentage of cyan and yellow, the chroma will intensify, but the hue will still not be an accurate match. However, a sea of colors can be reproduced through the CMYK color spectrum. This book and all the marks that appear within are built from this spectrum.

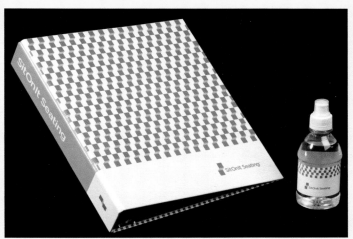

Diagram 6 Primary sets within their respective color theory. When a pure hue is applied to another paradigm, some hues become semipure or achromatic.

Traditional Color

Four-color Process

Additive Color

Subtractive Color

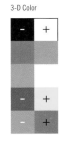

3-D Color

CMYK document calibration

In Photoshop or Illustrator different processes for color calibration are required. However, the starting point is the same: the PANTONE 4-color process guides. Color calibration requires that the hue on the screen be calibrated to something offscreen. In this case, PANTONE 4-color process guides give visual verification of hue appearance. Both Photoshop and Illustrator contain a multitude of color-management profiles from which to choose. To color calibrate using the standardized color-management profiles, follow these steps:

1. Purchase the PANTONE 4-color process guides. If a different ink-matching system will be used for visual verification, the revelant swatch book(s) will need to be purchased. If the swatch books are not affordable, see step 6.

2. In either Photoshop or Illustrator, create a 12-step color wheel using the following CMYK color builds (each one of these CMYK colors matches the builds of a PANTONE process hue found in their swatch books):

Red / C000 M100 Y100 K000
PANTONE DS 73-1-U

Red-Orange / C000 M070 Y100 K000
PANTONE DS 49-1-U

Orange / C000 M050 Y100 K000
PANTONE DS 32-1-U

Yellow-Orange / C000 M035 Y100 K000
PANTONE DS 18-1-U

Yellow / C000 M000 Y100 K000
PANTONE DS 1-1-U

Yellow-Green / C050 M000 Y100 K000
PANTONE DS 294-1-U

Green / C100 M000 Y100 K000
PANTONE DS 274-1-U

Blue-Green / C100 M000 Y050 K000
PANTONE DS 254-1-U

Blue / C100 M020 Y000 K000
PANTONE DS 225-1-U

Blue-Violet / C100 M050 Y000 K000
PANTONE DS 207-1-U

Violet / C100 M100 Y000 K000
PANTONE DS 184-1-U

Red-Violet / C050 M100 Y000 K000
PANTONE DS 164-1-U

3. Select Color Settings in either program. In Photoshop CS, Color Settings can be found under the Photoshop heading in the main menu. In Illustrator, select either Color Settings or Assign Profile. Either can be found under Edit in the main menu.

4. In the Color Settings or Assign Profile dialog box, choose either Working Spaces CMYK in Photoshop or Working CMYK in Illustrator. Both of these settings are scroll-down menus. Choose one of the following color-management profile settings:

· Colorsync CMYK-Generic CMYK profile
· Euroscale coated v2
· Euroscale uncoated v2
· Japan color 2001 coated
· Japan color 2001 uncoated
· Japan Web coated (Ad)
· U.S. sheetfed coated v2
· U.S. sheetfed uncoated v2
· U.S. Web uncoated v2
· 150-Line (PANTONE)
· Canon CLC500/EFI Printer
· Generic CMYK Profile
· Janpan Standard v2
· KODAK SWOP Proofer CMYK-Coated stock
· KODAK SWOP Proofer CMYK-Newsprint
· KODAK SWOP Proofer CMYK- Uncoated Stock
· Photoshop 4 Default CMYK
· Photoshop 5 Default CMYK
· SWOP Press
· Tekronik Phaser 111 Pxi

Cliffside Entertainment
Designer: Mark Sackett

Associative Color Response:
· mysterious, spatial: black
· luxuriant, stimulating: yellow-orange
· regal, classic: blue-violet
· refined, nostalgic: red-violet
· brilliant, energizing: red

Color Scheme: monochromatic plus continuous tone containing tints/shades (near-analogous, near-incongruous, and complementary)

Using both black and white and shaded red-violet, this one-color logomark shows superb sense of color through the orchestration of the stationery system. At first glance one might think this is a random color palette, but if you break this palette apart it is less random than you might think. Blue-violet, red-violet, and red make a near-analogous color palette (one step off). Blue-violet and red-violet are heavily shaded

to disguise this near-analogous color palette. Yellow-orange and blue-violet are complementary colors on a 12-step color wheel, and red and yellow-orange are a near-incongruous color scheme. Complex in its construction, and beautiful in its execution, this color palette is truly magnificent.

Note the color hierarchy found within the stationery system. The yellow-orange plays the most prominent role and is seen first in the hierarchical structure. The red continuous-tone image on the back of the letterhead is second in the hierarchical structure. The shaded red-violet and blue-violet play a tertiary role in this color palette. Little four-color images (a multitude of colors) are the least significant in the color palette, and are used as a visual magnet to draw the viewer in once he or she is close

enough. The hierarchical structure follows a clear path from warm to cool and from high-chroma to low-chroma.

5. Scroll down and select each profile setting in the swatch book. In a separate Word file, indicate the hues that are accurately represented within each profile setting. Some settings do better than others in each family of colors. No one color profile setting can accurately match every hue or even family of hues. Conduct a series of tests by printing out each profile setting to verify if color appearance is altered. Make sure that you write down the overprinting RGB and L*a*b* numbers from 10 to 100% in 10% steps.

6. Without a color swatch book, create two 12-step color wheel documents. The first is the same as above. However, the second document needs to be set up differently.

· In Photoshop and through the foreground color in the toolbox palette, select each individual PANTONE hue specified above. Write down both the RGB numbers and L*a*b* coordinates. For Illustrator, use RGB, and for Photoshop use L*a*b*.

· Create either or both the Photoshop or Illustrator document and save it. Both will create an accurate depiction of the hues specified with the exception of their chroma value; the colors will look right except for their brightness. Either document, Photoshop L*a*b* color document or Illustrator RGB document, can be used to match colors.

· Open both 12-step color wheel documents, either the L*a*b* or RGB document and the 12-step document, using the specified PANTONE hues above.

· Repeat step 5.

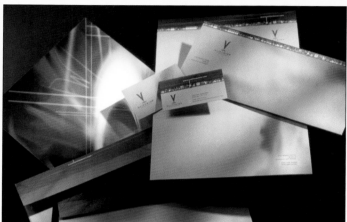

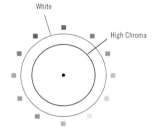

Diagram 7 Traditional 12-step color wheel.

White

High Chroma

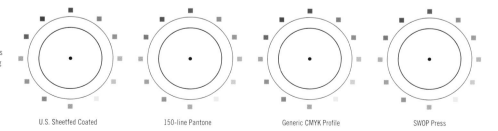

Diagram 8 These color wheels illustrate the various color renderings achieved through different color-management settings. Note how some of the colors display a very subtle shift depending on the management setting used.

U.S. Sheetfed Coated   150-line Pantone   Generic CMYK Profile   SWOP Press

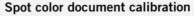

zango

Spot color document calibration

When creating marks in Photoshop or Illustrator utilizing spot colors that fall outside of the CMYK color gamma, the color-wheel verification document should be set up for the standard ink-matching system used. For example, if spot colors from PANTONE are specified, then the PANTONE Formula Guide Coated/Uncoated swatch book primaries/base colors should be used to create the color wheel. If another ink-matching system is utilized, the base inks/primaries that create the multitude of hues found within the system engender the color-wheel verification document. The base inks/primaries for the PANTONE Coated/Uncoated system are as follows:

For Coated Basic Colors

Primaries	RGB equivalent			L*a*b* equivalent		
Yellow C	R252	G225	B0	L89	A-4	B112
Yellow 012 C	R255	G214	B0	L87	A2	B114
Orange 021 C	R255	G92	B0	L63	A63	B95
Warm Red C	R252	G61	B50	L57	A71	B53
Red 032 C	R244	G42	B65	L54	A74	B41
Rubine Red C	R211	G0	95	L44	A78	B8
Rhodamine Red C	R229	G15	B159	L52	A79	B-19
Purple C	R183	G39	B191	L46	A68	B-48
Violet C	R79	G3	B169	L24	A54	B-74
Blue 072 C	R0	G25	B168	L19	A40	B79
Reflex Blue C	R0	G32	B159	L19	A32	B-74
Process Blue	CR0	G130	B209	L47	A-33	B-57
Green C	R0	G175	B138	L60	A-78	B2
Black C	R50	G44	B36	L18	A2	B6

For Uncoated Basic Colors

Primaries	RGB equivalent			L*a*b* equivalent		
Yellow U	R255	G229	B0	L91	A-2	B96
Yellow 012 U	R255	G220	B0	L89	A3	B94
Orange 021 U	R255	G113	B41	L67	A57	B66
Warm Red U	R255	G98	B93	L63	A61	B36
Red 032 U	R248	G81	B99	L60	A65	B28
Rubine Red U	R217	G61	B122	L52	A64	B3
Rhodamine Red U	R230	G75	B163	L57	A66	B-14
Purple U	R189	G84	B195	L53	54	B-39
Violet U	R113	G80	B178	L42	A31	B-48
Blue 072 U	R54	G65	B162	L31	A21	B-55
Reflex Blue U	R59	G77	B160	L35	14	-48
Process Blue U	R0	G125	B200	L48	A-17	B-51
Green U	R0	G163	B134	L57	A-61	B1
Black U	R87	G83	79	L36	A1	3

Zango
Studio: Hornall Anderson
Design Works

Associative Color Response:
· luxuriance, stimulating: yellow-orange
· whimsical, gregarious: orange
· intense, joy: red

Color Scheme: analogous and incongruous

The color selected for the Zango logo communicates a cheerful, stimulating response from the viewer. The formal attributes of the letterform "g" add to this response with the springlike manipulation of the looping descender. High in chroma value, the stimulating yellow-orange bounces off the page. When paired with a muddy red, an incongruous color palette is created. In this case, a color palette more unique than the typical incongruous color combinations is created. A typical incongruous color palette is

positioned, on a 12-step color wheel, so that the colors are five positions away from one another. For example, red-violet and yellow-orange are five steps away from each other on a 12-step color wheel, or three steps apart. In this case, the dirty-red and high-chroma yellow-orange are only two steps apart. Then, 50% black and 39% cyan are added to the red to shade and lessen the intensity, creating an earth-tone red.

In examining the 12-step color wheel, this type of color palette inherently creates a pleasing color combination that will not clash. In more typical incongruous color combinations, some clashing colors will occur.

Within the kit cover, envelope, and stationery system, broad expansive fields of color are utilized to engage

the audience in an aggressive and energetic way. The mark is placed on the page asymmetrically, adding to the liveliness and kinetic energy generated by the color palette. Screen tints of the dirty red and yellow-orange (on tabs) are utilized to stretch the color palette and create a better navigational system—truly a beautiful design and color palette.

Creating specialty inks

A specialty ink is a spot color not found in any standardized ink-matching system. Any four-color-process hue can be converted into a specialty ink by the offset or silkscreen printer. (Many high-end corporations have created custom inks to help brand their identity, including their mark.) For that matter, any six-color-process hue, or any hue found on any substrate, can be reproduced as a specialty ink if the hue is created through subtractive means. (There is a minimal cost involved in creating a custom color.) When creating a specialty ink, ask the printer for the L*a*b*, HSB, RGB, CMYK, and CMYKOG coordinates. With this information, accurate color swatches can be created in Photoshop or Illustrator.

When creating the electronic mechanical utilizing specialty inks, the mechanical is set up in an unorthodox manner. For example, if the mark is utilizing two specialty inks, when specifying the colors pick any two standardized spot colors—for example, PANTONE 300 and PANTONE 123. These colors should look very different from the intended specialty hues. In this way mistakes are unlikely because the custom colors look dramatically different from the two standard inks temporarily specified— a visual reference and reminder to properly indicate the two custom inks. After the electronic mechanical is set up for press, print out the separations on paper, for indication purposes only. Scratch out the names of the PANTONE colors and replace them with the names of each specialty ink. Along with the electronic mechanical, make sure that these printouts are supplied to the printer and are also indicated with an accompanying note. The electronic file should be created using four-color-process hues for the client's comprehensive. (This file does not go to press and is meant only as a comprehensive.) If the specialty ink falls outside of the four-color-process or six-color-process spectrum, higher-end comprehensive printing devices are necessary, and the hues may need to be indicated utilizing L*a*b* or RGB coordinates. Again, this is for comprehensive purposes only. The quality of proofs is set out below.

Full Moon Foods
Designer: Wayne Sakamoto
Art Director: Mark Sackett
Studio: Sackett Design

Associative Color Response:
· meditative, regal: blue-violet
· warm, radiant: yellow-orange/ yellow (gold)

Color Scheme: complementary/near complementary

This two-color logomark and collateral material are wonderfully presented through the use of color and symmetry. The logo is masterfully harmonious, and is a richly tranquil visual experience. The logo is classically laid out and the colors chosen for the mark and collateral materials harmonize with the ingredients and products they sell. This further adds to the classic tranquillity of the design work.

Again, color has context— these hues are derivatives of the experience one would find within a shop. With the exception of blue-violet, the color palette is directly pulled from the products produced or sold, thereby maximizing harmony. Blue-violet and yellow-orange/ yellow are complementary/near complementary and create the regal backdrops.

Diagram 9 When creating specialty inks the information listed below each color swatch is needed for the printer to create the ink.

Red

L*a*b*: 51.76 / 74 / 54
HSB: 356.407° / 100% / 100%
RGB: 237 / 28 / 36
CMYK: 0% / 100% / 100% / 000%
CMYKOG:
0% / 100% / 0% / 7% / 77% / 0%
XYZ: 30.88 / 17.23 / 5.26

Orange

L*a*b*: 70.98 / 33 / 71
HSB: 29.043° / 97% / 100%
RGB: 237 / 28 / 36
CMYK: 0% / 50% / 100% / 000%
CMYKOG:
0% / 0% / 35% / 20% / 85% / 0%
XYZ: 38.00 / 29.53 / 4.08

Red-Orange

L*a*b*: 56.86 / 62 / 59
HSB: 6.213° / 94.9% / 100%
RGB: 240 / 78 / 35
CMYK: 000 / 085 / 100 / 000
CMYKOG:
0% / 55% / 0% / 4% / 30% / 40%
XYZ: 37.04 / 22.85 / 4.34

Yellow-Orange

L*a*b*: 80 / 17 / 79
HSB: 41.655° / 98.2% / 100%
RGB: 253 / 184 / 19
CMYK: 0% / 30% / 100% / 000%
CMYKOG:
0% / 0% / 70% / 5% / 37% / 0%
XYZ: 55.74 / 50.56 / 7.61

Yellow

L*a*b*: 94.90 / -6 / 95
HSB: 59.997° / 100% / 100%
RGB: 255 / 242 / 0
CMYK: 0% / 0% / 100% / 0%
CMYKO6:
0% / 0% / 90% / 0% / 0% / 0%
XYZ: 72.34 / 78.47 / 6.01

Yellow-Green

L*a*b*: 68.62 / -44 / 49
HSB: 97.038° / 79.7% / 69.5%
RGB: 97 / 187 / 70
CMYK: 65% / 0% / 100% / 0%
CMYKO6:
0% / 100% / 0% / 7% / 77% / 0%
XYZ: 30.88 / 17.23 / 5.26

Green

L*a*b*: 57.25 / -74 / 30
HSB: 187° / 99.1% / 53.1%
RGB: 0 / 166 / 80
CMYK: 100% / 0% / 100% / 0%
CMYKO6:
0% / 0% / 35% / 10% / 0% / 100%
XYZ: 9.60 / 21.54 / 6.32

Blue-Green

L*a*b*: 59.21 / -63 / -9
HSB: 171.356° / 98.9% / 57.9%
RGB: 0 / 169 / 156
CMYK: 100% / 0% / 50% / 0%
CMYKO6:
65% / 0% / 0% / 2% / 0% / 75%
XYZ: 10.32 / 20.27 / 9.07

Diagram 10 (a–d) This diagram
is a demonstration of the temporary
composite (a), spot color 1 (b),
spot color 2 (c), and final composite
(d). Note that b and c are a film
positive facsimile.

allc⏻nnect

Quality of color proofs

The following color-proofing systems are ranked by quality from low to high. A crude breakdown of their expense is also given. Most often, quality relates to expense. The color-proofing systems outlined are commonly used within graphic design. With color-proofing systems, quality is related to how well a color system can match specified colors, including spot colors, and how well it demonstrates position and size.

Fiery

This is a low-end color proof that is digitally printed. This type of proofing system is not created using film and is meant to yield a crude estimation of color appearance. A Fiery is mostly used for client proofs and for working layouts. Since a Fiery is produced through digital means (an electromagnetic-heat-fusion process of colored pigments), the color proof can be unreliable for typographic composition, photographs, color, and line work. The cost is minimal. A Fiery can be acquired at most photocopy stores, service bureaus, and printers.

Ink-jet

This is a low-end color proof that is digitally printed. This type of color-proofing system is used to obtain a crude estimation of color appearance and for client proofs and working layouts. Some ink-jet color proofs have better color appearance than others, depending upon the manufacturer, the quality of equipment, and the number of ink color primaries used to create the full color spectrum. Ink-jet color-proofing systems are unreliable for typographic composition, photographs, color, and line work. They have a random mezzotint pattern to create continuous tone. The cost of an ink-jet color proof is minimal; it is generally the least expensive of all color proofing systems.

Iris

This is a low-end color proof that is digitally printed. This type of proofing system has a better color appearance than a Fiery or ink-jet, but does not show dot generation (it has continuous tone like a photograph). The dyes are highly light-sensitive and fade rapidly in sunlight. Iris proofs are meant for client proofs and for working layouts. Unlike any other color-proofing systems, an Iris is preferred for proofs with artwork that is meant to be displayed on a computer screen. The color spectrum is greater than with most other printed color-proofing systems, allowing for a higher color gamma. However, an Iris can be unreliable for typographic composition, photographs, and line work. An Iris is usually more expensive than a Fiery or an ink-jet, but the cost is still minimal.

---

allconnect
Studio: Hornall Anderson Design Works

Associative Color Response:
· quality, practical: gray
· fresh: green

Color Scheme: hue plus neutral

In this two-color logotype, color and shape are used very effectively. The color green indicates "on," which is reinforced by the "on" symbol substituted for the "o" in the word "connect"—a beautiful example of substitution, separation, and symbolism. In many logotypes, substitution to create metaphorical subjective or objective interpretation or representation is a highly effective way of creating a conceptual connection to the subject matter, accomplished through simile, irony, or parody. In this case, simile is achieved through the use of silhouette—the "o" in the "on" symbol for a computer has the same

basic (formal) similarity. The method of separation is used to partition the "on" in "connect" by marking out plainly the most meaningful part. Separation can be used both typographically and photographically to pull out the most meaningful part or parts found within content. Symbolism indicates "on" or "go" through the use of color. Also, in this case, an iconic representation of the green hue was used to reinforce the content and context—the green hue is used to light up the "on" computer button.

To clearly communicate each of these concepts, it would be wise to select the appropriate proofing device before press. Since composition is essential, a blue-line or composite proof would help to check registration. However,

composite proofs will not verify color. In this case, the Creo Veris Proof, Kodak Approval Proof, or Cromalin would accurately communicate the color.

T   To better understand what should be substituted within a logotype, a stream-of-consciousness mind map should be created. The key to any mind-mapping exercise is to not self-edit while processing the information. After the subject matter is fully exhausted (everything is written out on the mind map), editing takes place. If done correctly, a mind map should yield a multitude of images to substitute.

Blueline

This is a type of proof produced by film output. A blueline is a highly accurate proof for typographic composition, sharpness of photographs, registration, and line work. Since a blueline is produced by the job's actual film, the halftone screens are accurate as well. However, bluelines depict all information through tints of blue so they are unreliable for color proofing. This type of color proofing system is highly sensitive to light; after viewing, a blueline should be placed in a folder for protection. Because of this sensitivity, most printers substitute digital "bluelines," which are not made from the plates. Digital bluelines are essentially color prints and are meant only for checking imposition. Although the cost of a traditional blueline is minimal, they do cost more than Fiery, ink-jet, or Iris proofs.

Color Key

This type of proof is produced by film output. Color Key proofs are as accurate as bluelines for typographic composition, sharpness of photographs, registration, halftone screens, and line work. This type of color-proofing system yields fairly accurate color appearance for four-color-process jobs, but it does not depict spot colors well. Color Keys also have a hard time with accurate color appearance of purples. Each piece of film—cyan, magenta, yellow, and black—is overlaid on clear acetate, in register. A Color Key is more expensive than a blueline, but the cost is still minimal.

Diagram 11 In four-color-process printing the violet family is the most difficult to color prove. A violet hue can easily shift back-and-forth from warm to cool, and for that reason a Matchprint or higher should be pulled to color prove.

Matchprint

This type of proof is produced by film output. Matchprint proofs give an accurate color appearance of the four-color process and a limited range of spot colors, such as those from the PANTONE formula guides. This type of color-proofing system is an in-register composite and is accurate for typographic composition, sharpness of photographs, registration, halftone screens, four-color-process color, limited PANTONE colors, and line work. The Matchprint is moderate in cost and is a very useful color-proofing device.

Creo Veris Proof

This is a high-end color proof that is digitally printed. Although not created using film, the Creo Veris proofing system can be used for in-register composition. This system is accurate for typographic composition, sharpness of photographs, registration, four-color process, spot colors, and limited use of metallic inks. The Creo Veris proof is similar to the Kodak Approval proof (see below), but it uses an ink-jet delivery system, which makes it more economical.

Kodak Approval Color Proofing System

This type of proof is produced by film output. This system gives an accurate color appearance for the four-color process, spot colors, and metallic inks. The Kodak Approval system uses rolls of donor film to create spot colors and metallic inks. Donor film is a color-coated polyester film that, when exposed to lasers, transfers an image onto the stock, in register. It can also can overprint. Typically, these additional films are orange, green, and silver. In combination they do a decent job matching metallic colors, but the system falls short in matching the intensity of Day-Glo colors. Kodak Approval proofs use mylar laminated to the stock of choice. The process is similar to that used for a Matchprint or Cromalin. The Kodak Approval system is moderate in cost and is a very useful color-proofing device.

Creo Digital Matchprint

This is a high-end color proof that is digitally printed. The Creo Digital Matchprint delivers the same quality as a Kodak Approval proof and outperforms the Creo Veris proof. The Creo Digital Matchprint system is moderate in cost, falling somewhere between a Creo Veris and a Kodak Approval proof.

Morphosis Architecture Inc.
Designer: Sisi Xu
Art Director: John T. Drew

Associative Color Response:
· earthy, good: earth-tone red
· nature, versatility: green

Color Scheme: complementary tints and shades plus continuous tone

The logomark and logotype are designed to be easily recognized by the viewer, to be used in multiple sizes, both large- and small-scale, and to create a sense of interest through the use of gestalt. The use of color (four-color process plus spot) within the marks and collateral help to illustrate the dedication of the company to environmentally friendly businesses—their principal client base. To minimally assure this color rendition, it would be appropriate to select a proofing system that can nearly match the spot inks, such as a Creo Veris Proof. If photographic rendition is important, but spot

color is not a concern, then a Color Key or Matchprint would suffice. It is important to check all work before press with the most accurate proofing device available for the techniques used.

The use of an expanded sans-serif font in the logotype aids in the legibility of the mark—at smaller sizes and at greater distances, the logotype does not collapse in on itself, allowing for all anatomical parts to be clearly visible. Economy of line is utilized in the form/counterform relationships found within the logotype. In the logomark, the modular shapes help to establish a 3-D illusion on a 2-D plane. This 3-D illusion creates kinetic energy, activating the mark and creating greater viewer interest. The logomark's legibility is quite

high. The mark will not collapse in on itself because the counterform is basically the same shape and size, which gives the three major pieces of the mark the same visual angle. In other words, if the counterform of the mark were half as thin, the viewing distance would be dramatically limited, at about 50%.

In the initial conversations with the client, it was found that two basic objectives needed to be communicated: "environmentally friendly" and "strength." To ascertain the correct colors and color palettes to be utilized, the psychological and behavioral effects of color were researched to determine the most advantageous colors to meet these objectives. Shape was also considered to help emphasize the objectives. Although

the logomark is not organic in nature, the weight and modular units found within the mark help communicate the idea of strength. The selection of a bold sans-serif typeface with a green earth tone helps to communicate both objectives within the logotype.

Cromalin

This is produced by film output and is similar to a Matchprint. Cromalin, however, can reproduce accurate color appearance of PANTONE colors. This type of color-proofing system is an in-register composite and is accurate for typographic composition, sharpness of photographs, registration, halftone screens, four-color-process color, PANTONE color, and line work. A Cromalin is moderate in cost and is useful for color proofing.

Press Proof

A press proof is produced by film and printed on an actual press (usually a small press or an older model). A press proof is a highly accurate color proof. This type of color-proofing system uses the actual inks specified for the job and depicts accurate typographic composition, sharpness of photographs, registration, halftone screens, four-color-process color, PANTONE color, dot gain, and line work. A press proof is expensive, which means it is commonly used only for jobs with large print budgets.

Trapping

Trapping is when one plate (color) is choked or spread so that a small amount of ink is overlapping an adjacent hue. This is achieved through film or digital methods and implemented on the plate or directly on the digital printing press. Choking (down) or spreading (out) a color creates a slight overlap of adjacent hues so that a print job looks perfect.

Dark trapping involves reversing the order of cyan and magenta, a process that improves image quality, because the trap cannot be detected by the eye. These effects typically transpire in a visible color tint of the hue that was printed last. Depending upon the colors utilized, this effect can be slight or drastic. For example, printing black on top of yellow will create a neutral black, but printing yellow on top of black will create a warm black with a slight tint of yellow. Another example is printing 100% cyan over 100% magenta, which creates purple with a bluish tint. Reversing the order of printing creates purple with a reddish tint.

Most marks created today often utilize more than one hue. The trap needed to accommodate a mark can be drastically different depending upon the printing technique utilized, materials used, and/or substrate printed on. These factors are critical in determining the flexibility inherent in the color palette chosen to brand the mark, company, and/or product. For example, most silkscreen printers need between $\frac{1}{16}$ and $\frac{1}{4}$in (1.6 and 6.4mm) to hold the trap—in other words, for the job to appear in register without any unwanted paper color showing between printed hues. For transparent vinyl, the trap should be set at $\frac{1}{8}$ to $\frac{1}{4}$in (3.2 to 6.4mm). (Transparent vinyl is sometimes used to create backlit signs.) Typically a trap is much smaller for offset printing, and therefore not noticeable to the naked eye. With this said, a mark's color palette should be designed so that the hue scheme can accommodate different printing techniques.

PUNK MARKETING™

Punk Marketing
Designer: Nicolas Ammann

Associative Color Response:
· stimulating, dramatic: red
· strong, basic: black

Color Scheme: hue plus neutral

This logomark is used for a book cover design and all collateral material associated with its publication. To be in line with the title, *Marketing Renegades*, the graphics needed to be simple, bold, and rebellious. These simple, almost international symbols and pedestrian graphics needed a color combination that would amplify the meaning. Red and black were chosen for their stark, bold nature. The intensity of both colors harmonized well with the simple and bold graphics.

Diagram 12 (a–d) A wide variety of choke and spread settings. Note that as type is choked, the hairlines of letterforms become more compressed and therefore may lose some legibility 12b. in contrast, type that is spread may become thicker than was intended.

Diagram 12 (e–h) Optimal trapping conditions would be to balance the choke and spread of an image or mark so that each will be minimally affected. Generally, the background is choked down while the foreground, in this case type, is spread out. Type that is filled with 100% of a color that is built into the background will not need to be choked or spread. For example, yellow type on a red background (h) will not need to be altered because the red has yellow in it.

a

1-pixel Choke

c

2-pixel Spread

b

2-pixel Choke

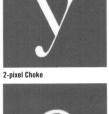

d

4-pixel Spread

e

f

g

h

Many color combinations will not be effective when using transparent vinyl, silkscreening, or any other type of printing that requires a trap setting of greater than .144pt. All printing inks are translucent and some are more translucent than others. The more pure the color is, the more translucent the color will be. In most cases, a color that is pure or semipure will create, when overprinted, an additional third hue that is noticeable. (See Overprinting, pages 148–151. Pigment additives can be mixed into ink to make it less transparent; however, these additives tend to alter the hue appearance.) When a large trap value is assigned, this third additional color may overpower the mark, creating legibility and readability problems, or making the product simply look hideous. Most logo designs are meant to be used for decades, and therefore require forethought to accommodate any printing technique or medium. Such planning will allow the client tremendous flexibility in the print delivery of the mark.

Diagram 13 (a and b) A change in printing order on a two-color job comprised of magenta and cyan. In a, the magenta is printed over the cyan; and in b, the cyan is laid over the magenta. In most cases, the image will subtly shift to the hue of the last printed color.

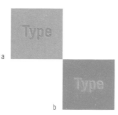

Diagram 14 Depending upon the order in which ink is laid down, even with very dark hues, color tinting will take place. In this case, the hue black will have a warm or cool appearance depending upon the printing order.

100% Black

100% Black + 100% Cyan

Diagram 15 As seen in this diagram, a, visible trap is created when using different printing processes. Note, the offset trap is unnoticeable due to the amount of choke and spread needed to hold the type in register.

.625 trap

.125 trap

.25 trap

offset trap

In 1994, we conducted a color study utilizing PANTONE-identified silkscreen inks (listed below). Although this study was originally designed to test color legibility, due to the printing method used some type and color combinations were illegible because the trapping area overpowered the legibility of the original two-color combination. Nonetheless, this color study indicates the basic color principles that govern the visibility of a trap. To ensure accuracy within our findings, we created an additional color study (in 2005) utilizing the hues found on the 12-step color wheel. (This also included 50% tints of the 12 hues and 20% tints of cyan, magenta, yellow, black, yellow/magenta, yellow/cyan, and cyan/magenta.) The general principles that govern the visibility of trapping are listed below. These guidelines are particularly important when using printing methods that require a trap setting from $\frac{1}{16}$ to $\frac{1}{4}$in (1.6 to 6.4mm) or greater.

· The cruder the method of printing, the more likely the trap will be visible.

· The higher the CVD, the less visible the trap.

· The higher the paper brightness rating, the more likely the trap will be visible (This applies to any substrate.)

· The lower the paper brightness rating, the less likely the trap will be visible.

· Printing on coated paper will make the trap more apparent than printing on uncoated.

· Using a color combination that is analogous will yield a virtually invisible trap.

· Using a color combination with the colors two steps away from each other (on a 12-step color wheel) will yield an invisible to visible trap;

however, in almost every case the trap is not overpowering. (See Diagram 16.)

· Depending upon the hue scheme, a color combination in which the colors are three steps away from each other will create a visible to overpowering trap. The exceptions to this rule follow. These color combinations tend to yield a virtually invisible trap:

· The violet family in combination with the blue-green family;

· The green family in combination with the yellow-orange family;

· The yellow family in combination with the red-orange family; and

· The yellow-orange family in combination with the red family.

· Any color combination that is created with a cool color and a warm color of the same visual intensity will create a trap that is overpowering.

· So long as black is printed with the proper ink density, the trap, with any other hue, is virtually invisible.

The best way to determine whether a potential color combination will yield a visible to overpowering trap is through the use of Photoshop or Illustrator. Select the spot colors in question. Photoshop and Illustrator allow use of any standard ink-matching system, as well as the choice of one spot color from one system and a second spot color from another. Put each spot hue on its own layer. After each hue is on a layer, select the Multiply feature. In Photoshop, Multiply is under the Layers dialog box, and in Illustrator it is under the Transparency dialog box. To determine visually how apparent the trap will be when printed, use Multiply. Creating

---

Croatian National Tourist Board
Designer: Boris Ljubicic

Associative Color Response:
· brilliant, energizing: red
· luxuriance, cheer: yellow-orange
· life, spring: green
· spaciousness, calm: blue
· meditative, tender: blue-violet

Color Scheme: additive primaries plus near analogous hues

Croatia has a warm Mediterranean climate, with crystal-clear water and more than 1,000 islands, and is a popular holiday destination The Croatian National Tourist Board wanted a mark that would symbolize these attributes. The client also wanted the logotype in many different languages, including its own language (Hrvatska). In writing "Croatia" in different languages, the fourth letterform "A" is consistently stable and therefore yielded an opportunity to embed metaphoric interplay.

The idea of substitution was used to represent the Adriatic Sea. The alternating squares symbolically represent Croatia (red, white, and blue are the country's colors), the sun rising (red) over the Adriatic Sea, and a sailboat (blue). The texture of the mark was created with a watercolor brush to help signify the connection between Croatia and the Adriatic Sea.

The color palette chosen was quite intense: high-chroma colors of red, yellow-orange, green, blue, and blue-violet. Designer Boris Ljubicic wanted to convey a Mediterranean paradise where people from around the world could come to relax and enjoy themselves.

 Color has context. If put into a sexy context, for example, color will have sexual overtones. Color works primarily on a symbolic level. Color needs shape in order to communicate a planned message. With that said, color can amplify the intended message like no other weapon in a designer's arsenal.

Diagram 16 A visual demonstration of hues that are two steps away from each other on a 12-step color wheel. Note how these hues yield a trap that is not overpowering.

a document that utilizes overprinting colors is a prudent choice if the trap is visually apparent. Understanding how the hues will overprint can yield innovative color designs/mechanicals that will print more effectively, considering the visual anomaly has been built into the design/mechanical. For example, instead of using the printing technique of trapping, one can simply knockout through the overprinted color to reveal the color that is laid down first on press.

The electronic mechanical will often have to be constructed differently when changing the designated ink order for printing. For example, when printing small yellow type on a black background, the mechanical will be set up in the traditional manner. However, to create yellow type on a warm black background with a yellow tint, the mechanical will need to be constructed differently. Either the black ink will need to incorporate a large percentage of yellow (50–100%, customizing the color), or the black plate will need a type reversal, and the yellow plate will need a solid overprint covering the black plate. The first option involves a change to the normal printing procedure and will create a more visible color tint. The scenarios above can be designated for a change in printing order. Both mechanicals are set up properly to accommodate this experience because the trap is eliminated or virtually undetected.

The printing order of inks is often defined because the print job tends to trap better with the darkest color printed last. However, in two-color jobs it is sometimes a toss-up as to which ink should be the hue that traps because the print job will not be adversely affected. In these cases, changing the printing order may create a printing effect whereby the colors being utilized create a more pleasant hue experience.

Diagram 17 These hues are an exception to the rule that states colors three steps away from each other will yield a visually overpowering trap.

Diagram 18 Color combinations with cool and warm hues of the same visual intensity will create a trap that is overpowering.

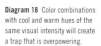

Diagram 19 When black is printed with the proper ink density the trap will be near invisible.

Diagram 20 Choking and spreading is unnecessary when building a composite in this manner.

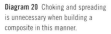

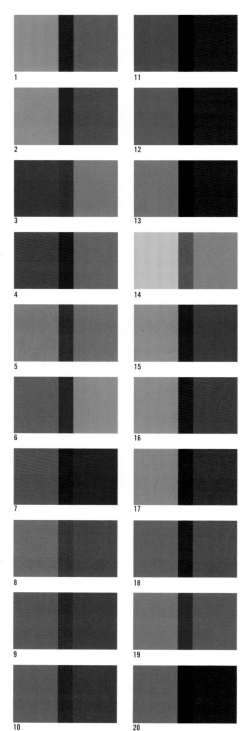

Extremely Bad Color Combination for Trapping

	PANTONE Hue 1	Y-T	CMYK	PANTONE Hue 2	Y-T	CMYK	CVD	Base Inks
1	PANTONE Red 032 C	21.79	0/91/87/0	PANTONE 348 C (K3%)	16.02	100/0/79/27	DT 5.77	1/3
2	PANTONE 416 C (K9.4%)	28.02	0/0/15/51	PANTONE 5473 C (K13.6%)	13.91	90/42/55/22	DT 14.11	3/3
3	PANTONE 288 C (K5.9%)	7.11	100/65/0/30.5	PANTONE 3272 C	29.95	100/0/47/0	LT 22.84	3/2
4	PANTONE 357 C (K20%)	12.52	79/0/87/56	PANTONE 431 C (K15.6%)	18.12	65/51/43/15	LT 5.6	3/3
5	PANTONE Process Blue C	17.40	100/0/0/0	PANTONE 485 C	18.22	8/98/100/1	LT .82	1/2
6	PANTONE 3005 C	22.11	100/30.5/0/6	PANTONE Red 032 C	21.79	0/96/74/0	LT .68	2/1
Average		**8.30**						

Poor Color Combination for Trapping

	PANTONE Hue 1	Y-T	CMYK	PANTONE Hue 2	Y-T	CMYK	CVD	Base Inks
7	PANTONE 335 C (K5.9%)	17.69	100/26/71/12	PA NTONE 295 C (K11.2%)	7.76	100/83/33/32	DT 9.93	2/3
8	PANTONE 334 C (K1.5%)	23.14	100/9/70/1	PANTONE 293 C	13.47	100/75/4/1	DT 9.67	2/2
9	PANTONE 327 C	20.34	100/20/62/6	PANTONE 286 C (K5.9%)	10.44	100/83/6/1	DT 9.9	2/3
10	PANTONE 186 C	17.54	11/100/85/2	PANTONE Blue 072 C (K1.5%)	2.92	100/92/2/2	DT 14.62	3/1
11	PANTONE 287 C (K3.0%)	8.27	100/83/16/5	PANTONE Black C (K100%)	3.77	63/63/70/66	DT 4.5	3/1
12	PANTONE 221 C (K5.9%)	11.73	32/100/50/20	PANTONE Black C (K100%)	3.77	63/63/70/66	DT 7.96	2/1
13	PANTONE 513 C	14.47	48/99/1/0	PANTONE Black C (K100%)	3.77	63/63/70/66	DT 10.70	2/1
14	PANTONE Orange 021 C	30.67	0/78/100/0	PANTONE 2727 C	30.67	76/53/0/0	0	1/2
15	PANTONE 485 C	18.22	8/98/100/1	PANTONE 2617 C (K5.9%)	7.53	84/100/20/15	DT10.69	2/3
16	PANTONE 485 C	18.22	8/98/100/1	PANTONE 343 C (K20%)	9.92	94/41/79/39	DT 8.3	2/3
17	PANTONE 192 C	19.63	2/100/66/0	PANTONE 2756 C (K11.2%)	2.31	100/98/24/17	DT 17.32	2/3
18	PANTONE 253 C	17.41	45/92/0/0	PANTONE 287 C (K3%)	8.27	100/83/16/5	DT 9.14	2/3
19	PANTONE 334 C (K1.5%)	23.14	100/9/70/1	PANTONE 293 C	13.47	100/75/4/1	DT 9.67	2/3
20	PANTONE 300 C	16.20	100/56/2/0	PANTONE Black C (K100%)	3.77	63/63/70/66	DT 12.43	2/1
Average		**9.63**						

Y-T = Y tristimulus value
CVD = Color value differential

PANTONE Colors displayed here are process simulations and do not match the solid PANTONE-identified standards. Consult current PANTONE Color Publications for accurate color.

Diagram 21 This is a visual facsimile (simplified) of the color study conducted in 1994. Note, the information has been organized by quality of trap.

Good Color Combination for Trapping

	PANTONE Hue 1	Y-T	CMYK	PANTONE Hue 2	Y-T	CMYK	CVD	Base Inks
21	PANTONE 4525 U (K1.7%)	50.00	22/27/51/0	PANTONE Blue 072 U	2.92	100/92/2/2	LT 47.08	4/4
22	PANTONE 294 C (K5.8%)	9.45	100/82/25/16	PANTONE Black C (K100%)	3.77	63/63/70/66	DT 5.68	3/1
23	PANTONE 142 C	53.70	5/27/84/0	PANTONE 2756 C (K11.2%)	2.01	100/98/24/17	DT 51.69	3/3
Average	**17.87**							

Excellent Color Combination for Trapping

	PANTONE Hue 1	Y-T	CMYK	PANTONE Hue 2	Y-T	CMYK	CVD	Base Inks
24	PANTONE 266 C	11.42	73/85/0/0	PANTONE Black C (K100%)	3.77	63/63/70/66	DT 7.65	2/1
25	PANTONE 430 C (K87.5%)	30.16	51/38/33/2	PANTONE 280 C (K5.9%)	7.10	100/88/21/17	DT 23.06	3/2
26	PANTONE 107 C	73.50	4/5/92/0	PANTONE 356 C (K5.9%)	17.10	100/28/100/19	DT 56.4	3/3
27	PANTONE 216 C (K20%)	11.30	38/96/54/33	PANTONE Black C (K100%)	3.77	63/63/70/66	DT 7.53	3/1
28	PANTONE 320 C	26.31	100/13/35/1	PANTONE 2738 C	2.65	100/96/3/3	DT 23.66	2/2
29	PANTONE Yellow 012 C	70.95	3/12/100/0	PANTONE Reflex Blue C	17.40	100/90/8/5	DT 53.55	1/1
30	PANTONE Red 032 C	21.79	0/96/74/0	PANTONE Black C (K100%)	3.77	63/63/70/66	DT 18.02	1/1
31	PANTONE 199 C	19.03	8/100/73/1	PANTONE 287 C (K3%)	8.27	100/83/16/5	DT 10.76	2/3
32	PANTONE 165 C	31.74	0/77/100/0	PANTONE Black C (K100%)	3.77	63/63/70/66	DT 27.97	2/1
33	PANTONE 347 C	20.73	100/10/100/2	PANTONE Black C (K100%)	3.77	63/63/70/66	DT 16.96	2/1
34	PANTONE 153 C (K5.9%)	21.62	20/67/100/7	PANTONE Black C (K100%)	3.77	63/63/70/66	DT 17.85	3/1
35	PANTONE Yellow 012 C	70.95	3/12/100/0	PANTONE 199 C	19.03	8/100/73/1	DT 51.92	1/2
36	PANTONE 226 C	18.88	13/100/17/0	PANTONE Black C (K100%)	3.77	63/63/70/66	DT 15.11	2/1
37	PANTONE 420 C (K1.1%)	62.75	19/15/16/0	PANTONE 477 C (K5.9%)	8.95	40/77/78/52	DT 53.8	3/4
38	PANTONE 485 C	18.22	8/98/100/1	PANTONE Black C (K100%)	3.77	63/63/70/66	DT 14.45	2/1
39	PANTONE 321 C (K1.6%)	20.84	100/27/41/4	PANTONE Black C (K100%)	3.77	63/63/70/66	DT 17.07	3/1
40	PANTONE 206 C	19.16	10/100/60/1	PANTONE Black C (K100%)	3.77	63/63/70/66	DT 15.39	2/1
41	PANTONE 109 C	65.73	2/16/100/0	PANTONE 2593 C	9.86	62/97/0/0	DT 55.87	2/2
42	PANTONE 185 C	21.02	2/100/82/0	PANTONE 286 C	10.44	100/83/6/1	DT 10.58	2/2
43	PANTONE Warm Red C	26.78	0/90/85/0	PANTONE Reflex Blue C	17.40	100/90/8/5	DT 9.38	1/1
Average	**25.35**							

Y-T = Y tristimulus value
CVD = Color value differential

PANTONE Colors displayed here are process simulations and do not match the solid PANTONE-identified standards. Consult current PANTONE Color Publications for accurate color.

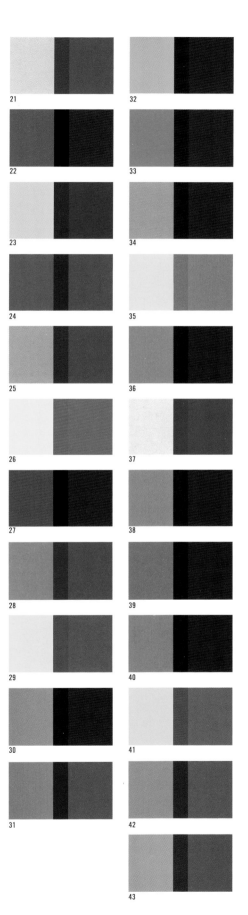

Color Correcting

In today's marketplace, logomarks, logotypes, and simple symbols can take on an array of continuous tones and gradients. With gradients, the control from light to dark, including split-fountains, is easily achieved. The blend of the gradient is of concern when preparing a job for press. To safeguard against any unwanted banding, make sure the blend steps are maxed out at 256 steps. Banding is especially evident when using the 3-D feature in Illustrator. Assuring that the blend steps are maxed out will help to alleviate any problems.

To color correct continuous-tone marks for press, whether four-color, grayscale, monotones, duotones, fake duotones, or tritones, the tonal values from light to dark must be set up correctly. For press there are six major concerns when dealing with color correcting:

· The quality of the original image.

· The quality of the scanned image (if applicable).

· Ensuring proper contrast from light to dark within the photograph. Without this the image will look flat. Typically, a lack of contrast is caused by the overall image being too light, too dark, or too even (a lack of lights and darks). When continuous-tone marks appear flat, the color primaries throughout the overall image tend to be relatively proportionate.

· Avoiding the light areas dropping out.

· Preventing the dark areas filling in (dot gain), both of which cause a loss in detail and an improper tonal range from light to dark.

· Compensating for the printing process, including the paper being utilized.

With duotones, fake duotones, and tritones there is usually a seventh factor: maintaining tonal range when overprinting takes place. This can be achieved through the curve settings in the duotone dialog box.

The quality of the original image is the primary criterion that determines whether it will print well—what you start with is what you get. An image that is flat, out of focus, or constructed incorrectly will never yield a mark of high quality. The image in question must be in focus, be properly color balanced, and have the proper tonal range from light to dark, including grayscale marks that have gradients or continuous tones.

Having the right tool to color correct photographs is paramount, and there is no better application program for this than Photoshop. Once the image is scanned and saved in the right color mode (RGB, CMYK, or grayscale), determine the proper contrast. There are several ways to achieve this through Photoshop. The first step is to try using the Auto-contrast and Auto-level features under Image in the main menu. This is accurate 50% of the time. For press, however, dropout and dot gain must be taken into account. If these automated features do not properly color correct the image for press, open the Information dialog box under Windows in the main menu of Photoshop. The Information dialog box reads the color builds found within the image at any given point, including grayscale. For press, the highlights and lowlights or shadow areas within the image should be properly determined, and their builds should be retrieved. The general rule for highlighted areas is no less than 2–3% of color information for each channel,

---

itself otherwise. Although this is a commonly used phenomenon, the choice of the type and shape of the boxes creates intrigue in the design that is truly not mindless. When used in different color combinations, the design subtly changes but the gray circles are dramatically altered.

Diagram 22 The higher the quality of printing, the more likely banding will be noticeable. To safeguard against it, set the banding features to their highest settings.

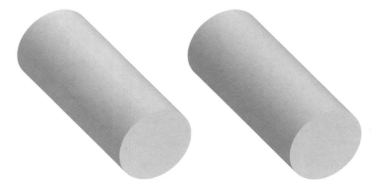

totaling no less than 8%. (Color information is the amount of image data found on each channel—use the Information dialog box under Window in the main menu to retrieve this information.) Correcting the image to fall within this percent range will alleviate most of the dropout on press. On press, 2–3% typically translates to 0% color information. In other words, if the image is not properly adjusted for press, a 5% highlight area will appear on press anywhere from 0–2%, resulting in the dropout of a considerable tonal area.

For press, the general rule for dark areas is no more than 98% color information. By properly adjusting the contrast to achieve this percentage, dot gain will be counteracted on most coated and less absorbent papers. If using a highly absorbent paper, a maximum of 94–97% is recommended: on absorbent papers, these areas will completely fill, creating a solid, 100% color-field. If these general rules for press cannot be met through the automated features mentioned above, the Brightness and Contrast feature under Image in the main menu of Photoshop will need to be adjusted. Using this feature, along with the Information dialog box, will ensure that the image has the proper contrast and color for press.

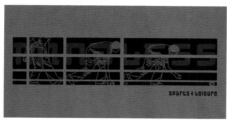

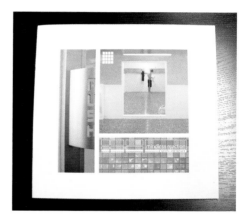

Diagram 23 This diagram demonstrates an image that has been properly color corrected, and one that has not. Using the steps outlined above will safeguard against improper color balance.

TravelP⊙⦿⦿T

Duotones, fake duotones, and tritones

For duotones, fake duotones, and tritones, a few more steps must be taken in order to properly color balance and color correct continuous tone within the mark. Prior to the mid-1980s, duotones were created with two separate pieces of film, one for each color. Each piece was taken from the original image and exposed to light differently to create the base art. In Photoshop, this is no longer the case. A duotone is created from one piece of film or one channel and split into two pieces of film for press. Therefore, color correcting a duotone, fake duotone, or tritone in Photoshop creates visual verification problems. In other words, when using two spot colors, including black and one other, what appears on the computer screen is not what will appear on press.

Verifying Spot Colors

You can use several methods to create a document, all of which allow for visual verification when color correcting a duotone, fake duotone, tritone, or setup for press. The first is to refer to a color guide. PANTONE offers a duotone guide for both coated and uncoated colors—the PANTONE Studio Edition Duotone Guide. Each duotone color combination offers four distinct, curved setups for black and another spot color, and the guide offers a comprehensive compilation of 11,328 setups, with an explanation of how to work with duotone curves in Photoshop. This information is excellent when working with duotones created with black and another color. However, many duotones are created with two spot colors, such as PANTONE 102 and PANTONE 2415.

Both PANTONE hues— PANTONE 102 and PANTONE 2415—fall within the CMYK color gamma. The method listed below works only with spot colors that fall within the CMYK color gamma. (A method for dealing with spot hues that cannot be matched by the four-color process is described later in this chapter; see page 174.) There are two ways to verify whether a spot color falls within the CMYK gamma. The easiest is to check in one of the color guides that display which spot colors meet this requirement. The PANTONE colorbridge™ guide is such a book.

A less expensive way to visually verify whether a spot color falls within the CMYK gamma is to use the QuarkXPress Colors features under Edit. Photoshop CS or higher will also allow you to verify if a spot color falls within the gamma or not. Using the Colors features in QuarkXPress, you can simulate any solid-to-process guide for any color-matching system, including PANTONE, Toyo, TRUMATCH, and Focoltone.

1. Open the Default Colors dialog box by clicking on Colors under Edit in the main menu.

2. Within this dialog box click on New, choose the spot color to be verified, and click OK to return to the Default Colors dialog box.

3. Choose Edit within this to return to the Edit Colors dialog box.

4. Choose the CMYK mode under Model. The spot color along with the four-color-process equivalent will appear in the New and Original color swatch section within this dialog box, allowing for visual verification. If the two colors match, the spot color can be created within the CMYK gamma. If the

---

Travel Port
Design Studio: Hornall Anderson
Design Works

Associative Color Response:
· brilliant, energizing: high-chroma red
· life, motion: high-chroma green, orange
· lively, pleasant: high-chroma blue
· quality: neutral gray
· powerful, basic: black

Color Scheme: primary and secondary plus neutral

This primary and secondary color palette, with neutral gray, yields a very vibrant and interesting logotype. On a 12-step color wheel, the red and green and the orange and blue are complementary to one another, which creates a vivid, high-chroma color palette. Color is intensely utilized within all collateral materials. Grays and blacks are juxtaposed to the bright primary and secondary colors, which produces

a popping sensation to the eye when viewed. The red, orange, and green are classified on the warmer side of the color palette, and when juxtaposed with gray and black these colors move forward. This stationery system and collateral material demonstrate a highly effective use of color.

The collateral material utilizes fake duotones that give the work more of a graphic nature. The black and gray graphic armatures unite the stationery system with the collateral material. Through the use of high-chroma fake duotones and graphic armature, continuity and diversity are achieved to create a brilliant and energizing work.

Diagram 24 A demonstration of how a duotone is created.

 +  =

two colors do not match, then the method listed below will not give an accurate color appearance. In this case, the method for dealing with spot colors that fall outside of the CMYK gamma should be used.

Duotones Within CMYK Color Gamma

When creating a duotone for a logo with two spot colors other than black, follow the method below in order to create an accurate color appearance for final output. The PANTONE Studio Edition duotone curves can also be used with any image in Photoshop by loading the setting.

1. Create a duotone using the spot colors, for example PANTONE 102 and PANTONE 2415, in Photoshop.

2. Open up the original grayscale image and create a monotone using PANTONE 102.

3. Create a PANTONE 2415 monotone using the same grayscale image as for Step 2.

4. Copy each monotone into a new CMYK document in Photoshop. There should be two layers each having a monotone image and a background layer (white).

5. Click on layer 2 to make it active, then apply Multiply under Normal in the Layers dialog box to see how the two spot colors are overprinting in Photoshop in process color. At this point, a difference in color between the Photoshop duotone and the hybrid facsimile just created should be discernible. Check any PANTONE coated or uncoated spot colors against the PANTONE colorbridge guide to see if they match (the newer swatch

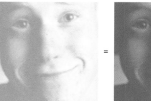

Diagram 25 A demonstration of how a fake duotone is created. A fake duotone is when one of the two channels is utilized at 100% of color to create a flat color-field. The darker of the two colors used (in this case, cyan) creates the continuous-tone image. A fake duotone is an excellent way to make an image more graphically inclined.

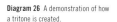

Diagram 26 A demonstration of how a tritone is created.

clearw ̇re

books indicate whether a PANTONE color can be matched through CMYK means), or use QuarkXPress/Photoshop to determine color gamma. The duotone facsimile created in the CMYK mode is more color-accurate than the Photoshop duotone and can be used as a guide to color correct the Photoshop duotone image for press. (The CMYK duotone facsimile is created from two grayscale images, unlike its Photoshop counterpart, thus creating a color facsimile closer to what will appear on press.)

6. If the spot colors match the CMYK color gamma, color correct each layer in the Curves dialog box (only), under Image in the main menu of Photoshop, and save both curve settings. Keep the image in CMYK mode and do not add any channels.

7. Click back on the Photoshop duotone and reopen the duotone setting under Image in the main menu.

8. Click on each duotone Curve setting individually. The duotone curve matrix will appear.

9. Load the Curve settings saved for each color. The duotone will be properly color corrected.

Creating Duotones Outside CMYK Color Gamma

When creating a duotone for a logo outside the CMYK color gamma, the computer monitor will need to be set up differently so that it holds, or emits, only the colors that are specified for creating the duotone. A large percentage of spot colors are outside the CMYK color gamma. The primaries that make up these colors have a higher chroma rating than those that can

be created through process colors. Therefore, the computer monitor's color space needs to be changed to accurately reflect the chroma value of each individual duotone. Two of the CMYK color primaries within Photoshop must be altered each time a duotone is created, as outlined below.

1. Open a grayscale image or convert a CMYK image to grayscale.

2. Convert the grayscale image to the duotone setting under Image in the main menu of Photoshop.

3. Select the Duotone mode in the Duotone Options dialog box.

4. Select the two spot colors to create the duotone. Do not adjust the curve settings.

5. After selecting the two spot hues, click back on each color and then click on Picker and write down the individual L*a*b* values for each spot color.

6. Click on the overprinting setting at the bottom of the Duotone Options dialog box.

7. Click on the color swatch found in the Overprinting dialog box and then click on the Picker and write down the L*a*b* values of the overprinted hue.

8. Open the duotone.

9. Under File in the main menu, scroll down to Color Settings and select the CMYK setup.

10. Under the CMYK Setup dialog box, select Custom within the Ink Colors slot. (For each Photoshop version, the process of acquiring the Ink Colors dialog box is somewhat different. However, it is usually found under Preferences or Color Setup under File in the main menu of Photoshop.)

clearwire
Design Studio: Hornall Anderson
Design Works

Associative Color Response:
· dignified, pleasant: high-chroma blue
· new growth, sharp: high-chroma yellow-green

Color Scheme: near incongruous

The clearwire logotype, featuring a near incongruous color palette, is an energetic and refreshing change from the past. This new growth industry is clearly depicted within the logotype and reinforced through the color scheme. The art of subtraction and economy of line are clearly evident within the "i" of "wire." The stem of the lowercase "i" is subtracted from the logotype to reinforce the concept of "clear" and to help create a focal point (the dot of the lowercase "i") within the logotype to symbolize disseminating information. The unique solution for this logotype is worth studying.

 In preparing to create a logotype, a clear understanding and analysis of the anatomical structure of each letterform, both uppercase and lowercase, is essential. For most logotypes, substitution or gestalt plays an important role in creating intrigue. Understanding what anatomical parts can be deleted, elongated, cropped, connected, or substituted will help create better solutions. Printing out the alphabet, including punctuation and numbers of the typeface or typefaces intended to be used, will help the designer understand what can be subtracted, elongated, cropped, connected, or substituted. Within both the uppercase and lowercase letterforms used to create the logotype, circle the anatomy that is similar to the other letterforms comprising the mark. Next, indicate the areas of each letterform that are not necessary in order for the letter to be clearly readable—in some cases

this is not much. Finally, indicate the punctuation marks (make sure to include all the punctuation marks and symbols associated with the font) that could be substituted anatomically.

11. Click on the L*a*b* coordinates at the bottom left of the dialog box. The L*a*b* setting must be activated in order for this process to work.

12. In the Ink Colors dialog box, enter the L*a*b* values for the first duotone color in the three cyan slots.

13. Enter the second duotone color in the three magenta slots.

14. Enter the overprinting duotone color in the three cyan/magenta slots.

15. Click on OK in the Ink Colors dialog box.

16. Save the ink color settings by clicking on Save in the CMYK Setup dialog box and then click OK.

17. Open the original grayscale image, copy it to the clipboard, and then close the grayscale image.

18. Open a new CMYK document in Photoshop. Copying the original image on the clipboard will prompt Photoshop to automatically create a document the size of the original grayscale image.

19. Paste the original grayscale image into the cyan and magenta channels.

20. Select and delete any information found on the yellow and black channels within the document. Do not delete the channels. Instead, erase the information on them.

21. Click on the composite CMYK channel to view the facsimile duotone. If the spot colors chosen are outside of the CMYK color gamma, the Photoshop duotone, already open on the computer screen, and the facsimile duotone color composite should

Diagram 27 (a and b) As is clearly demonstrated, this method will yield a better understanding of how the image will print on press.

Standard Duotone

 +  =

a

Duotone within CMYK Color Gamma

 +  =

b

TERRAVIDA COFFEE

look dramatically different. The facsimile duotone is an accurate color representation for press.

22. Within the facsimile duotone, click on the cyan channel and open the Curves dialog box.

23. Adjust the curve setting and save it to the appropriate folder.

24. Once the cyan channel curve setting has been saved click OK.

25. Repeat steps 22–24 for the magenta channel.

26. Within the Photoshop duotone, load the curve settings for each spot color and save the document. The duotone is now mechanically ready for press.

PANTONE has done an outstanding job in compiling 11,328 different duotone curve settings for use with its colors. These settings can also be used by loading the desired settings in steps 23 and 26. Furthermore, they can be used with other ink-matching systems, such as TRUMATCH, Focoltone, and Toyo. To use these curves effectively, select colors that are similar in value and chroma. The hue does not need to match. By altering the two hues that create the duotone, the secondary and tertiary colors and their corresponding tints will be different.

Creating Fake Duotones

For fake duotones only one curve setting needs to be saved, not the solid color. Under Duotones in Photoshop, set the curve setting for the spot-color solid. In the duotones matrix set the "0" setting at 100 and the "100" setting at 100. This will ensure that the second color

of the duotone prints 100% of color. When creating fake duotones, the darker of the two colors should always be the continuous-tone image. The process for color verification and mechanical preparation is as described above.

TerraVida Coffee
Design Studio: Hornall Anderson
Design Works

Associative Color Response:
· gentle, enticing, good spirit: mid-range orange

Color Scheme: monochromatic with shading

This two-color logotype, featuring a monochromatic color palette with shading, is a wonderful point of departure for the basis of all color use throughout the collateral material, packaging, interior design, and advertising. Simple yet effective, the textural aspects found within the mark are transferred into all aspects of design. There is a sea of color, from high-chroma pure and semipure hues, to low-chroma earth tones, that creates an environment that is lively and energetic—a place where people can meet and make new friends.

Note, the bags, paper cups, napkins, and coffee sleeves are printed in two colors. This is a cost-cutting measure that is virtually undetectable when placed within the environment. These products are the most expendable and the most consumed and have the highest number of reprints. Also, the coffee bags are printed in four colors. At first glance, this would seem to be an expensive proposition, but the designers of Hornall Anderson have been clever. They also printed the crack-and-peel coffee labels in four colors—giving each type of coffee a completely different color palette. In doing so, all offset coffee bags are printed with the same graphics, allowing the client to print one giant press run. The larger the press run, the cheaper each bag.

The crack-and-peel coffee labels are relatively small and can be ganged up on press, on the same paper, to be printed at one time—thereby cutting costs. The large graphics (the posters) in the windows of the coffee shop can be printed, one off, on an oversize plotter printer to further reduce costs.

When designing and pricing a job like this, it is always prudent to inventory all items that need to be designed, including the environmental graphics and interior space, in terms of most consumed to least consumed. This should yield insight into which items need to be analyzed for cost-cutting measures.

 When used appropriately, texture acts as a magnet to draw the viewer or consumer into the design. Adding texture, in most cases, creates curiosity within viewers—they want to figure out what they are looking at. Texture, therefore, can be placed strategically within the design to navigate the viewer.

Diagram 28 A demonstration of how a fake duotone is created. Note, the lighter of the two hues has been used as the background color.

 +  =

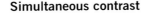

Simultaneous contrast

Simultaneous contrast is a strobing effect resulting from the use of unequal portions of colors. Simultaneous contrast is most pronounced with an imbalance of large and small areas of color. A pronounced simultaneous contrast of color opposites can cause an unpleasant strobing effect.

To some degree, simultaneous contrast occurs with all colors, but it is most pronounced when pure complementary colors are juxtaposed. This phenomenon is caused by retinal cone fatigue. The photoreceptor cells found within the cones near the fovea of the eye become overworked because each cell can process only one color at a time. The resultant switching back and forth overstimulates the photoreceptor cell (for example, the cell responsible for green- and red+) thereby creating the visual phenomenon of simultaneous contrast.

This is a natural phenomenon, regardless of the medium used. However, we can use it to our advantage. As stated above, pronounced simultaneous contrast is predictable when using pure complementary colors. As the complementary colors become less pure, the effect lessens, which means we can control the degree of the strobe. Learning to utilize this effect can lead to innovative color work. For example, we can create a logomark that utilizes this back-and-forth motion—a perfect scenario for any company associated with movement-oriented activities such as sports. The possibilities are tremendous. However, simultaneous contrast must be considered every time logotypes or logomarks with detail are created within a color-field. To read when pronounced simultaneous contrast occurs can

be difficult or impossible. Getting the mark off the computer and testing it in different light sources is the best safeguard for predicting outcome. Remember, the computer screen lies for print. Pull accurate color proofs and verify the color combination in different light sources. For example, view the mark outside in the daylight, under fluorescent lighting, under incandescent lighting, and on a computer screen.

In print-based graphics it is much harder to predict the outcome of simultaneous contrast. Due to the design process and the production phases associated with print-based graphics, it is far more complicated to visualize the final outcome without viewing the finished work. The quality of the printer will affect the result. If the area in question is made up of four-color-process builds, it is easy to predict outcome. If the mark is made up of spot colors that fall outside of the CMYK spectrum, a more accurate color proof should be pulled (such as an Iris, Cromalin, Matchprint, Fuji Final Proof, Agfa Print, Waterproof, or Kodak Approval color-proofing system). An Iris proof matches most spot colors for the lowest price.

Today, application programs for graphic design have a color component built in. This feature allows designers to retrieve the color builds of any hue used within the document. As we know, pronounced simultaneous contrast occurs when pure complementary colors are juxtaposed. By reading builds of the hues in question, we can predict the amount of simultaneous contrast that will occur and then make the appropriate adjustments.

Forum 21
Designer: Boris Ljubicic

Associative Color Response:
· brilliant, intense, energizing: high-chroma red
· life, motion, growth: high-chroma green
· powerful, basic: black

Color Scheme: complementary plus neutral

This logo for the nonprofit Forum 21, for The Association of Electronic Media Journalists, represents a new beginning to make information public in Croatia. Prior to the breakup of the Soviet Union and Yugoslavia, information airwaves were controlled by the state. The client wanted to replace the traditional gray tone mark with a logomark that would represent positive change within the information airways of broadcast television. Designer Boris Ljubicic decided to use transparent colors

to symbolically represent the free exchange of ideas and information in the 21st century. The primary colors of additive color theory plus black were used to represent broadcast television. Using the fonts Times and Futura, sunglasses are made from a typographic manipulation of "2001." Times is used for the arms of the sunglasses and the font Futura is used to create the frame. In this case, the arms of the sunglasses metaphorically represent the clout and outreach of the association.

 When used as an actual pair of sunglasses, these colored gels of red, green, and blue create interesting optical illusions—they can create a 3-D effect and make objects disappear. To make an object "disappear," make sure the object is the same color as one of the gels used in the sunglasses. Typically, cyan, magenta, or yellow work best.

Diagram 29 A visual depiction of the color primaries for 3-D color theory. A photoreceptor cell responsible for detecting color within the human eye can only process one color at a time. The photoreceptor cells found within the rods can process black, white, and shades of gray at the same time. This is why simultaneous contrast does not occur to any great degree in black and white form.

3-D Color

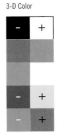

Several strategies can be employed to adjust the amount of simultaneous contrast occurring within a piece:

· Add a portion of one color to another by setting up a color matrix with 10% increments. This matrix will help to determine the point at which simultaneous contrast does not affect the readability or legibility of the color combination in question.

· Tint the color combination in question with a third color; this also requires the building of a color matrix. (Use the mark or part of the mark in place of type to determine legibility.)

· Shade the color combination with black to reduce the amount of simultaneous contrast, again building a logo and color matrix.

· Combine all of the above.

· Switch the color combination to a harmonious color palette—one that has an equal portion of one color running through both color-fields (for example, a yellow mark on a green background). This combination is harmonious because the amount of yellow is stable in both the foreground and the background.

In print-based graphics, the first, second, and fifth techniques will still create a two-color combination, and no additional ink is necessary to complete the job. In other words, if the paper is white, the job is still considered two-color and not three-color. When tinting or shading one or both of the colors, select a color swatch that has additional white, black, or another color. In addition, a color percentage of one of the two hues found within the combination would still be considered a two-color job.

Diagram 30 These techniques can be utilized to decrease or increase simultaneous contrast.

Tinted Red Type/Green Background
100%;90%;80%;60%;40%;20%;10%;0%

Shaded Red Type/Green Background
5%;10%;15%;20%;25%;30%;35%;40%

Tinted Green Type/Red Background
100%;90%;80%;60%;40%;20%;10%;0%

Green Type/Shaded Red Background
5%;10%;15%;20%;25%;30%;35%;40%

Red Type/Green Background with Percentages of Magenta
10%;20%;30%;40%;50%;60%;70%;80%

Tinted Green Background/Red Type
100%;90%;80%;70%;60%;50%;40%

Green Type/Red Background with Percentages of Cyan
10%;20%;30%;40%;50%;60%;70%;80%

Tinted Red Background/Green Type
100%;90%;80%;70%;60%;50%;40%

Red Type/Shaded Green Background
5%;10%;15%;20%;25%;30%;35%;40%

Clashing colors

Often corporations and companies want their mark updated—not necessarily a completely new design. In these cases, color is a dramatic tool that can evoke more accurately the current and future intent of the client or company. However, the client may feel uncomfortable abandoning a color scheme that has been used for decades to help identify the company. In these cases, most often there is a transitional period in which the color palette changes slowly over time. In these types of scenarios clashing colors are most often generated. (The scenario is also applicable to any collateral material the corporation or company may be producing within this transitional timeframe.) Another scenario may be that the client wants a color combination that clashes and simply cannot be talked out of it.

Incongruous color palettes most often generate clashing colors—a color palette that makes a discordant combination. These color palettes are often very energetic and unique, but if one is not careful a clashing color combination can arise. On a 12-step color wheel, an incongruous color palette is two to three steps to the right or left of its complementary. These types of color palettes have little color harmony and therefore have a greater potential to clash with one another.

If a color combination is clashing, the easiest way to rectify the situation without changing the two hues in question is to overprint the hues, creating a bridge that harmonizes with both colors, unifies the palette, and creates no additional cost. For example, take the worst clashing two-color combination you can think of and place the two hues, on their own layers, in Illustrator or Photoshop. After this is completed, select the Multiply feature and watch a hideous color combination turn into a palette everyone can live with. The bridge can be weighted to one side or the other by altering the opacity settings. This will help to create emphasis if needed. With clashing colors, creating a bridge is the key to creating something that is aesthetically beautiful.

SMS Foods
Designer: Boris Ljubicic

Associative Color Response:
· life, growth: green
· quality: neutral gray
· brilliant, intense, energizing: high-chroma red
· healing, growing, happy: high-chroma orange

Color Scheme: near analogous with complementary accent and neutral

The slogan for SMS Foods is "A Message from Nature." It represents a true gastronomic delight that uses only natural products (fish, olives, vegetables, and fruits) from the coastal region of Dalmatia. The color use in this SMS logotype is both symbolic and iconic. The two gray hues and two green hues iconically reference fish scales and olive leaves, whereas the red and orange symbolically represent edible foods. Both the high-chroma red and orange have an excellent appetite

rating, with an associative taste of very sweet. Gray and green have no known associative tastes, but green is a good color choice for products other than meat. With red and orange hues, the higher the chroma, the sweeter the association. A color palette that reflects the company's slogan and promotes good health was the main objective. Through the use of color, the company wanted to reflect the natural ingredients they use.

The application of the mark and its colors changes with the materials and ingredients that make up the product. This creates a highly kinetic package design that suits each product. This is a macro/micro relationship that is well thought out and beautifully executed.

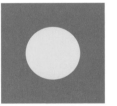

Diagram 31 Harmony is created through the use of yellow: yellow is utilized to build both hues.

Olive leaf

Fish tail

Diagram 32 By overprinting to create a harmonizing bridge, virtually any clashing color combination can be harmonized to create a pleasing arrangement.

When creating any food package design, make sure to understand both the associative taste and appetite rating for each hue used. (This information can be found in *Color Management: A Comprehensive Guide for Graphic Designers.*)

HORNALL ANDERSON DESIGN WORKS

Type and Color

When setting up a document for press, the little formal details are the elements that cause printers to have fits. They are most often also the elements overlooked by designers, and they tend to create readability, legibility, and registration problems. Some simple rules, when applied properly, can facilitate the process of setting up the mechanical for press.

Reversals

A reversal is when type or a mark is dropped out to the color of the substrate from a solid color. A reversal can also be dropped out of color tints and shades. For example, a type and/or mark reversal with a color tint or a solid orange on white paper will more than likely not be legible because either the color tint or the solid orange does not have a 40% differential from the white paper. In this scenario, the mark would be presented rather small on the page. The same phenomenon would happen if the mark were viewed at a great distance. Each paper stock has a brightness rating or color value number that can be obtained from a paper representative or a paper swatch. The color in which the mark

reverses is also an issue with reversals. There is not usually a problem if the color is pure, semipure, or a spot color, but there can be a problem mechanically when dealing with four- and six-color processes. If the color is made from all process primaries, it will be very difficult to hold the job in register on press, especially with small type, small marks, or detail found within a logo. The solid color background in which a reversal takes place should not be made from more than two of the process primaries. This may seem limited, but with the addition of color tinting there are thousands of colors from which to choose. If color shading (the addition of black) is desired, one of two strategies can be employed to create a proper electronic mechanical. If two colors already make up the solid background, then color shading should be applied uniformly to both the background and the reversal. In this case, the type or mark is no longer a reversal, but rather, a knockout, and registration is still held to only two plates. Because black is uniformly applied, registration is not a problem. The second strategy is to eliminate one of the two colors and replace the second color with the shading addition of black.

Hornall Anderson Design Works
Studio: Hornall Anderson Design Works

Associative Color Response:
· quality: neutral gray
· healing, happy: high-chroma orange
· dignified, pleasant: blue

Color Scheme: complementary with neutrals

This identity system communicates at first glance a professional company with an upbeat attitude through color and form. When looking closer, we can see that this is reiterated in the nuance and humor implied throughout the system. Each element of the design is open to change and customization through check boxes and blank areas to fill in.

Diagram 33 As shown here the color value differential (CVD) is critical in determining if the object can be seen or not at a distance. With that said, some hue combinations that have a 2% CVD or less are perfectly legible. The 20% CVD rule is good for normal eyesight. However, a 40% differential will alleviate any doubt and is more inclusive.

Diagram 34 (a–c) This diagram illustrates the difficulty of holding numerous plates in register when on press. In other words, the more plates that are used to create the specified knockout or reversal, the more chances the job will not be in register.

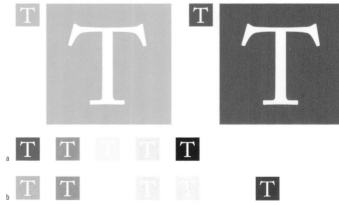

Knockouts

Knockouts are when type or a mark is cut out of a background color and replaced with another hue. For example, a white mark on a red background is a reversal (white being the color of the paper), whereas a purple mark on a red background is a knockout. This example is one that is easy to hold on press. As each color, purple and red, is built from 100% magenta, there are no registration issues with this plate, only with the cyan and yellow plates. The two-color rule also should be applied in these scenarios, using pure and semipure colors. If the background color is so dirty or muddy that a large percentage of black is being utilized (giving a color value of 0–20%), construct a decent trap to negate the two-color rule, allowing all process primaries to be utilized. (See Trapping on page 164 to better understand the factors involved in creating a decent trap.)

When using small text type, graphic elements, or a mark with tints and shades, the most typical scenario is black on a background that has 80–100% color value. Black has a color value rating, in printed form, of 10–15%, creating a CVD of no less than 65%. This scenario is always a safe bet because it eliminates registration problems, and legibility issues are not a concern. The rule to apply when using a solid color, other than black, on a tinted background is to keep the CVD to a minimum of 40%, but this may not eliminate registration problems. To guard against both legibility and registration problems, the background color should always have a color value rating of 80% or higher, and the type or mark color should always have a rating of 20% or less. This creates a 60% CVD, which

eliminates registration problems. The type or mark color will be so dark that it can be overprinted with little adverse effect.

Building colors that are made up from more than two primaries can lead to registration problems on press. You should always take this into consideration when deciding where to place which colors on the electronic mechanical. Most often, simple adjustments to the electronic mechanical will make the press person's job much easier and eliminate costly mistakes.

Diagram 35 A visual depiction of a knockout. The two-plate rule is still intact. Only the cyan and yellow plates are held in register.

Diagram 36 A visual depiction of a knockout using a spread and choke to create the composite. The two-plate rule is still intact.

Diagram 37 A visual depiction of a knockout. There is no choke or spread in this scenario, nor is there any critical registration.

Color coding for navigational purposes and brand identification is an excellent way to utilize color. Coding speeds up recognition—the very definition of readability. Readability is different from legibility. Readability is a clear depiction of all anatomical parts when viewed at the prescribed or designed distance.

When choosing a typeface to display information on electronic devices such as television sets and computer screens, three simple typographic studies can be conducted. One: create a typographic study, in Photoshop, by applying different motion blurs to determine how well the font will hold up while in

motion. Two: zoom out in Photoshop to determine the minimum size needed for the font to be legible. Three: set the computer monitor at different resolution settings: 256, thousands, and millions of colors. Millions equates to a high-definition television. Make sure the font works in all three settings.

Type in Motion

In print form a mark is physically static; however, through the use of color it can take on a life of its own. Color, the most profound tool a designer has, can stimulate the mind and activate the soul through psychological and/or learned behavioral effects. The mind is stimulated by color and light and this needs to be carefully thought out to optimize the human perception and interaction of color while in motion. If not, viewers can be over- or understimulated, with unwanted consequences.

A printed logomark can be affected by motion, either by the observer being in motion while viewing the static mark or by the mark being placed on something that is in motion. In either case, color plays an important role in viewer comprehension of the mark and in legibility and readability. Color has a direct effect on the distance at which we can see objects, and the Y tristimulus value is the key to understanding that distance. (The Y tristimulus value represents the relative lightness to the mind's eye, and is the mathematical equivalent of that representation.)

For example, PANTONE Purple C has a Y value of 16.64; PANTONE Violet C has a Y value of 4.09; and PANTONE 395 C has a Y value of 74.70. The lower the number, the further the distance at which we can see the color. In other words, if all things are equal, PANTONE Violet C can be seen at a distance that is 70.61% greater than PANTONE 395 C. If the size of a mark is limited, CVD will play a role in determining if the viewing public comprehends the logomark, logotype, or simple symbol. The Americans with Disability Act of 1990 prescribes a minimum CVD of 40% and in this case it is a good rule to follow.

With this said, the reaction time that is needed to pick the mark up and comprehend it is critical in determining whether or not an object is registered in the mind's eye. Without the proper amount of reaction time, the mark will simply go unnoticed. Overkill is better. If the logo is going to be placed on an object that is moving—say, a tail fin or the fuselage of an airplane—the reaction time needed and the viewing distance of the mark are critical in successfully identifying the company. In other words, the further away the mark can be seen the more reaction time is granted. Choosing a hue that has a low Y tristimulus value or a color combination that has a CVD of 40% or greater can dramatically increase the viewing distance, thus increasing the reaction time.

Using these basic principles described above along with the rules outlined in Chapter 8 will allow a designer to properly prepare a mark for motion.

HRT Croatian Radiotelevision
Designer: Boris Ljubicic

Associative Color Response:
· brilliant, energizing: high-chroma red
· dignified, lively: high-chroma blue
· clean, cool, innocent: white

Color Scheme: two hues of a primary triad plus neutral

HRT is the national radio and television broadcasting system in Croatia. In 1990, when Croatia split from Yugoslavia, a new broadcast system celebrating national identity and independence was created. The two red squares reference the historic Croatian coat of arms, which consists of 25 red and white squares. The squares of the mark change according to the three organizational branches: blue represents television; black represents radio; and white represents joint services. In 3-D form, the two squares become cubes,

and when applied to motion graphics the squares become animated. This is clearly the most important part of the logotype. The logotype is a visual code for national unity, solidarity, and independence, and it is branded on each of the three television channels owned by HRT (Channels 1, 2, and 3).

The mark needed to be clearly legible due to the different media and substrates in which it would appear (broadcast television, Web, environmental graphics, and print). However, the mark's appearance on screen had priority in the evolution of the mark. (The font used to create the logotype is Futura Bold.) The branding of the mark is quite comprehensive, from cars, trucks, cameras, audio mikes, and stage design, to hats, T-shirts, a Web site, CDs, DVDs, and many other

print-based graphics. This is a complicated branding system that is held together primarily through the use of color.

Diagram 38 (a–c) If all things are equal, the lower the Y tristimulus value, the greater the distance at which the hue can be seen. This statement assumes that the hue would be illuminated.

a   b   c

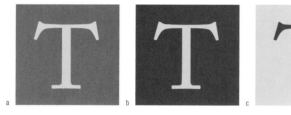

Diagram 39 (a–c) It is a myth to believe it makes a difference which color is the foreground and which hue is the background for viewing at a distance. For example, in b and c, the viewing distance is the same. In other words, the "T" can be seen at the same distance.

a   b   c

a   m   a   n   g   a   h

Line Weight

The weight of a line, or stroke width, is one of the most overlooked elements in the construction of a mark. Several factors must always be considered when using a line(s) within a logomark, logotype, or simple symbol. These factors involve the thickness, or stroke width, of the line(s) and the color indicated for it.

A line weight that is perfectly appropriate for a 3-inch (76mm) logo may fall apart when the mark is reduced down to a half-inch. Likewise, that same line weight indicated for a 3-inch (76mm) mark may be grossly overstroked when the logo is used on a large scale (on a building, storefront, billboard, or any oversized venue). Do not let the computer automatically scale the line weight to size—visually verify the work in numerous sizes. A minimum stroke of .33pt is a prudent rule to follow for offset printing. However, the stroke width is too small for silkscreen, for which the minimum stroke width is from 1 to 1.5 points. The greater the stroke width, the easier it is to hold on press no matter what type of printing procedure.

The color of a line is not particularly important, but how it is constructed is critical. (This is not an issue with one-color logomarks, logotypes, and simple symbols.) When constructing a mark of two or more colors, how many plates are used to construct the color is important. The fewer plates/screens utilized to construct the color, the easier it is to hold on press. For example, many colors can be simplified to eliminate additional plates/screens so that a minimal amount is utilized in the printing process. A muddy/dirty yellow-green (C021; M012; Y100; K023) is a good example.

This hue can be simplified two ways. The first is to reconstruct the hue using three plates (C015; Y100; K035), for which there would be no additional cost. The second is to create a specialty ink of the muddy/dirty yellow-green, thereby reducing the plates/screens utilized to create this hue to one. Printers charge extra to create a custom ink, and when run with four-color process the job would be considered a five-color job (four-color process with an additional spot color).

In most cases, a logomark, logotype, or simple symbol can be placed on almost any surface utilizing almost any type of printing available. This chart demonstrates the appropriate software and setup for preparing files for press.

Diagram 40 These are the different point sizes needed for line work for different types of printing.

————————————————————	.33 pt
————————————————————	.5 pt
————————————————————	1 pt
————————————————————	1.25 pt
————————————————————	1.5 pt

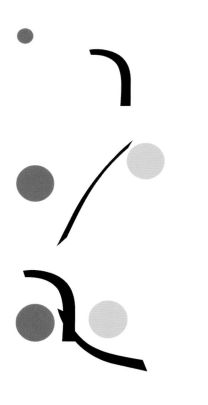

a m a n g a h

Diagram 41 (a and b) As shown in
a, there is an inappropriate color
use. In b, color adjustments have
been made in order to make the
line work easier to hold in register
on press.

(a)

	.33 pt
	.5 pt
	1 pt
	1.25 pt
	1.5 pt

(b)

	.33 pt
	.5 pt
	1 pt
	1.25 pt
	1.5 pt

Type of Job	Software
Package Design (paper)	Illustrator/Freehand
Poster	Illustrator/Freehand
Logomark	Illustrator/Freehand
Logotype	Illustrator/Freehand
Masthead	Illustrator/Freehand
Billboard	Illustrator/Freehand
Broadside	Illustrator/Freehand
Stationery System	Illustrator/Freehand/QuarkXPress
Magazine Ads	Illustrator/Freehand/QuarkXPress
CD Package (out of paper)	Illustrator/Freehand
CD Inserts (letter, accordion fold, or saddle stitch)	Illustrator/Freehand
DVD Package (out of paper)	Illustrator/Freehand
DVD Inserts	Illustrator/Freehand
Brochures	
Palm Brochure	Illustrator/Freehand
Gatefold Brochure	QuarkXPress/InDesign/PageMaker
Accordion-fold Brochure	QuarkXPress/InDesign/PageMaker
Extended Brochure	QuarkXPress/InDesign/PageMaker
Self-mailing Brochure	QuarkXPress/InDesign/PageMaker
Roll-fold Brochure	QuarkXPress/InDesign/PageMaker
Single-fold Brochure	QuarkXPress/InDesign/PageMaker
French-fold Brochure	QuarkXPress/InDesign/PageMaker
Double Parallel Brochure	QuarkXPress/InDesign/PageMaker
Publication Design (Magazines, Books, Manuals, and Catalogs)	
Interior Design	QuarkXPress/InDesign/PageMaker
Saddle-stitch	QuarkXPress/InDesign/PageMaker
Perfect Bind (cover, separate document)	QuarkXPress/InDesign/Illustrator
Smyth Sewn (cover, separate document)	QuarkXPress/InDesign/Illustrator
Spiral Bind	QuarkXPress/InDesign/PageMaker
Hardback (cover, separate document)	QuarkXPress/InDesign/Illustrator
Newsletter	QuarkXPress/InDesign/PageMaker
Dust Jacket	QuarkXPress/InDesign/Illustrator/Freehand
Cover/Spine/Back Cover for Book	QuarkXPress/InDesign/Illustrator/Freehand
T-Shirts	Illustrator/Freehand
Aluminum Cans	Illustrator/Freehand
Bottles	Illustrator/Freehand
Bottle Labels	Illustrator/Freehand
Banners	Illustrator/Freehand
Signage (on paper)	Illustrator/Freehand
Plastic Packaging	Illustrator/Freehand
Baseball Caps (using ink)	Illustrator/Freehand
Pocket Folder/Kit Cover/Media Kit	Illustrator/Freehand
Photographs*	Photoshop
Rasterizing Images**	QuarkXPress/Illustrator
Finishing	
Foil Stamp	QuarkXPress/InDesign/Illustrator/Freehand/PageMaker
Spot Varnish	QuarkXPress/InDesign/Illustrator/Freehand/PageMaker
Flood Varnish	QuarkXPress/InDesign/Illustrator/Freehand/PageMaker
Emboss	QuarkXPress/InDesign/Illustrator/Freehand/PageMaker
Deboss	QuarkXPress/InDesign/Illustrator/Freehand/PageMaker
Blind Emboss	QuarkXPress/InDesign/Illustrator/Freehand/PageMaker
Fonts	QuarkXPress/InDesign/Freehand/PageMaker
Outlined Fonts	Illustrator
Photoshop Fonts***	Photoshop

Sheetfed Lithography/Flexography
Webfed Lithography/Sheetfed Lithography/Silkscreen Printing
Webfed Lithography/Sheetfed Lithography/Flexography/Silkscreen Printing
Webfed Lithography/Sheetfed Lithography/Flexography/Silkscreen Printing
Webfed Lithography
Sheetfed Lithography/Silkscreen Printing
Sheetfed Lithography/Silkscreen Printing
Sheetfed Lithography
Webfed Lithography/Sheetfed Lithography
Webfed Lithography/Sheetfed Lithography/Flexography
Webfed Lithography/Sheetfed Lithography/Silkscreen Printing
Sheetfed Lithography/Silkscreen Printing
Webfed Lithography/Sheetfed Lithography/Silkscreen Printing

Webfed Lithography/Sheetfed Lithography
Webfed Lithography/Sheetfed Lithography
Webfed Lithography/Sheetfed Lithography
Webfed Lithography/Sheetfed Lithography
Webfed Lithography/Sheetfed Lithography
Webfed Lithography/Sheetfed Lithography
Webfed Lithography/Sheetfed Lithography
Webfed Lithography/Sheetfed Lithography
Webfed Lithography/Sheetfed Lithography

Webfed Lithography/Sheetfed Lithography
Webfed Lithography/Sheetfed Lithography
Webfed Lithography/Sheetfed Lithography
Webfed Lithography/Sheetfed Lithography
Webfed Lithography/Sheetfed Lithography
Webfed Lithography/Sheetfed Lithography

Webfed Lithography/Sheetfed Lithography

Webfed Lithography/Sheetfed Lithography
Webfed Lithography/Sheetfed Lithography

Silkscreen Printing
Flexography
Flexography
Webfed Lithography/Sheetfed Lithography
Sheetfed Lithography/Silkscreen Printing
Silkscreen Printing
Flexography/Silkscreen Printing
Flexography
Sheetfed Lithography/Silkscreen Printing

Webfed Lithography/Sheetfed Lithography/Flexography/Silkscreen Printing
Webfed Lithography/Sheetfed Lithography/Flexography/Silkscreen Printing

Webfed Lithography/Sheetfed Lithography/Flexography/Silkscreen Printing
Webfed Lithography/Sheetfed Lithography/Flexography/Silkscreen Printing
Webfed Lithography/Sheetfed Lithography/Flexography/Silkscreen Printing
Webfed Lithography/Sheetfed Lithography/Flexography/Silkscreen Printing
Webfed Lithography/Sheetfed Lithography/Flexography/Silkscreen Printing
Webfed Lithography/Sheetfed Lithography/Flexography/Silkscreen Printing

Webfed Lithography/Sheetfed Lithography/Flexography/Silkscreen Printing
Webfed Lithography/Sheetfed Lithography/Flexography/Silkscreen Printing
Webfed Lithography/Sheetfed Lithography/Flexography/Silkscreen Printing

*This includes grayscale, monotone, duotone, tritone, quadtone, CMYK 4-color process, and CMYKOG hexachrome process.

**In QuarkXPress all images need to be saved at 300dpi, TIFF mode, and actively linked. In QuarkXPress font usage should be actively linked as well. If using Illustrator as a support file within QuarkXPress, the document should be exported as a TIFF. Do not save image as EPS. In Illustrator all images need to be saved at 300dpi, PSD mode, and embedded into the document. Do not save image as EPS. Fonts being used for the job need to be outlined.

***Photoshop document must be saved at 300dpi, at 100% of size (end use) in order for font quality not to degrade (less than a 300dpi document will have the jags on press). This includes backlit kiosk signs/advertisements typically found at airports.

Color Management Across Applications

No matter if a mark is created using one color or an array of colors, different technical issues will arise depending upon the medium and/or the type of printing. What may work for Web-based design may not always work for print-based design, or even through a fax machine. Understanding the full potential of a mark, the context in which it is used and will be used in the future, is critical for design longevity. Without a proper understanding of the numerous factors that are involved in the versatility and longevity of a mark, the end result will surely create a colorful mess. Color sells the product, but not at the expense of everything else.

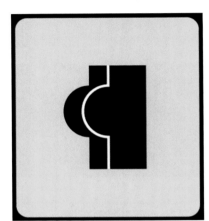

Logo Lo-con
Designers: Bryan Cantley and Kevin
O'Donnell

Associative Color Response:
· aggressive, stimulating: yellow-
  orange
· heavy, sober: black

Color Scheme: one hue plus neutral

This series of lo-cons (logo + icon)
was created to provoke a visual
cue—an anchor as a counterpoint
for lectures. Designers Cantley and
O'Donnell wanted to create a series
of symbols or icons that were slightly
ambiguous for the notation of the
architectural design process. This
communication paradox created a
navigation system that was clearly
legible, but vague in its meaning.
This intentional ambiguity helped to
create visual appeal.

Yellow and black were chosen to
mimic the Occupational Safety
and Health Administration (OSHA)
hazard-stripes at points of danger.
Designed as visual magnets, this
paradoxical relationship of "look
at me, but stay away" is carried
out through the misinterpretation
of each lo-con. These lo-cons are
strategically placed throughout the
client's lectures, on architectural
drawings (in pencil outline form),
on the Web, and on their models
as decals.

From Print to Web

Depending upon the medium—in this case Web-based or print-based—different format configurations should be taken into consideration in the design process. If, for example, a logomark is created in a style that is highly reductive, a vector-based mark is the most appropriate. If typography accompanies the mark and/or a logotype is created, the typography should be outlined into vector form. This allows the mark to be 100% vector art with no accompanying font files.

The mark will need to be saved differently if the same mark is going to be used for both Web-based and print-based design. For Web-based design, the vector art will need to be converted to a Graphic Interchange Format (GIF) file so that the image can be compressed to the maximum amount without altering the color or injecting color anomalies. (A GIF document compresses better than a JPEG format for flat-pattern art work.) For print-based design, the file should be saved as an Encapsulated Postscript File (EPS), allowing for multiple use within almost any print-based software application, and a spot hue or hues should be specified. For print-based graphics, the artwork will be ripped to a minimum amount of film. If the mark uses more than three specified inks then a four-color or six-color process typically is used.

If both mediums are going to be used in the practical application of the mark, Web-based and print-based, color choices should be carefully thought out. Designers have several options to control color outcome, and if matching color is of critical concern the options become very limited. With vector-based logomarks, the color palette is limited

to the 216 colors found within the Web-safe Color Cube. However, not all of the hues found within the cube are reproducible through print-based means. (See Color-Matching Hues on pages 196–197) for Web-safe hues that can be reproduced using different ink-matching systems.) Expanding the color palette beyond the "browser-safe" color cube will create color shifting not only within the Web environment, from platform to platform, but also from Web to print.

If the client can accept some color shifting, choosing a hue through a standard ink-matching system, four-color process, or six-color process will create a far greater color palette for dissemination. It is easier to match a subtractive color on an additive color device such as a computer than to try to match an additive hue through a subtractive medium. (Four-color process can match over 60% of the PANTONE MATCHING SYSTEM® Colors—40% of the colors fall outside of the CMYK color spectrum. A great number of additive hues fall outside of any standard subtractive ink-matching system.)

Diagram 1 (a and b) The primary colors on one wheel are secondary colors on the other. However, the additive color wheel has a greater color spectrum which creates chroma that cannot be reproduced through subtractive means.

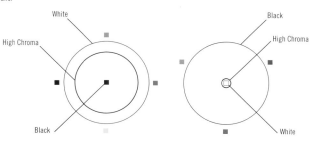

(a) Four-color process, subtractive color wheel

(b) Web, additive color wheel

Insite Works
Studio: Hornall Anderson Design Works

Associative Color Response:
· communication, dramatic: orange
· authoritative, service: blue

Color Scheme: complementary

The orange "I" creates visual interest and balance within this logotype; it is visually indicative of a cursor on a page. The dots that create the "I" seem to flash much like a curser does in a stationary position, waiting for the writer to add new meaning to content. In this case, the meaning brought to the content is "site design"—a play on the partial name of the firm: Insite. This is visually indicated through the color coding of the design. The position of orange type, stating "site design" is halfway through the blue tagline, just as the orange "I" is placed halfway through the logotype.

Color coding visual information is an excellent method of unobtrusively adding meaning to a design. Through color coding, the designer influences how the audience pairs the information. For example, site design and architecture development are seen independently of each other or as one continuous statement. This is another use of gestalt.

8ballmultimedia.com

A JPEG configuration is the most appropriate for continuous-tone marks used for the Web. A JPEG is designed to capture continuous-tone objects, including marks with gradients, with a minimal amount of color loss or shifting. When converting a mark into this format, experimenting with multiple compression settings will allow a greater understanding of the degree a mark or object can be compressed with no observable color loss. JPEG formatting allows a spectrum of compression settings. When designing for the Web, the more the mark can be compressed, the faster the object will load.

If the continuous-tone gradient mark will be used for both print- and Web-based design, the mark needs to be set up differently for print. For a mark created in Photoshop, the logo should be saved in CMYK mode with an EPS setting, and a duplicate file should be saved in RGB mode with a JPEG setting for use on the Web. If the mark is going to be placed in QuarkXPress, a TIFF format should be used—this type of formatting is native for QuarkXPress. Color comprehensives will print better with no color anomalies, and printers prefer TIFF files in Quark for RIPing film (Raster Image Processed). Make sure you create the print-based file first. When converting a CMYK document to RGB mode there is no color loss. This is not always the case when converting RGB documents into CMYK mode.

It is best to create a mark with a gradient in a vector-based program and then convert the mark for Web use. Using these guidelines will ensure better color management when logos are used in print- and Web-based design.

Diagram 2 (a–f) This diagram indicates the steps needed to move a mark from print to web.

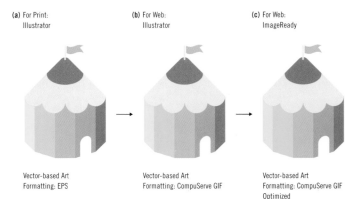

(a) For Print:
Illustrator

(b) For Web:
Illustrator

(c) For Web:
ImageReady

Vector-based Art
Formatting: EPS

Vector-based Art
Formatting: CompuServe GIF

Vector-based Art
Formatting: CompuServe GIF
Optimized

(d) For Print:
Illustrator

(e) For Web:
Photoshop

(f) For Web:
ImageReady

Vector-based Gradient/
Continuous-tone Image +
Outlined Type
Formatting: EPS

Vector-based Gradient/
Continuous-tone Image +
Outlined Type
Formatting: JPEG/72dpi

Vector-based Gradient/
Continuous-tone Image +
Outlined Type
Formatting: JPEG/72dpi Optimized

8 Ball Multimedia
Studio: 8 Ball Multimedia

Associative Color Response:
· spatial, strong: black
· authoritative, service: blue

Color Scheme: two primary hues
plus continuous tone

Shown here are sketches for, and
frames from, a self-promotion,
motion-graphic work for the studio
8 Ball Multimedia. A reflection of
the "8 ball," in frame five of the
piece, can be seen within the moving
eye. The black-and-white mark is a
vector-based graphic that is easy to
recognize and quick to download over
the Internet. New depth is brought to
the mark when it is communicated in
a simple Flash animation. Although
the Flash animation is continuous
tone, it is highly controlled so that it
will work well on the Web. The color
choice is shallow and selected so
that it will communicate clearly on
all platforms. In addition, memory is
minimized by the range of action and
intent of the animation. Therefore,
the number of frames needed to
communicate the animation is low.

From Static to Motion

In the early 1990s, our industry witnessed the emergence of a new medium—the Web. This medium transformed the way that studios, advertising agencies, and universities conducted business, created infrastructure, and disseminated information. In the past, designers did not have to consider that the mark they created might be put into motion. Up until the 1990s, most logos were static and could be placed in motion only by applying them to moving objects. Today this is not the case: more and more logomarks bounce, flip, twist, spin, and fly across the screen. No longer does a logomark need to be in 3-D space for it to move. However, the way in which humans see motion has not changed, and the same principles apply.

Human perception of form is classified and organized through the simple, complex, and hypercomplex fields located in the primary visual cortex of the brain. These photoreceptive fields classify visual information for interpretation by the primary visual cortex and other parts of the brain and help us to detect shape, contour, mass, orientation, direction, edges, and slits of static and moving objects. For both the simple and hypercomplex fields, position and length of stimuli is critical. In other words, the size of an object and the way the object moves are critical in determining whether humans can see it or not. Understanding the way in which humans see can yield extraordinary insight into the shape that an object needs to take and the way it moves across the screen.

Simple fields of vision

Photoreceptor fields that are parallel to one another and work best with moving stimuli.

Complex fields of vision

The mechanics of perceiving the location and orientation of an object. Complex fields respond best to moving slits, edges, and dark bars. The position of the stimulus is not critical.

Hypercomplex fields of vision

Matrix fields of photoreceptor cells within the brain that respond most favorably to moving objects that behave with a set direction and definite position or pattern. The physical or spatial design delimitations required for today's cross-media marks are as follows. If used properly, these three simple rules will ensure that a mark can be designed for almost any context. (See following page for a fuller explanation of these guidelines.)

Rule one The mark should be designed for viewing at any distance, be it small or great.

Rule two The anatomy of the mark should incorporate the way humans view objects.

Rule three The way a mark moves should correspond to the way in which humans view moving objects.

Second Annual World Military Games
Designer: Boris Ljubicic

Associative Color Response:
· surging, hope: red
· powerful, neutral: black
· dignity, energetic: blue
· motion, life: green
· anticipation, welcome: yellow
· purity, balance: white

Color Scheme: primary plus one hue and neutral tints and shades

The Second Annual World Military Games are similar in spirit and content to the Olympics. As a point of departure and inspiration, five interlocking rings were chosen as the basic geometric shapes. In contrast to the Olympic design, these rings were tightly grouped and rendered three-dimensionally into the shape of an open flower—an oxymoron of strong and delicate. Each color (red, blue, yellow, green, black, and white) signifies the major colors

found on the flags of all nations, and the red or white squares signify the geographical location of the games—in this case, Croatia. The role of the colors and shape of the mark are aesthetically functional. The World Military Games are very unpopular, and designer Boris Ljubicic was charged with creating an aesthetically pleasing mark, a positive image, that could be easily translated and produced on many different surfaces using a multitude of materials (including metals, cloth, paper, and plastic) and media, such as static, collateral, or motion.

Diagram 3 Simple fields of vision respond best to moving stimuli.

Diagram 4 Complex fields of vision respond best to moving slits, edges, and dark bars; position is not critical.

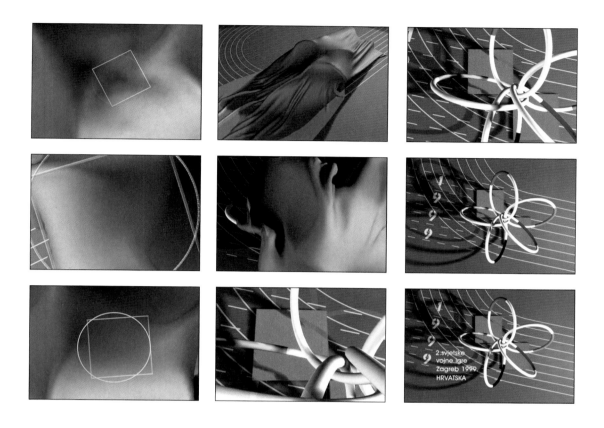

Diagram 5 Hypercomplex fields
of vision respond best to moving
objects with a set direction and
defined pattern.

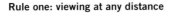

Rule one: viewing at any distance

After creating the mark, print the logo out at reduced sizes. All the anatomical parts of the mark should be clearly discernible at a size of half an inch. If the mark can be reduced down to one-half inch or smaller, the mark's anatomy will be legible at almost any distance. (This exercise should be done in the final color(s) for the mark.) This simple exercise demonstrates both at what size and how far the mark can be seen.

Rule two: anatomy of a mark

When developing the anatomy of a mark, the form/counterform relationships are critical for viewing both at a distance and in motion. If the form/counterform relationships found within the anatomy are not constructed properly, the mark will collapse in on itself when viewed at extreme distances, both small and great, and when the mark is in motion. For optimal viewing at a distance, the counterform must be, at a minimum, the same size as the form. For example, the counterform of an uppercase "E" should be at least the same width as the stroke (see Diagram 7). When viewing at a distance the visual angle is the same—meaning both the stroke of the letterform and counterform will disappear from sight at the same time. (A simple printout test of this scenario will verify these results.) Different viewing angles are created if the logomark or logotype has thick and thin relationships found within the forms and counterforms. This will mean that different parts of the mark will disappear at different distances, possibly leading to

illegibility at extreme or not-so-extreme distance. If this cannot be helped, viewing distance is determined by the smallest or thinnest form or counterform, and testing these parts will determine the distance at which the mark can be viewed in a given size. (This exercise should be done in the final color(s) for the mark.) Color has a bearing on the distance at which an object can be seen.

Rule three: a mark in motion

When developing the anatomy of a mark that is going to be placed on an object in motion, or the mark itself is in motion, the form/counterform relationships must be reconfigured to accommodate this phenomenon. In short, the mark's counterforms need to be opened up. For example, using an extended cut of a letterform instead of a roman or regular typeface typically yields better anatomical results for movement. With today's technology, it is easy to test how well a mark will hold up when in motion by simply placing the logomark, logotype, or simple symbol in Photoshop and applying different degrees of motion blurs to the mark. Typically, the counterforms found within the mark should be adjusted so that the counterform is greater than the average stroke width of the mark. This type of test yields information about how fast a mark can actually move.

As was stated above, all three photoreceptor fields (simple, complex, and hypercomplex) respond best to moving stimuli. However, the orientation, direction, and predictability influence how well humans can track an

eos Airlines
Studio: Hornall Anderson Design Works

Associative Color Response:
· pleasure, peace: blue
· gentle, inviting: green

Color Scheme: complementary

The openness of the counterforms is an integral part of the design for this logotype and, along with the tapering strokes of the letterforms, suggests freedom of motion.

Diagram 6 As shown here, the openness of the counter forms found within this logotype are well suited for motion. Each example indicates the mark from static to progressively faster speeds of travel.

Diagram 7 (a and b) These three capital "E"s demonstrate a ratio of one-to-one (stroke width to counterform width). Each letterform has one visual angle. At a minimum, a one-to-one is required for type in motion and for viewing at a distance.

(a)

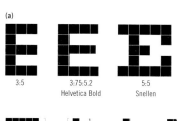

3:5   3:75:5.2   5:5
       Helvetica Bold   Snellen

1   1
5
5   5   Helvetica Bold   1

(b)

Diagram 7 (c) The counterforms shown here have been opened 30-40% to accommodate motion.

Diagram 7 (d) In this diagram the typography has not been manipulated and therefore the letterforms are not as anatomically sound for motion.

(c)

motion

(d)

motion

object—in this case, a mark. To bounce, flip, twist, spin, and fly a mark down a street or across the screen needs forethought, planning, and testing. Humans love pattern and predictability—it is the way we make sense of the world. From the layout of a city to the way in which we fold cloth, pattern and predictability provide us with comfort. If, for example, we create a mark that is random in motion, the eye will have a much harder time tracking the object, and frustration will soon set in.

For the most part, marks that move in our environment move in a predictable manner, but on the computer screen, TV screen, or motion-picture screen this may not always be the case. Understanding gestalt theory, as applied to graphic design, will shed some light on how objects should move. Too much predictability in the pattern creates boredom and an overall lack of visual interest. Not enough predictability in the movement leads to chaos and frustration. The key to creating kinetic movement is to have the right amount of variation and predictability imbedded in the underpinning structure. A simple test of pattern forming can yield great insight into the structure of kinetic movement.

Three-circle Test

Draw a circle on a piece of paper and ask any person what will be drawn next. Most people will reply, "I have no idea." Draw another circle beside the one already drawn, and ask the same question. A majority of people will say a circle, but there will still be quite a few individuals who will say something other than a circle. Draw another circle beside the two already drawn, and ask the same question. The answer will always be "another circle." Vary this test by

drawing a circle, then a square, then a circle, and so on. Typically, an individual will need two circles and two squares in order to understand the pattern. Keep varying the test by adding more complexity to the pattern, for example, circle, square, circle, circle, and circle. The subject will not comprehend the pattern until the pattern starts to repeat itself. This is the quickest way for subjects to comprehend kinetic movement.

When dealing with marks that are moving at great speeds, the predictability of the movement needs to be increased. As an object moves faster and faster, the ability to track the object becomes more difficult. If an object is moving slowly, then more complexity can be built into the underpinning structure.

**VIII Mediterranean Games,
Split, 1979**
Designer: Boris Ljubicic

Associative Color Response:
· stirring, dignity: blue

Color Scheme: monochromatic tints and shades

The VIII Mediterranean Games were held in Split, Croatia, in 1979. The logomark and environmental graphics are still considered an exceptional example of design for an international sporting event. In fact, due to the resounding approval of the mark within the international community, since 1979 the International Committee of the Mediterranean Games has used this mark as its logo. Therefore, each subsequent event has used the logomark as the primary branding element alongside the host country's secondary symbol. This event, comprised of 18 countries participating in 25 sporting events

and akin to the Olympics, is fundamentally shaped by its location along the Mediterranean. The history, culture, participating countries, and body of water that defines the Mediterranean determine the shape of the mark and the colors.

The shape of the mark references an earlier sign of the Mediterranean Games, in which three regular circles connect horizontally—similar to the top row of the Olympic logo. The lower half of each circle was developed through sketch, direct observation, and photo reproduction techniques aimed at maintaining the accuracy of the drawing while creating the illusionary form of a circle immersed beneath the surface of the Mediterranean Sea. The colors of the original symbol were blue, black, and yellow, so referencing

the Olympic logo. Boris Ljubicic's mark is executed in one color (blue), and in 1979 was applied across all event material through a systematic palette of five hues (blue, green, yellow, red, and gray) expressed in two values each—one lighter (tint) and one darker (shade)—to create ten colors. The conceptual genesis of the color model was to mimic the tonal quality of Mediterranean light as it reflects off the sea. By changing the mark to one color, unity among nations was stressed and the sea connection was emphasized. Over the years, the blue mark has brought a sense of stability and professionalism to the organizing committee. When reversed out of a field of color to white, the logomark takes on a delightfully optimistic nature rather than a strictly professional tone.

The palette of 10 colors used in 1979, which referenced the participating nations, alluded to the mission of the Games to build friendship and peace in the spirit of sport throughout the Mediterranean. In addition, the color plus the reflective water quality brought to the lower half of each circle differentiates the mark from the Olympic symbol. Given the prominence of the project, the identity was well supported internationally, and therefore the color choices were not limited by budgetary constraints. This provided for great diversity and allowed the designer to organize the information in distinctive ways throughout a variety of platforms, including environmental graphics, print media, and broadcast.

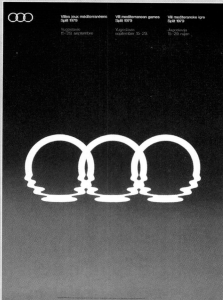

Diagram 8 The movement within this mark is irrational, unnatural, and therefore hard for humans to track. If placed in motion this would ultimately lead to frustration for the viewer.

9 Resources

Glossary

Absorbed light: Light that is absorbed by an object; the opposite of transmitted light.

Achromatic: Hues made from black, gray, and white.

Additive color theory/mixing: Combining lightwaves to create colors.

Afterimage: Illusions occurring when retinal cones and neurons become fatigued or overstimulated.

Analogous colors: A color grouping in which the colors are to the near left and right of each other.

Bronzing: An effect that develops when some inks are exposed to light and air: this creates a false reading in the calculation of color.

Chroma: Color intensity. Sometimes referred to as the color's brightness, chroma is another word for the Y tristimulus value in 3-D color theory.

Chromatic colors: A series of colors arranged in set increments.

CMYK: The four hues used in subtractive four-color-process printing—Cyan, Magenta, Yellow, and Black.

Color contrast: The difference between lightwaves detected by the apparatus of the eyeball.

Color gamma: The spectrum of color within a system.

Color mixing: The process by which different pigments, dyes, colorants, or lightwaves are mixed to create a new hue.

Color purity: The absence of white, black, or gray from a hue.

Color rendition: The phenomenon of two colors appearing the same in one light source, but very different in another.

Color saturation: The richness of a hue.

Color scheme: The color combinations selected for a particular design.

Color shading: Adding black.

Color temperature: The degree of warmth or coolness that a color suggests.

Color tinting: Adding a small amount of one color or white pigment to another color.

Color toning: Adding one complementary color to another.

Color value: The relative lightness or darkness of the color as perceived by the mind's eye.

Color wheel: A matrix comprised of primary, secondary, and tertiary hues or colors.

Complementary colors: Hues that are found on opposite sides of the color wheel.

Complex fields of vision: The mechanics of perceiving the location and orientation of an object.

Complex subtractive mixing: The process of removing lightwaves through absorption and scattering.

Cones: The receptor cells responsible for our perception of bright light and color.

Duotone: A one-color photograph that is reproduced using two hues.

Electromagnetic radiation: The transfer of radiant energy as heat and light, through air, water, or vacuums.

Fake duotone: A one-color photograph that is reproduced in two hues—one halftone image overprinted on top of a solid color.

Fixation points: Discrete points at which the eye is in focus.

Fovea: A small spot on the retina that provides our narrow, central field of focused vision.

Fugitive colors: Colorants, pigments, or dyes that change or lose color rapidly when exposed to light and air.

Harmonious colors: Two or more colors that have a sameness about them.

Harmony of analogous colors:

· **of scale:** color tones that are produced through a single scale;

· **of hue:** colors that have the same relative lightness to the mind's eye (color value rating);

· **of dominant color:** hues that are related to the factors involved in color contrast.

Harmony of contrast:

· **of scale:** two colors with the same or near same color value rating, but different hues;

· **of hue:** chromatic colors with distinctly different color value ratings mixed together in stepped increments;

· **of color temperature:** two colors with the same or near same color value rating, but different color temperatures.

Hue: A classified or specified color.

Hypercomplex fields of vision: Matrix fields of photoreceptor cells within the brain that respond most favorably to moving objects that behave with a set direction and definite position or pattern.

Illuminant: Light, physically realized or not, defined by spectral power distribution.

Incongruous colors: Colors that make a discordant combination.

Integrated sphere: A hollow sphere used to collect all of the light reflected from the surface of a color sample.

Invariant pairs: Color samples or objects having an identical spectral reflectance curve and the same color coordinates.

Iris: The portion of the eye that helps to focus an image, adjust the amount of light passing through the pupil to define depth of field, and gives eyes their color.

Knockouts: Type or marks that are cut out of the background color and replaced with another hue.

Light energy: Light distinguished by the human eye as colors.

Metameric pairs: Pairs of colors with different spectral reflectance curves (see spectral power distribution curve) that have the same appearance in one light source, but not in another.

Monochromatic colors: Hues consisting of one color, including screen percentages of tints, shades, and combinations of tints and shades (see *color tinting* and *color shading*).

Muddy/Dirty hues: Colors that are made up from three or more inks, one of which is black.

Neutral color: A hue with a near-equal screen percentage of one or more colors, including its complementary.

Overprinting: Printing one or more colors (inks) over the top of another ink that has already been printed.

Parent colors: Two or more hues that are used to create or build an array of colors.

Primary colors: Pure hues that create the foundation of all color spectrums.

· **Subtractive primaries:** Cyan, magenta, and yellow are used to create a full color spectrum. In four-color process mixing black is added as a fourth primary to ensure color saturation and richness.

· **Additive primaries:** Red, blue, and green. Traditionally, additive color primaries create a wider color spectrum than their print-based counterparts: light is transmitted directly from its source into the human eye.

· **3-D primaries:** Three sets of primaries constitute subsets of 3-D color theory. The International Commission on Illumination (CIE) primaries are red, green, and blue. Light sources of average daylight are set at: U.S. standard, known as Source D50, 5,000 K; European standard, known as Source D65, 6,500 K; tungsten filament lamp, known as Source A, 2,854 K; and noon sunlight, known as Source C, 4,800 K. There is no Source B. The Young-Helmholtz theory, also known as the trichromatic color theory, includes three sets of primaries (blue-/yellow+, green-/red+, white-/black+-), and the opponent–process theory, developed by Ewald Hering, has four sets of primaries (blue-/yellow+, green-/red+, white-/black+, purple). In both theories, negative and positive stimuli are used in the calculation of color perception.

Primary visual cortex: A portion of the brain located at the end of the visual pathway, devoted to the input for and interpretation of sight.

Pupil: The pupil is the black point in the center of the eye through which light travels in order to strike the retina. It operates like the leaf shutter of a camera, opening and closing in a circular pattern.

Pure hues: Colors that are made up from one ink

Retina: The region at the back of the eyeball where the ganglion cells, cones, and rods are located.

Reversals: A reversal is when type or a mark is dropped out to the color of the substrate from a solid color.

Rods: Photoreceptors responsible for night vision.

Scattering: A phenomenon that occurs when light strikes an object with a rough surface, causing lightwaves to reflect in many directions.

Secondary colors: Hues formed by adding equal amounts of two primary colors to one another.

Simple fields of vision: Photoreceptive fields that are parallel to one another and work best with moving stimuli.

Simple subtractive mixing: The process of removing lightwaves through the absorption process.

Simultaneous contrast: A strobing effect resulting from the use of unequal portions of colors.

Specialty ink: A hue that is custom-made and not found in a standard ink-matching system.

Spectral power distribution curve: The spectrum of color seen by the human eye; when combined this makes white light.

Split complementary colors: Two or more hues on or near opposite sides of the color wheel.

Spot color: Hues that are specified in a standard ink-matching system.

Standard observer: A set angle of observation that affects the response of normal color vision.

Standard source: A light source for which the characteristics—wavelength, intensity, etc.—have been specified.

Subtractive color mixing: The process of removing lightwaves or matter in physical space to create additional colors.

Tertiary colors: Colors produced by mixing equal amounts of a primary and a secondary color.

Transmitted light: Light that is reflected.

Transparent: If light travels through an object uninterrupted, the object is said to be transparent.

Trapping: Trapping is when one plate (color) is choked or spread so that a small amount of ink is overlapping an adjacent hue.

Tristimulus values: X, Y, and Z tristimulus values refer to the amount of light the eyes see from the three primaries—red, green, and blue—of 3-D color theory. These values are determined by multiplying the power (light source) by the reflectance by the standard observer (the equivalent of normal color vision within humans). The three most typical standard light sources are Source A (tungsten filament lamp), Source D50 and/or D65 (U.S. and European standards for average daylight), and Source CWF (fluorescent lighting).

Tritone: A one-color photograph that is reproduced using three hues.

Undercolor addition (UCA): A method of adding color to improve image quality.

Undercolor removal (UCR): A method of removing color to improve image quality.

Visual pathway: The pathway from the eyes to the back of the brain, the primary visual cortex, to which the electrical impulses travel to be recognized and interpreted in the mind's eye, instantly, and right side up.

Warm colors: Colors that produce the appearance of an object being nearer the observer than it is.

Wavelength range: The visual range within which humans can distinguish the color spectrum.

Web-safe Color Cube: An arrangement of the 216 hues, at 20% intervals, that can be depicted accurately with most common computer platforms. This includes black and white, and their shades and tints (see *color shading* and *color tinting*).

Y tristimulus value: A measure indicating the relative lightness of a color to the mind's eye.

Bibliography

Albers, Josef. *Interaction Of Color.* New Haven and London: Yale University Press, 1963.

Alpern, Andrew. *Handbook of Specialty Elements in Architecture.* New York: McGraw, 1982.

Arnheim, Rudolf. *Art and Visual Perception.* Berkeley and Los Angeles: University of California Press, 1974.

Berryman, Gregg. *Notes on Graphic Design and Visual Communication.* Los Altos, California: William Kaufmann, 1984.

Billmeyer, Fred W., Jr. *Principles of Color Technology.* New York: Wiley-Interscience, 1981.

Binns, Betty. "Readability and Legibility in Text." *Step-By-Step 6* (1987), pp 56–61.

Birren, Faber. *Color & Human Response.* New York: John Wiley and Sons, 1978.

___. *Color Psychology and Color Therapy.* New Jersey: Citadel Press, 1950.

___. *Color Perception in Art.* New York: Van Nostrand and Reinhold Company, 1976.

Blatner, David and Steve Roth. *Real World Scanning and Halftones.* California: Peachpit Press, 1993.

Bleier, Paul. "Comprehensive Sign Plans: An Alternative to Restrictive Sign Ordinances." *Messages,* Summer 189: pp 7–9.

Bopst, Harland. *Color and Personality.* New York: Vantage Press, 1962.

Bowles, Susan, David S. Travis, John Seton, and Roger Peppe. "Reading from Color Displays: A Psychophysical Model." *Human Factors 32* (1990), pp 147–156.

Bringhurst, Robert. *The Elements of Typographic Style.* Vancouver: Hartley and Marks Publishers, 1992.

Byrnes, Deborah A. "Color Associations of Children." *The Journal of Psychology: The General Field of Psychology.* Massachusetts: The Journal Press Provincetown, 1983.

Carter, Rob. *Working with Computer Type, Volume 3: Color and Type.* Switzerland: RotoVision, 1997.

Carter, Rob, and Philip Meggs. *Typographic Design: Form and Communication, Second Edition.* New York: Van Nostrand Reinhold, 1993.

Carter, Rob, and Philip Meggs. *Typographic Specimens: The Great Typefaces.* New York: Van Nostrand Reinhold, 1993.

Claus, Karen and James R. *Visual Communication Through Signage: Design of the Message, Volume 3.* Ohio: Signs of The Times Publishing Co., 1976.

—. *Visual Communication Through Signage: Perception of the Message, Volume 1.* Ohio: Signs of The Times Publishing Co., 1972.

Craig, James. "Techniques for Display Type." *Step-by-Step 6* (1987), pp 62–65.

DeMao, John, John T. Drew, Ned Drew, and Sarah A. Meyer, eds. *Design Education In Progress: Process and Methodology Volume 3, Visual Thinking.* Virginia: Center for Design Studies, 2003.

Drew, John T., Ned Drew, and Sarah A. Meyer, eds. *Design Education In Progress: Process and Methodology Volume 2, Type and Image.* Virginia: Center for Design Studies, 2003.

Duke-Elder, Sir W. Stewart. *Textbook of Ophthalmology.* St. Louis: The C. V. Mosby Company, 1938.

Easterby Roland, and Harm Zwaga, eds. *Information Design.* New York: John Wiley and Sons, Ltd., 1984.

Eiseman, Leatrice. *Color for Every Mood.* Virginia: Capital Books Inc., 1998

Eiseman, Leatrice. *Pantone Guide to Communicating with Color.* Florida: Grafix Press, Ltd., 2000.

Ewald, Willam R., and Daniel R. Mandelker. *Street Graphics and The Law.* Chicago: Planners Press, 1988.

Executive Committee AIGA/New York Chapter. *Press Wise.* New York: American Institute of Graphic Arts, 1995.

Fehrman, Cherie and Kenneth R. *The Secret Influence.* New Jersey: Prentice Hall, 2000.

Finke, Ronald A. *Principles of Mental Imagery.* Cambridge, Massachusetts: The MIT Press, 1989.

Fishenden, R. B. "Type, Paper and Printing in Relation to Eye Strain." *British Journal of Ophthalmology 30* (1946), pp 20–26.

Fleury, Bob. "Combining Type and Color." *Step-by-Step 6* (1987), pp 66–69.

Follis, John. *Architectural Signing and Graphics.* New York: Whitney Library of Design, 1979.

Goethe, J. W. "Moral Effects of Colour." *Goethe's Theory of Colour.* Great Britain: New Knowledge Books, 1970.

Hamid, Nicholas P. and Adrienne G. Newport. "Effect of Color on Physical Strength and Mood in Children." *Perceptual and Motor Skills 69* (1989), pp 179–185.

Hannaford, Steven and Richard Imbro. *An Introduction to Digtal Color Prepess.* Agfa Educational Publishing.

Henrion, F. H. K., and Alan Parkin. *Design Coordination and Corporate Image.* New York: Reinhold Publishing Corporation, 1966.

Hoeksma, Jan B. and Mark M. Terwogt. "Color and Emotions: Preferences and Combinations." *The Journal of General Psychology 122* (1995), pp 5–13.

Karp, Eric M. "Color Associations of Male and Female Fourth-Grade School Children." *Journal of Psychology 122* (1988), pp 383–388.

Kosterman, Wayne. "Turning Type Into Signs." *Step-by-Step 6* (1987), pp 90–93.

Long, Michael E. "The Sense of Sight." *National Geographic* (November 1992), pp 3–41.

Luke, Joy T. *The New Munsell Student Color Set: The Munsell Color System; A Language for Color.* Fairchild Publications, 1946/1994.

Lüscher, Dr. Max, Ian A. Scott. *The Luscher Color Test.* New York: Random House, 1969.

Mahnke, Frank H. and Rudolf H., "Color and Light in Man-made Environments." Van Nostrand Reinhold, 1993.

Mikellides, Byron. "Color and Physiological Arousal." *Journal of Architectural and Planning Research Volume 7 #1* (1990), pp 13–19.

Miyake, R. "Comparative Legibility of Black and Colored Numbers." *The Journal of General Psychology 3* (1930), pp 340–343.

Neal, Kane, Ed. SEGD Education Foundation. Cambridge, Massachusetts, 1992: 3.

Pantone, Inc. *Pantone: Duotone Studio Addition, Colors and Black.* Ohio: Pickerbook Publishing Co., 1998.

Pantone, Inc. *Pantone: Process to Solid Guide.* Ohio: Pickerbook Publishing Co., 1998.

Pantone, Inc. *Pantone: Two Spot Color Mix Guide.* Ohio: Pickerbook Publishing Co., 1998.

Peery, Brady. *Fast Track to Duotone Success.* Ohio: Pickerbook Publishing Co., 1998.

Pipes, Alan. *Production for Graphic Designers.* New Jersey: Prentice Hall, 1993.

Preston, K. "Effect of Variations in Color of Print and Background on Legibility." *The Journal of General Psychology 6* (1932), pp 386–390.

Pring, Roger. *www.Color: Effective Use of Color in Web Page Design.* New York: Watson-Guptill, 2000.

Pye, David. *The Nature and Aesthetics of Design.* New York: Van Nostrand Reinhold Company, 1978.

Reger, Joan A. *Feeling States Evoked by Color Lighting.* Wisconsin: University of Wisconsin, 1967.

Rehe, Rolf F. *Typography: How to Make it Most Legible.* Indianapolis: Design Research Publications, 1972.

—. *The Visible Word.* New York: Hastings House, 1968.

Robson, Stephani K. "Turning The Table: The Psychology of Design for High Volume Restaurants." *Cornell Hotel and Restaurant Administration Quarterly 40* (1999), pp 56–58.

Rose, F. Clifford, ed. *The Eye in General Medicine.* London: Chapman & Hall, 1983.

Sharpe, Deborah T. *The Psychology of Color Design.* Chicago: Nelson-Hall, 1974.

Shinsha, Kawade S. *Designer's Guide to Color: Volume 3.* San Francisco: Chronicle Books, 1986.

Shinsha, Kawade S., and James Stockton. *Designer's Guide to Color: Volume 2.* San Francisco: Chronicle Books, 1984.

___. *Designer's Guide to Color: Volume 4.* San Francisco: Chronicle Books, 1989.

___. *Designer's Guide to Color: Volume 5.* San Francisco: Chronicle Books, 1991.

Sidelinger, Stephen J. *Color Manual.* Englewood: Prentice Hall, 1985.

Stanziola, Ralph. *Colorimetery and the Calculation of Color Difference.* New Jersey: Industrial Color Technology.

Stockton, James. *Designer's Guide to Color: Volume 1.* San Francisco: Chronicle Books, 1984.

Summer, F. C. "Influence of Color on Legibility of Copy." *Journal of Applied Psychology 16* (1932), pp 201–204.

Taylor, Cornelia D. "The Relative Legibility of Black and White Print." *The Journal of Educational Psychology 8* (1934), pp 560–579.

Tinker, Miles. A. "The Effect of Color on Visual Apprehension and Perception." *Genetic Psychology Monographs 11* (1932), pp 459–461.

Tinker, Miles. A., and D. G. Paterson. "Studies of Typographical Factors Influencing Speed of Reading." *Journal of Applied Psychology 15* (1931), pp 241–247.

Traxler, Arthur E. "The Relation Between Rate of Reading and Speed of Association." *The Journal of Educational Psychology 8* (1934), pp 357–365.

West, Suzanne. *Working with Style: Traditional and Modern Approaches to Layout and Typography.* New York: Watson-Guptill Publications, 1990.

Whitehouse, Roger. *The Americans with Disabilities Act White Paper.* Cambridge, Massachusetts: SEGD, 1992.

Wisniewski, Agnes M. *The Influence of Color and Figure-Ground Patterns on Target Accuracy.* Smith College, 1973.

Wong, Wucius. *Principles of Color Design: Designing with Electronic Color.* New York: John Wiley and Sons, 1997.

Wyszecki, Gunter and W. S. Stiles. *Color Science.* New York: John Wiley & Sons, 1967.

Zwimpfer, Moritz. *Color: Light, Sight, Sense.* Pennsylvania: Schiffer Publishing Ltd., 1988.

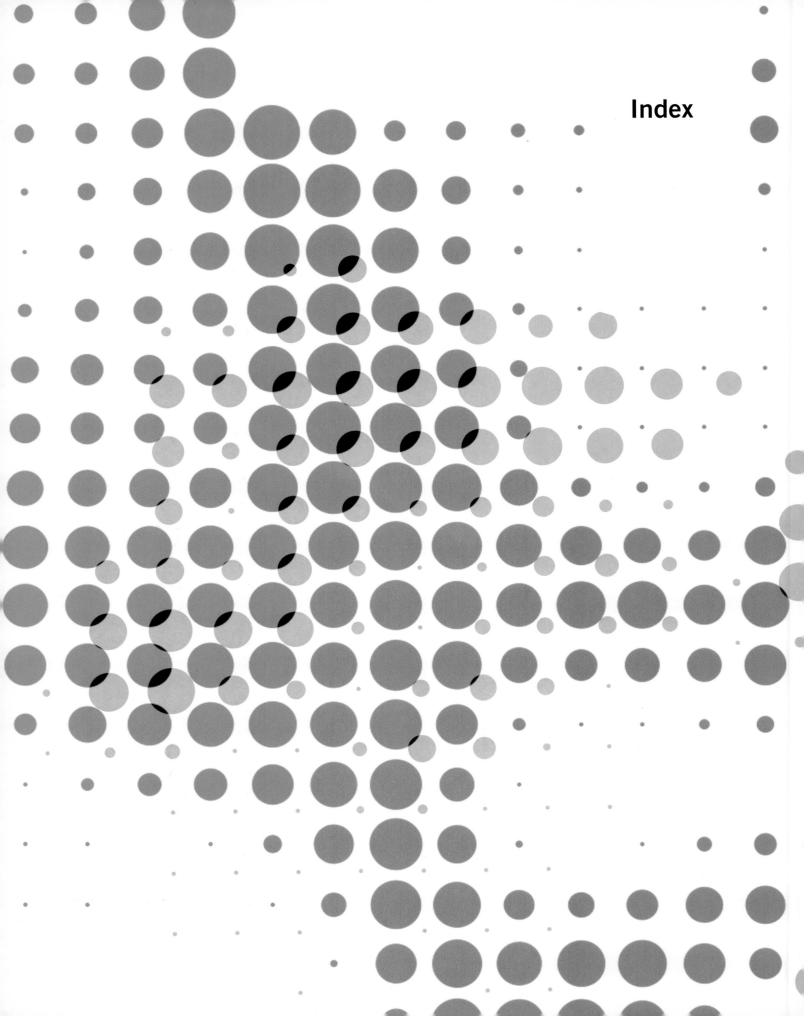

Index

Acknowledgments

We would like to thank all those who have contributed to and made this book possible. So many people have shown generosity and insight that it is impossible to list them all. Our deepest gratitude goes to: Christine Pickett, for making us sound like geniuses; John Randolph Carter (master poet); Tanya Ortega and Carlo Irigoyen for their help in the international call for entries; the International Council of Graphic Design Association (ICOGRADA) and the American Institute of Graphic Arts (AIGA), for supporting the call; all our students who have inspired us to think differently; the people at RotoVision, especially Lindy Dunlop, for her continued support; and finally everyone who answered the call and may or may not appear in this book. *Color Management for Logos* would not have been possible without your participation.